HUGH DOUGLAS
One Man's Ministry

HUGH DOUGLAS
One Man's Ministry

The Life and Work of
The Very Revd H O Douglas KCVO, CBE, DD, LLD

Introduction and Epilogue by
Professor John McIntyre

Edited by
Colin Forrester-Paton

SAINT ANDREW PRESS

First published in 1993 by
SAINT ANDREW PRESS
on behalf of Mrs Isabel Douglas

Copyright © Mrs Isabel Douglas 1993

ISBN: 0–86153–158–2

British Library Cataloguing in Publication Data
  A catalogue record for this
  book is available from the
  British Library.

The copyright owner acknowledges financial assistance from The Drummond Trust towards the publication of this volume.

Cover design by Mark Blackadder.

Typeset by J&L Composition Ltd, Filey, North Yorkshire.

Printed in Great Britain by Athenaeum Press Ltd, Newcastle upon Tyne

CONTENTS

LIST OF CONTRIBUTORS

The Very Revd R A S Barbour, KCVO, MC, DD, BD, STM, formerly Professor of New Testament Exegesis in the University of Aberdeen.

The Revd David M Beckett, BA, BD, Minister of Greyfriars Tolbooth and Highland Kirk, Edinburgh.

D Bruce Cannon, Secretary of the Church of Scotland Board of Communication.

Mrs Isabel C Douglas, MA, wife of the late Dr Hugh Douglas, former National President of the Church of Scotland Woman's Guild.

The Revd Colin Forrester-Paton, MA, BD, formerly Church of Scotland Missionary in Ghana and former Minister of Burnfoot Parish Church, Hawick.

Mrs Jean L Forrester-Paton, BA, Secretary of the Committee on Christian Marriage and Family Life, Christian Council of Ghana 1961–72.

The Revd William Henney, MA, DD, Minister of Hope Park Church, St Andrews.

The Very Revd John McIntyre, CVO, DLitt, DD, Dr *h.c.*, DHL, FRSE, formerly Professor of Divinity in the University of Edinburgh.

The Revd Alan Main, MA, BD, STM, PhD, Professor of Practical Theology at Christ's College, Provost of the Faculty of Divinity, and Head of the Department of Practical Theology in the University of Aberdeen.

The Revd Colin R Martin, MA, BD, Minister of St Ninian's Church, Corstorphine, Edinburgh.

Mrs Martha Steedman (née Hamilton), OBE, MA, formerly Church of Scotland Missionary in the Eastern Himalaya, and former Headmistress of St Leonard's School, St Andrews.

The Revd Gordon G Stewart, MA, Minister of St Leonard's in the Fields and Trinity Church, Perth, and Clerk to the Presbytery of Perth.

The Revd D H Alec Watson, BA, BD, Minister of Anstruther Church.

The Revd D H Whiteford, CBE, PhD, formerly Deputy Chaplain General, Army, and former Minister at Gullane.

The Very Revd James A Whyte, MA, LLD, DD, formerly Professor of Practical Theology and Christian Ethics in the University of St Andrews.

FOREWORD

Principal Hugh Watt in 1926, in a book of the same title, made his selection of *Representative Churchmen of Twenty Centuries*. With hindsight denied to the author, who after all had only a quarter of the century to select from, we would not go far amiss in proposing the name of Hugh Douglas as a candidate for the twentieth century, as far as the Church of Scotland is concerned. The choice would be based on the range and comprehensiveness of Hugh's ministry, founded as it was solidly in the parishes and the congregations to which he was called, but reaching out to touch the wider community and the nation and the national Church. This book seeks to do justice to Hugh's ministry in a series of steps, and by a variety of means.

Part I consists of biography. It follows a predictable pattern and describes Hugh's boyhood, school and university days, his work in Govan Old Parish Church with the then Revd Dr George MacLeod, and his ministry in the parishes of St John's, Leven, North Leith and Dundee (St Mary's), together with an account of his very fulfilling pastoral ministry as Associate in Hope Park Church, St Andrews, after his retirement. In writing those sections of Part I which take the narrative up to the end of Hugh's ministry in St John's, Leven, John McIntyre was greatly assisted by the availability of a draft of an autobiography which Hugh had extensively revised but had not been able to complete.

In this biography two objectives are kept in mind: first of

all, rather than providing simply a historical record, it aims to set out the perspectives within which Hugh's very full ministry was exercised, and his message communicated; second, it aims to facilitate an understanding of his ministry and message by showing how they were seen, heard and appreciated by those who came within their influence, and who observed them at close quarters.

Part II of the book has evolved from an examination of many of Hugh's writings, sermons, broadcasts and recorded talks, which were soon seen to fall into certain identifiable categories. These categories, in most cases, answered to the different aspects of his many-sided ministry, and so came to form the chapters of Part II. Each chapter consists of two sections, the first being an introduction to the particular theme of the chapter, based both on the writer's own knowledge of Hugh's work, and upon his perusal of relevant portions of Hugh's writings. The second section of each chapter in Part II consists of a selection, made by the writer except in two cases, of Hugh's actual preaching, lecturing, writing or broadcasting, on the theme of the chapter, or on subjects closely related to the main theme.

In the face of the mass of written and recorded material which Hugh left, major selection has been inevitable. A limited amount of editing has been done, particularly to the many sermons reproduced here from manuscripts which he had not revised for publication. Two sermons, 'Personal Responsibility' in Chapter 6 and 'You are the Man' in Chapter 8, have been taken from tape-recordings of the services at which they were preached, and something of the style of Hugh's delivery is reflected there. Notional titles have been supplied for some sermons and addresses, taken almost invariably from a phrase or an idea in the original.

The form and method of this presentation of Hugh Douglas's ministry was suggested by John McIntyre, and Isabel Douglas and Colin Forrester-Paton worked with him in compiling it. The general editorship was carried out by Colin Forrester-Paton, who had the additional special responsibility of supervising the selections for Part II, and of trying to ensure that they were truly representative. All three wish to thank most warmly the contributors of Parts I and II. They all responded immediately to the invitation to contribute, and the alacrity of their response clearly sprang from the affection in which Hugh was held by them.

Isabel C Douglas
John McIntyre
Colin Forrester-Paton

Acknowledgements

I am very conscious of the debt I owe to two friends without whom it is unlikely this book would ever have been written.

Colin Forrester-Paton agreed to be editor when a collection of sermons and addresses was envisaged. When a biographical volume was agreed upon, his work certainly doubled in every way. Nevertheless, it is still stamped by his notable attention to detail and meticulous care.

It was John McIntyre who suggested a biographical volume and was kind enough to undertake that task. It is not difficult to detect in this John's characteristic ability to interweave a serious subject with a lightness of touch which can be most refreshing.

I am grateful to the friends (see pages viii–ix) for their willingness to introduce the various Sections, to Jean McIntosh and Evelyn Hood for their patient typing, to Jim Douglas and Ron Fergusson for ideas and tips from their journalistic professionalism, and to other friends who have greatly encouraged and assisted the production of this book.

In these days of stress and strain, sorrow and sadness, poverty and despair, I hope this book may encourage all who seek to proclaim the Gospel of Christ and the coming of His Kingdom.

Isabel Douglas

Acknowledgements are also due to the following for their kind permission to reproduce material in this book:

Extracts from the Authorised Version (AV) of the Bible (The King James Bible), the rights in which are vested in the Crown, are reproduced by permission of the Crown's patentee, Cambridge University Press.

Extracts from the New English Bible (NEB) © 1970 by permission of Oxford and Cambridge University Presses.

Extracts from the Revised Standard Version (RSV), copyright 1946, 1952, © 1971, by the Division of Christian Education of the National Council of the Churches of Christ in the USA, and are used by permission.

Extracts from the Church Hymnary Third Edition (CH3), © The Church Hymnary Trust, Oxford University Press, London, 1973.

Extracts from the Revised Church Hymnary (RCH), © Oxford University Press, London.

The British Broadcasting Corporation for the use of 'It Can't Happen To Me!' on pp 213–219, a BBC TV broadcast on Sunday 5 March 1965; 'The Minister Calls—At The End of The Year' on pp 219–228, a BBC TV broadcast in the 'Meeting Point' series on Sunday 29 December 1957; 'Afraid to Die?' on pp 228–229, from the BBC TV programme 'Victory Over Death', July 1967.

The poem by G A Studdert-Kennedy on pp 81–82 from *The Rhymes of G A Studdert-Kennedy*, Hodder & Stoughton, 1910, acknowledged with thanks.

The Expository Times, T & T Clark, Edinburgh, for the use of 'Religion in the Middle Years' on pp 146–149, March 1990; 'Our Whole Lives for God' on pp 131–134, September 1987; 'Citizens of Heaven' edited version, on pp 259–264, October 1987 (original 12 May 1974).

Trinity College Bulletin, Faculty of Divinity of the University of Glasgow for the use of 'The Work of a Central City Parish' on pp 252–256, November 1966.

'In hoc Signo' on p 82, from *Through The Christian Year*, SCM Press, London, 1933.

Thanks are also due to 'Charles' for allowing the use of correspondence on pp 128–131.

PART I
Biography

INTRODUCTION

John McIntyre

Scotland has never been short of *theological* accounts of the nature of the Christian ministry, as the ministry of Word and Sacraments, of the apostolic tradition within which that ministry stands, or of the authority of that ministry in the judgment of the Church's ecumenical partners. Such authenticity, formally impeccable and wholly supportable in the cut-and-thrust of conciliar debate, however, does scant justice to the richness, variety and range of such ministry, as it was practised, or rather, as it was lived out, in the churches, the parishes, and homes of the country. In fact, the characterisation of the true face of the ministry in Scotland has in this century been exceedingly scant. There have been written in that period scarcely a dozen readable biographies or autobiographies of ministers of the Presbyterian Churches in Scotland; while, of the three thousand or so sermons preached every Sunday in Scotland, amounting to 150,000 in any one year, many of them written out fully, a small handful survive beyond twelve noon or eight o'clock of a Sunday evening. Here indeed are ephemera of a highly volatile order, and with such ephemera vanishes a massive volume of perception of the entire spectrum of the human condition in its political, economic, social, moral and spiritual dimensions, as well as the Church's understanding of the substance of the faith. Add to that loss the disappearance of the diaries of ministers, and their records of pastoral visits, or more grandly, their case-books, or still more grandly, their filofaxes, and the extent of our true ignorance of what the Church does, thinks, believes and plans, and of the part which the Christian ministry plays in these various enterprises, begins to emerge. Yet these things form the blood and bones, the flesh, muscles and sinews, the body, mind and spirit of the Church, and without them, and without the story of the people whose being they are, the Church and its ministry become fictions of theological reflection. Denied access to these all-important ephemera, we have to make-do with the 'paper Church', the construct of the official General Assembly Reports, 'the Blue Books', as we call them in Scotland, and pretend to knowledge of what the Church was 'thinking' in the twentieth century, with a certainty bred of hearing only one side of a case, or a story. Maybe, as Church historians, we should have been much more agnostic of the past than by nature we are, when we realise just how little of it has been preserved.

It would be wrong to create the impression that these two levels of operation—the ministerial/parochial and the General Assembly/Blue Book—are disparate and unconnected or, worse still, alien to one another. The minister is the conductor, or the semi-conductor, between the two levels, but a once-in-four-years membership of the General Assembly provides insufficient indoctrination or illumination to ensure effectively that the recorded word, whether of Assembly Reports or official journals, is a safe guide to what the Church is thinking at any one time, even if there were an entity which might be regarded as the Church's uniform thinking. Pluralism is not the pre-emptive right only of the world religions to co-exist. It may also be a characteristic of the thinking and behaviour of groups within the Church.

Our intention here is to endeavour to preserve the shape of 'one man's ministry' and its content, always within touch of that officialdom, with its structured records. The method of doing so will be to provide a basic biography, defining the contours within which that ministry took place, the infinite variety of the environment with which it re-acted, and to some extent helped to determine. But the biography by itself might be in danger of being historical reconstruction, two-dimensional perhaps and even third-personal, if the figures will mix. So, to provide the third dimension, the first-personal immediacy, there will be opportunities to read what Hugh Douglas himself had to say on a comprehensive range of topics. By being able to pin-point the occasions on which the talks, addresses or reflections were delivered, we are in a position to ensure that the actual thinking and decisions, attitudes and actions of one member of the Christian ministry in the twentieth century have been fairly faithfully preserved. What will also emerge will be that the reality which is this 'one man's ministry' is a much more heterogeneous entity than could ever have been comprehended within theological formulae.

It comes as no surprise that this should be so, when we learn of the richness of the preparation of this 'one man' for his ministry. The phrase, 'preparation for the ministry' is often taken in the limited sense of the six or seven years which the candidate for the ministry spends at the university, or additionally, the one or even two years' probation, the narrow band of time in which he is thought to receive the skills and techniques, if not the wisdom, of his profession. For Hugh Douglas the picture was otherwise. He had a controlling notion in his thinking about life which he called 'Providence and the individual'—in fact he wrote quite a lengthy manuscript illustrating it—so that whatever overtook him was related in his interpretation to what God had in mind for him. It would be unwise to try to establish, even with all the advantages of hindsight, any one-to-one correlation between the preparation for the ministry which Hugh had, and the detail of its eventual unfolding and fulfilling. Nevertheless his ministry, in its broad outlines, interests and emphases can be traced to different aspects of his younger days. But the story of these years of preparation is interesting in and for itself.

CHAPTER 1

Hugh Douglas—
Early Years and University
John McIntyre

In an age in which family roots are widely researched, Hugh Douglas had a fairly clear picture of his, and the clerical flavour was strong, in that his father and his grandfather were both ministers. His grandfather, the Revd Peter Douglas, himself the son of a landscape gardener, decided to study for the ministry through the influence of the Revd Robert Murray McCheyne of St Peter's, Dundee. After attending St Andrews University and New College, Edinburgh, he was called to the Free Church, Inverkip on the Clyde and inducted in 1851, later in that same year marrying Ann Weir Bishop, whose father was a lawyer in Coatbridge. Peter Douglas ministered at Inverkip until ill health led to his retirement in 1880. Two interesting human contacts which occurred in that Inverkip ministry are recorded. He was presented with a family clock bearing the inscription:

To
The Rev Peter Douglas
from
The Highlanders of Skye
Labouring on the Wemyss Bay Line
In grateful recollection of his many labours
For their
Temporal and spiritual welfare

The second interesting contact of the Inverkip ministry was the decisive influence which Peter Douglas had on a young railway porter at Inverkip station. That was John McNeill. He helped to strengthen the faith of one who was to win world-wide fame as a minister and an evangelist. Hugh himself was later to encounter Mr McNeill, by then an old man, when Hugh, as a student, attended his meetings in Glasgow. McNeill's wit, as well as his lively illustrations, impressed him. In fact, if Hugh's record is true, McNeill must have been the original purveyor of 'holy wit'. For example, at a businessmen's lunch-hour meeting, he began by saying, 'They tell me that money talks. The only thing it has ever said to me is "Goodbye".' Another time, when a heckler shouted, 'Who was Cain's wife?', McNeill replied, 'My advice to you, young man, is never to be too interested in other men's wives'.

Ann Weir Bishop had died in 1874, having borne nine children of whom Hugh's father, Robert Baillie Douglas, was the youngest. On retirement, Peter Douglas had gone to live in Pollokshields, and his son, Robert Baillie Douglas, went to school there, entering Glasgow University at the age of fifteen. Graduating MA with Honours in Philosophy in 1890, he went on to Trinity College, Glasgow, for his ministerial formation. It was Trinity's heyday, with T M Lindsay in the Church History Chair, A B Bruce in New Testament, George Adam Smith in Old Testament, Henry Drummond in Natural Science, and James Candlish followed by James Denney in Systematic and Pastoral Theology.

Robert Douglas was ordained in 1894, and took up his appointment as a district missionary based on Jalna, in India, some 250 miles east of Bombay. The activities of the Free Church Mission consisted of medical care, education and evangelism. In 1903 he was married to Mary Osborne, having proposed to her by letter, being somewhat too shy to 'pop the question'. Thereby arose for the Douglas family what, in the next generation, Hugh was to call 'the prolific Osborne connection', including, notably, Osborne Mavor ('James Bridie'), Elizabeth Osborne, author of *The Ladies of Llangollen*, and Jack Osborne, a well-known elder in Cramond Kirk. The newly-weds returned to live in Alibag, situated on what was then wasteland between the mountains and the sea, south of Bombay. Hugh's mother had returned to Glasgow for the birth of Hugh, which took place on 11 September 1911, and returned to Alibag with him when he was two months old. Thereafter followed for the small family years of broken relationships dictated by the conditions obtaining then in missionary service: notably, the five-year tour, with furloughs punctuated by regular deputation responsibilities. From Alibag, Hugh's father supervised a large district, with a High School in the town, district primary schools, and two nearby Leprosy Asylums. Hugh and his mother returned to Glasgow in late summer 1914, to be joined later by his father. In the interval before the father's arrival, Mrs Douglas had been attempting to keep the memory of his father fresh in Hugh's mind by asking him to look at and kiss his father's photograph which stood on the mantelpiece. When father did arrive, Hugh waking to find him in the room, put to him the puzzled question, 'Why aren't you on the mantelpiece?'

In 1915 the family returned to Alibag, of which Hugh had some abiding memories—of learning to swim, of watching the harvesting of the coconut crop, and of a constant stream of guests fleeing the heat and humidity of Bombay. Two interesting guests were Dr J H Moulton, known to generations of divinity students for his *Introduction to the Study of New Testament Greek*, who was sadly lost at sea in 1917 when his ship was torpedoed on his voyage home; and Dr Winifred Rushforth, previously a medical missionary of the United Free Church, but perhaps better known for her work in the Davidson Clinic in Edinburgh, both during and after the Second World War. In 1917 the family moved into Bombay and spent some time in residence in Wilson College, but the climate was so debilitating in the city that Hugh was sent to Kodaikanal School run by American missionaries. Since he was not happy there, when given the choice of returning to it, or going back to Glasgow, to live with his aunts, Nancy, May and Edith Osborne, he elected to join the aunties. So Hugh in January 1919 was dispatched home, under the care of fellow-missionaries of his parents, Mr and Mrs W G Wilkie Brown, returning home on furlough with their family of five.

So began Hugh's Scottish schooldays, and he remained at Glasgow Academy until he entered the University of Glasgow. On the whole he enjoyed school, although to begin with he was ahead of his class age-group and, being physically less tough than some of his peers, he came to rely on the sharpness of his tongue to enable his escape from a tight corner. Nor did he take kindly to the regimented dress of the kilt, the tweed jacket and the Eton collar.

But the masters, beginning with the Rector, seem to have left with him a not altogether unfavourable impression. The Rector, Edwin Temple, 'Ted' to the lads, reigned from 1899 to 1932, and in that time amassed around him apparently more anecdotes, fables and myths than is the sad lot of most Heads. To one offender, by name Smith, he said, 'Up on the form, you miserable fellow, Smith. You'll live to be hanged! You'll live to be hanged!' Quite a few years later, at the School Sports, he met up with Smith again, and said, 'Ah Smith. Not hanged yet? Not hanged yet?' He knew all the boys personally when they were at school, but, even more remarkably, he remembered them years afterwards. Jack Buchanan, a very well-known star of musical comedies in the years between the two World Wars, was appearing in the Glasgow Alhambra as top-billing, with all the attendant publicity. Calling on the Rector of his old school, he was recognised at once; and after recalling incidents in Buchanan's school career, the Rector asked, 'And tell me, Buchanan, what are you doing now?' The Rector himself taught Scripture and led worship in the gymnasium each morning. Before leaving school eventually, each boy received from the Rector the prayer, 'Teach us to stand for the hard right against the easy wrong'. Of him Hugh was to say, 'I owe him much'.

The subject of English produced some interesting characters. One Peter Couper instilled a proper use of the language by the exposition of his own little blue *Academy English Grammar for Beginners*, and brought accurate pronunciation to Clydeside in the dead of winter, by insisting that his young charges said, not 'Feb-yoo-ary', but 'Feb-roo-ary'. His successor was Walter Barradell-Smith, who doubled as a writer of school stories under the pseudonym of Richard Bird. He encouraged anyone with the least talent for writing, and prescribed large sections of Shakespeare and Palgrave's *Golden Treasury* to be memorised.

Hugh enjoyed his years at Glasgow Academy, where, despite having contracted mumps on the eve of the Higher Leaving Certificate Examinations, he was awarded the Certificate on the basis of orals. He left school with a solid grounding in Latin, Greek and English, which was to stand him in good stead both at the university and in his ministry. He had always been bright at school and it was no surprise when he was joint-dux medallist. Rugby had proved to be an absorbing pastime, stimulated no doubt by the fact that the mid-twenties were successful years for the Glasgow Academicals.

Three other circumstances from the school years deserve mention. First, during these nine years Hugh lived at nine different addresses, sometimes with his aunts, and for a period of four years with his mother, and even then the address changed. This experience of having 'no fixed abode', on the one hand, must have deprived him of the sense of security and stability which is synonymous with the word 'home'; in fact he said that he had 'no real home' until his parents purchased a house at Cove on the Clyde in 1933. On the other hand, this absence of an abiding home in his own youth made his own home, in three manses, all the more dear to him in later years, and ensured that it was a homely place for all who visited it.

Second, in view of the absence of his parents for long periods in India, Hugh did not get to know them very well— his mother who was at home for extended furlough from time to time perhaps better than his father, whose mission tours were normally five years in duration. In fact, to run on ahead, it was not until Hugh was 24 years of age, in 1935, that his father finally came home from India, after 41 years of service.

Even then, despite their efforts to get to know each other better, father and son remained shy with each other and they did not achieve a close relationship.

Third, Hugh confessed to no great interest in the organised religion of the Churches. His diversity of addresses enabled him to gain a range of experience of the preachers of the day, among whom, rather perceptively, he selected Adam Burnet of Westbourne, and later of St Cuthbert's, Edinburgh, as most outstanding. He found no fellowship in the congregations themselves (a situation for which he rather honestly accepted some of the blame, because of his shyness), and the ministers in their conventional garb of frock-coats and silk hats, even on weekdays, proved off-putting. What saved the day for Hugh, as for so many schoolboys of his and immediately following generations, was the Scottish Schoolboys' Club, 'SSC' for short. Several aspects of SSC appealed to schoolboys. It had a remarkably fine group of leaders, such as John Kerr, one of the finest batsmen in the history of Scottish cricketing, Willie Boyd and Dougie Smith, in addition to famous rugby players of the international standing of Max Simmers and Malcolm Allan, with Stanley Nairne, the founder of boys' and men's clubs in Scotland, being the inspiration of the whole movement. These leaders, and only a few have been mentioned, held Sunday afternoon meetings usually in their own homes, the meetings taking the form of discussion of the nature of Christianity, and its relation to the issues of the day. There was never any coercion to conform. Another attractive feature of SSC was the annual Easter camp, attended by over 300 boys when Glasgow and Greenock schools only were involved, and by some 650 when the Edinburgh schools also participated. Discussion groups were part of the forenoon ritual, as well as games, while each evening, after a rousing sing-song in the big marquee, the challenge of the Christian faith was presented in a direct and attractive way by one or other of the leaders. The story has yet to be written of the way in which the SSC, with its sensitive and understanding approach, literally saved for the faith hundreds of boys who had had Hugh's experience of the organised Church.

Glasgow University: Arts and Divinity

Hugh entered Glasgow University in 1928 to study for an honours degree in Classics, and during that first year he was able to stay with his parents, his father being home on one of his rare furloughs. He confessed to studying with greater industry when at home, for he was anxious to win scholarships, as his father had done, and thus ease the financial pressure on parents whose income from a missionary's stipend was not extensive. In this regard, he was very successful. Those were the days when Classics classes were much larger than they are now, the diminution being due largely to the dropping of Latin as a compulsory subject in the so-called Ordinary Arts degree, and, to a lesser extent, the disappearance of Greek from the BD degree. Latin I had 200 students, and Greek 60 students, small perhaps by comparison with the 600 in MacNeile Dixon's English I class. The size of such classes seriously reduced contacts between professors and students, which was only partly atoned for by the sociability of some of the junior staff.

Rugby, which Hugh had played at school up to the level of the second XV, now served to provide him with a number of things. In the teams for which he played, he found an immediate camaraderie of a robust and extrovert type. Progressing within a year from the fifth XV to the seconds, he finally played for the firsts for his last four seasons and was awarded his first XV Colours, which gave him standing among his peers in the university. By the time he was known to be a candidate for the ministry, his sporting prowess did the image of the ministry no harm. He has left us an amusing combination of the sacred and the secular in a record of an exchange during a game, in which the frustrated forwards complained to the backs in the suitably amended words of a well-known hymn, 'Courage, brother, do not fumble'. They received from the backs the sharp reply that the forwards supplied them with so little 'good ball' that the opportunity to 'fumble' never occurred.

From Hugh's perspective, the university social life was an even-keeled affair. There was little regular or heavy drinking, probably because students were not, in those years when the depression was biting, at all affluent. Drugs were unknown, and tobacco, still considered to be a harmless indulgence and cheap in whatever form, one of the few of life's comforts. Hugh's perception of the sexual life of his contemporaries was that it was fairly restrained, extra-marital sex being much less common than today, and students not contemplating marriage until they felt themselves sufficiently secure financially to maintain a wife and family. It is difficult to resist the conclusion that during these seven years in the university, Hugh was firming up the attitudes to sex and marriage which were to be so convincingly presented when he wrote the pamphlet *What is Christian Marriage?* for the Iona Community in 1944, and in many later sermons, addresses and broadcasts.

Though Hugh had gone up to the university with the intention of becoming a lawyer, despite the hopes of his parents that he would be a minister, he seems never to have lost his faith even though he was not over-enthusiastic about the organised Church. His faith was sustained and challenged in a number of ways. For example, he came under the influence of the Student Christian Movement, which, supported by two outstanding figures in the university, the Revd Archie Craig, Chaplain to the University, and Professor A A Bowman of the Chair of Moral Philosophy, spoke with no uncertain voice concerning the meaning of the faith and its implications for person and nation.

Also, his social conscience was quickened, almost in preparation for the Govan days to come, by his work with a small Boys' Brigade company attached to the Anderston mission of the Claremont Church, which he was at that time attending. Although already aware of some of the difficult conditions which obtained in Glasgow from visiting in Partick with his mother, he was nevertheless deeply shocked by what he encountered in Anderston, in the vermin-infested, insanitary hovels in which some of the boys lived, with single stair-head toilets for six families, and one cold water tap in the kitchen to serve the whole household for all purposes.

But it was in the context of the SSC, to which we have already referred, that the deepest change was to come. The members of the Sunday Meeting, which he had been attending over the winter, were to have a summer camp at Portavadie on Loch Fyne in the summer of 1931, and Hugh was given the task of arranging a programme for the evening talks, a regular feature of such camps, around the theme of 'Vocation'. As he worked on his assignment, it began to come home to him that he had not thought, in such terms, about the career in law which he was planning for himself. He had drifted into it. So for three weeks he was under considerable pressure, as if God were leading him in a direction which he wished earnestly to avoid. Finally, in his own words, 'Not without a good deal of inner conflict, I made up my mind to study for the ministry'. Looking back on this decision, Hugh saw it as no 'Damascus Road' blinding illumination, but as part of a plan and purpose which God in his providence had been working out in his life. All that had gone before, and what was still to come, was his preparation for the ministry.

But that one decision led to some immediate actions—the returning of scholarships which he had been awarded as a law student, and, more urgently, study for the entrance examinations in divinity for Trinity College, in the subjects Hebrew, English Bible and Moral Philosophy. Meanwhile, the Classics Finals were looming close as the summer of 1932 approached. The event was a happy one, with thirteen of the finalists, including Hugh, receiving Firsts; among the others, there were many names which were to become distinguished in later life: such as Robert Cross, later Professor of Logic in Aberdeen University, Annie Robertson, later a leading authority on Scottish Roman archaeology, James McGuinness, a future Under-Secretary of State at St Andrew's House (the Scottish Office), and Charles Stewart, the outstanding Secretary of the University of Edinburgh for many years.

After the pressures of an Honours classics course, Hugh

did not find himself unduly burdened by the intellectual responsibilities imposed upon him by Trinity College, Glasgow. A number of circumstances eroded the attention which he might have given to his studies. For example, despite his skill in Classics, he was not greatly attracted to the discipline of Hebrew, and it is a 'discipline' in both senses of the term. A passing enthusiasm for the subject had been stimulated in him by the lively teaching of Professor John Edgar McFadyen, but his death in 1933, and the less fascinating, if equally scholarly, didactic method of Professor W B Stevenson, failed to keep the flickering flame of interest alive.

The other members of staff at Trinity made their peculiar contributions to the store of Hugh's memories, with no single one catching his imagination, or enthusing him with an integrated theological set of convictions. Professor A J Gossip of the Department of Christian Theology and Practical Theology was an outstanding preacher, and—a fact which endeared him to Hugh—a regular spectator of the rugby matches at Westerlands, the University ground. A not unobservant spectator either, for, on one occasion, after watching the annual match between Trinity and New College, Edinburgh, he remarked that Hugh had 'played Christian football', a compliment or an insult, Hugh could not decide which.

His formation in the field of Practical Theology came from a different Professor, Dr Archibald Main of the chair of Church History, who had engaged Hugh as his Reader (or assistant) when Dr Main was interim moderator at Hillhead Parish Church. They had long talks on Sunday evenings, when, with Mrs Main and their daughter, Maisie, the Professor entertained him to supper. The then Principal, Professor W M Macgregor, Hugh admired more for the literary quality of his sermons than for the kindness of his wit, which appears to have had an acerbic flavour, which could on occasion be hurtful.

What, perhaps more than any academic considerations, robbed Hugh of the concentration which would have led him to master Senior Hebrew and pass the second year degree examinations in the subject, was an invitation by George MacLeod to become his assistant at Govan Old Parish Church in September 1934. Professor G H C MacGregor, to whom Hugh was apologising for failing to qualify for the BD Finals, through not passing the second year BD examinations in the subject, and so being unable to specialise in New Testament with Garth, said in reply that, 'the Govan experience was worth the loss of a BD'. Thus began what was to be the most influential period of Hugh's preparation for the ministry.

CHAPTER 2

Hugh at Govan

John McIntyre

It is perhaps best to regard Hugh's period at Govan as a continuum, even though he began in 1934 as a student assistant—he had still one year of study to do in order to complete the course at Trinity College—was licensed to preach the Gospel by the Presbytery of Glasgow in 1935, was ordained in 1937, was a member of the Govan team from the beginning, but carried a special responsibility when George MacLeod left to found the Iona Community in 1938. There were, as there still are, two elements in the Govan situation—the Church of St Constantine, or colloquially, Govan Old Parish Church, and the Pearce Institute (these two elements being differentiated only in name, for they were regarded then, again as they still are, as a united fellowship, making a single witness to the Gospel in the Clydeside parish of Govan).

The Pearce Institute, commonly known as the 'PI', adjacent to the Church, had been gifted by Lady Pearce, widow of Sir William Pearce, a ship-builder, 'for the religious, educational, social and moral welfare of the inhabitants of Govan generally'. A codicil to her will, however, bequeathed the property to the minister and Kirk Session of Govan Old Parish Church. When George MacLeod was called to Govan in 1930, he chose to live, not in the manse in Paisley Road West, but in the top flat of the Pearce Institute, having it converted to living quarters for himself and his bachelor assistants. Because of liberal endowments to the Church for the securing of assistants, and George's own generosity in making part of his own stipend available for subsidising the work of the team, the Church and the PI benefited from the services of a much larger staff than any other congregation in the Church of Scotland.

Over his five years in Govan, Hugh worked closely with colleagues who later became famous in a variety of contexts. Harry Whitley, who distinguished himself as leader of the boys' and men's clubs, was the senior assistant on Hugh's arrival, and left soon after to take a charge in Port Glasgow, and of course to be elected eventually to the High Kirk of Edinburgh. Duncan MacGillivray had what 'Hugh himself once called 'a mild appearance and a quiet manner', veiling however resolute determination and powers of administration, linked to expertise in matters artistic and symbols ecclesiastical. David Cairns was also there for a short time after Hugh arrived, but departed for his first charge in Bridge of Allan, arriving eventually in Aberdeen in the Chair of Practical Theology in Christ's College. Andrew Easton, who had come as the other student assistant with Hugh, had been in business before entering the ministry, and despite a rather cherubic appearance was very competent in handling awkward situations in the boys' club or the Boys' Brigade. Joining the team later came Walter Hendrie to take over the boys' club, to be joined, in Hugh's final year, by Uist Macdonald, giving him support in the difficult months after George's departure.

But the half hath not been told. For, in addition to the men, there were lady members of the team: Elizabeth Craig, a senior Church Sister, who ran the women's organisations with efficiency; May Mackinnon, a cheerful and reliable secretary; and Isabel Rutherford, who later married Hugh, was in charge of the Girls' Club, with eventually 300 members and 60 voluntary workers. Hugh wrote later that though Miss Rutherford's 'trim figure and apple-blossom complexion' had not gone unobserved, she and he had no inkling, 'vibes' we would call them nowadays, that one day their relationship would be much closer than that of two team members, not infrequently engaged in arguments over the use of rooms for their respective clubs. They did eventually co-operate as well as argue, when they joined forces to run a Community Dance Club on Saturday evenings, being the PI answer to the sleazy, unattractive local dance halls which provided the only entertainment for the young folk in the parish.

The leader of this team, whose composition seemed to change annually and to remain nevertheless on a uniformly high level of efficiency, was George MacLeod, the constant factor sustaining it both by inspiration and example. His story has been told with much perception and wit by Ron Ferguson in his biography, *George MacLeod* (Collins: London 1989) and it is unnecessary to trace George's life-story up to the point which we have reached in Hugh's, except where it is of interest to see the events at Govan from 1934 to 1939 through a different pair of eyes, and still from within the situation. What Hugh has conveyed in telling about his time in Govan is the impression which George made on those who worked closely with him by day, and shared the fellowship of the top flat when the day's labours were ended. For example, when we recall the lukewarmth with which Hugh had regarded ordinary Church life in his years at school and at the university, finding a substitute in the SSC and the SCM, we realise that it was George who gave him the vision and the experience of the reality of the Church fulfilling God's purpose in the world, in the distress, in the social depravities and the unemployment, together with the excitement of Govan. It was ministerial formation of a high quality, combining the firm, but kindly, word of correction, the truth spoken in love, with the confidence that tasks could be delegated and accomplished without fussy interference or irritating supervision. From the start Hugh was caught up in the climax of the Mission of Friendship (21–28 October 1934); and with Robin Scott of the Barony Church as missioner, he was introduced to a style of comprehensive evangelism which brought folks of all ages into Govan Old, morning, noon and night, and to a warmth of fellowship which he had nowhere previously encountered. Congregational members, greatly fearing, went out into the parish, only to return with a sense of release and joy. Membership increased, but for George and the team the most significant consequence was the change in the life of the congregation itself. This experience provided the framework within which Hugh's work was to be set, and it set a standard for his own ministry.

But the grim reality of the social context remained and Hugh felt it deeply. Clyde shipbuilding had brought distinction to Scotland and to the Govan parish over decades, but the depression in the early 1930s took its sad toll of the spirit of men whose craftsmanship was no longer required. As he visited in the squalor of over-crowded and insanitary housing and witnessed personally the plight of young people in the extremes of tuberculosis induced by these conditions, he realised that 'ambulance work' was never going to solve such drastic problems. Solution would lie in the hands only of an elected government. Forever after, Hugh was convinced that the Church must be articulate on political issues; so much so that, in a BBC television interview with Ronnie Falconer in December 1969, he said, 'All that was happening to help the unemployed [in Govan during the Depression] didn't seem to be radical enough. It obviously needed a political solution and that's one reason why I've voted soundly Labour ever since'. It is interesting to think, against the new background of the 1989 General Assembly's talk about 'the theology of the poor', that in 1935 Hugh was saying that 'the Church had to speak out on behalf of the poor and the underprivileged'. One wonders how his view, carrying with it all the weight of the subsequent Iona Community, came to be lost in the intervening years. I cannot believe that it was, for indeed the seemingly new emphasis coming from South America and Liberation Theology, which is the present-day source of the 1989 General Assembly's 'theology of the poor', is only the repetition of a theme which has been in the Govan-Iona tradition for fifty years and more.

But there were positive things happening all the time in

Govan which stretched Hugh's understanding of the ways in which the Church might tackle the soul-destroying conditions of unemployment and ill-housing. The Fingalton Mill project, which Ronald Ferguson describes (*George MacLeod*, pp 124ff) so fully, became not only a conference centre, but a fun-place, as we would call it now, for crowds of Govanites who had had scant acquaintance with the open countryside, and who greatly enjoyed the ride in the bus driven by George Adie and the dip in the pool at the end of it. The official opening of the pool, an occasion for which a large crowd of Govanites had turned out, was not without its moment of special excitement. An ample matron accidentally fell into the pool minutes before the little ceremony began, and it fell to Hugh to drive her home to Govan in George's car. Her neighbours looked upon her 'with wild surmise' as she emerged from the car, dripping, and scantily wrapped in George's dressing-gown. In 1935 the Mill housed the first camp of Borstal boys, and proved to be an earnest of the development for similar purposes of a Community centre in the next decade at Camas on the island of Mull across the Sound of Iona from the Abbey.

Out of the Fingalton Mill project grew the organisation known as 'The Vanguard', headed by Hugh. It was a small Christian movement in answer to the many movements attracting the loyalties of the young in the 1930s. It was for men, under 35 years of age, who committed themselves to attend church every Sunday, meet fortnightly for a half-hour talk, a half-hour discussion, and a half-hour of physical training, with no smoking and no 'attractions'. Twenty members of 'The Vanguard' formed the hard core of Christian Highway, founded by Duncan MacGillivray under the aegis of the Home Board of the Church of Scotland, to mingle with the crowds of hikers and bikers who thronged the roads and by-ways of the West Highlands, from Loch Lomond north-wards. Duncan held services at the Youth Hostels which were the natural gathering-places for the young.

Living within the team led by George MacLeod, Hugh

inevitably imbibed the leader's views of the value of parish mission, of the integration of the sacred and the secular, of work and worship, and of religion covering the whole of life and not being only a part of it, or even *apart* from it. Of all of these major subjects, Hugh's own understanding gradually stabilised, but it was not a kind of blind following, or simply an acceptance of the brilliant philosophies of the charismatic prophet of Govan. On the contrary, not only did George expect his assistants to carve out their own line in the areas of their responsibility, but also Hugh had ample empirical opportunities to put these philosophies to the test, not least of all when George eventually decided to leave Govan for Iona and invited Hugh to carry on in the parish to ensure continuity in the implementation of all of the enterprises for which Govan was now famous.

The times at Govan were not without their lighter side for Hugh. He appreciated Clydeside humour, which some of us believe is among the richest in the world. He tells of how, one night at the Boys' Club, two members, Jimmy Laurie and James Elder, brought to him a new recruit with 'an infectious grin, and a head slightly tilted to one side'. On asking his name, Hugh received the answer, 'He's Awtie Jackson'. Not immediately recognising the Christian name of which 'Awtie' was an abbreviation, Hugh had to pursue his enquiries after the original, only to be told, 'His real name is Donald, but we cry him "Awtie". Cin ye no' see his heid's *awtie* yin side?' Awtie was to have a bright future as a member of the Club and later of the Church, eventually becoming a resident of California.

In a different context, in 1937 Glasgow University resolved to honour George MacLeod with an honorary DD. The Govan congregation was delighted, sharing, as it were, in the honour. It did create problems of comprehension, however. One old lady whom Hugh visited could not understand the honour at all, and asked, 'Whit's this the Yoonie's daein' tae Mr MacLeod?' 'They're giving him a DD', answered Hugh. 'Whit fur? He's no' been sittin' oany exams, his 'e?' 'No, no.

This degree is for merit, not for passing exams'. 'Merit, merit? Mr MacLeod's no' merri't, he's a bachelor'.

It was perhaps the very success of the many enterprises at Govan which finally brought to a head George's decision to move on to a wider field of action. But it was not a course of action which he 'entered upon lightly or unadvisedly'. Ron Ferguson has told of the agonising that preceded the final decision to leave Govan; but for Hugh the agonising was something that he lived with, in its acutest stages from the summer of 1937 until the final departure in 1938. He was party to the endless discussions about the relation of the new Community to the Church of Scotland, as well as about the availability of water in the Abbey precincts, to mention only two matters of paramount importance. For Hugh, there was still greater stress to follow.

Of immense strength to Hugh as he faced the task of holding the fort at Govan, as well as the joy which it brought to them both, was his engagement to Isabel Rutherford, whom we have already encountered as a member of the team from the earliest of Hugh's days in Govan, and as the leader of the Girls' Club. The story of the actual engagement is worth hearing for itself, for it is not an undue invasion of privacy, and because it brings out once again the shyness and diffidence in Hugh which he had always acknowledged in himself. He had decided to take Isabel to meet his mother, who by this time was living at Cove. In an understandable pre-occupation he forgot that the Craigendoran steamer did not stop at Cove, so he and Isabel were compelled to go on to Dunoon, returning to Cove somewhat later. The visit over, Isabel and Hugh were returning by train from Craigendoran to Glasgow, and Hugh chose an early point of the journey to propose to Isabel, when they were alone in the carriage. The proposal and the acceptance were only just completed when the train stopped at a station, and they were joined by some half-dozen passengers, who unwittingly but no less effectively inhibited any farther exploration of mutual feelings, attitudes and affection. Thus inauspiciously began what Hugh was later to describe as 'a partnership which was one of the greatest rewards of [his] years in Govan', a partnership which was a constant and inspiring component in all their joint achievements in the long years of ministry which lay ahead of them.

In the period after George's departure, Hugh had the support over the summer of 1938 of George Balls, prior to his departure for Union Theological Seminary, New York, and also of Uist Macdonald, one of the first of the young ministers to join the Community, with Walter Hendrie still continuing to be in charge of the Boys' Club. Quite apart from the responsibility to 'keep the show on the road', there arose extra-curricular problems in the shape of a petition raised by some of the younger members of the congregation, to present to the Presbytery, urging that George be allowed to return to Govan as minister, assisted by a competent colleague, while remaining as leader of the Iona Community. Govan would be the urban centre for the practical earthing of the challenge of Iona, the *praxis* to match its *theoria*. Opposition to the petition came, on the one hand, from elements in the congregation, who, despite their paucity of numbers, lingeringly still opposed what George had been doing in Govan; and, on the other, officially from the Interim Moderator and the Presbytery, who in the end had two cards to play. One was that the list of signatories to the petition, of whom there were 2,000, included names of persons no longer on the Govan roll, thus rendering the petition invalid. The second was a statement of George's that, rather than allow the matter to be protracted through debates by Presbytery, he would be willing to accept the decision of the Business Committee of the Presbytery, which in the event was that it was not competent for George to be both leader of the Iona Community and minister of Govan Old Parish Church. The story has been told, and rightly, from George's and the Community's side, and, with hindsight, the lost opportunity occasioned by the legalist decision stands revealed as damaging to the advancement of the Gospel in urban communities for years to come, as well as to the imaginative re-designing of ministerial formation in the second half of the twentieth century. But we must also spare a thought for Hugh, who was himself never one for self-pity. For, in the middle of what had become a national as well as a Church *cause célèbre*, and of the bitterness which such controversy inevitably generates, he had to maintain all the ordinances of the Church, weekdays and Sundays, at the old pitch. But he had the additional burden of being the go-between for George and his supporters, and he had to do so within the bounds of even-handed neutrality. Even then he was under suspicion from George's opponents.

Undoubtedly, the arguments had begun to affect the spirit of the congregation by Christmas 1937. It had always been one of the happiest of the Christian festivals at Govan, but that year it seemed to have lost its sparkle. There was a typical Glasgow pea-souper depressing everyone; but worse, the persons normally responsible for the Christmas decorations in the church had failed in their duty. Hugh himself was afflicted with incipient tonsillitis, but Isabel and he made a desperate last minute effort to introduce some greenery. Even so, they were themselves not in the greatest of spirits, when out of the fog appeared Robin Yellowlees, a sheep-farmer from Strachur. He had brought with him legs of mutton and lamb, with potatoes and other vegetables. Armed with the names and addresses of the most needy in the parish, he went off to distribute his largesse. War was soon to break out, and Robin, joining the RAF, lost his life early on a training flight. His family donated the candelabra in Iona Abbey in memory of him.

These months in Govan after George's departure left Hugh not a little disillusioned, aware as never before of the unsavoury aspects as he saw them of inflexible Church practice and procedure, resolved that he would never allow himself to be involved in a similar situation. Accordingly, he submitted his name to the Probationers Committee, willing to go where they, in their wisdom, would send him. He was, in the event, sent as one of three probationers to preach for the vacant charge of St John's, Leven, to which he was duly elected, and was inducted in February 1939.

As we reflect on these years which Hugh spent with George at Govan, on the quite remarkable degree to which he absorbed the ethos and inspiration of what George was doing and seeking to do, it is hard to understand why one solution was not sought to the impasse created by George's wish to retain a Govan connection and the Presbytery's intractability through its Business Committee. I refer to the proposition that Hugh himself should have been called to the charge of Govan Old. Admittedly, there were in Scotland, and furth of it too, no doubt, many who were casting envious glances in the direction of the Govan charge. But, given 2,000 supporters of the petition, there existed a corporate will towards a solution which would retain, and allow, George's interest in Govan. Hugh was sufficiently 'his own man' by 1939, indeed had been encouraged by George to be so, not to be simply a tool in the hands of the Community or its leader. In his office as minister of the charge and with his sympathy for the Iona Community, he would have facilitated all the developments of ministry in the urban community, which had been George's dream. No doubt the possibility must also have crossed Hugh's mind; it was a measure of his disillusionment that it went no farther. Govan was the loser, and in some senses also the Iona Community.

CHAPTER 3

St John's, Leven
(1939–42)

John McIntyre

Hugh was inducted to the charge of St John's, Leven in February 1939, a charge which has since united with others. Isabel and he were married in April, but before they had properly settled in to the manse and the parish, the Second World War began. Within weeks of the declaration of war, he was deeply concerned about whether he ought to become an Army Chaplain. He had lived too close to George MacLeod for four years not to be aware of the force of the pacifist argument. He recognised that war was the worst method of resolving international confrontational crises. But he appreciated that there is a degree of self-contradiction in the pacifist who accepts the safety provided by the armed forces or the police force, and that, *a fortiori*, there would be no place for a pacifist in the ranks of the Chaplains. Yet there was building up in his mind a sense that he could not be happy staying at home, and that he 'should have to bear the consequences of the nation's and [his] own sin, by enduring the consequences of war'. So by the beginning of October, he had almost reached the point of decision to become an Army Chaplain, arrangements having been tentatively made for his father to become *locum tenens* in his absence. With his customary discretion, Hugh decided to air the proposal unofficially with some of the members of the Kirk Session, and it was immediately clear that they did not wish him to go. The call to Hugh and the immediate success of his ministry had brought to an end a rather difficult time in the history of the Church, and the return to a period of unsettlement with no fixed minister would soon undo the good already achieved. But, generously, they would not stand in his way. To settle the matter in his own mind, he said that he would write to the Chaplains' Committee to discover whether they had a lengthy waiting-list. His decision was to stay in St John's, not with any feeling that it was a second best, but rather because of his conviction that he was 'doing as valuable a piece of work as [he] could do anywhere—*just now*'.

What is remarkable, from the perspective of fifty and more years on, is the extent to which the normal ordinances of the Church were sustained through these early war years, and in some directions extended. Despite the exigencies of war-time conditions, a second service was held on Sundays, sometimes in the St John's hall at six o'clock; and when that provided only limited space for the numbers attending, it was held in the church at that hour in the summer, and at three o'clock in the winter. Hugh was writing in October 1939 about the daily services being regularly attended by 15 to 20, and sometimes as many as 30, people. The Woman's Guild went forward in strength, inviting mothers with young children to bring them to meetings, and arranging one evening meeting a month for those who could not come in the afternoon. Here surely was the hand of Isabel, who was to make her mark with such distinction in the Guild in later years. She had had a good apprenticeship.

The Girl's Association and the Girls' Guildry seemed to thrive alongside one another. The adjustment of age-range for both, the former for girls from 16 to 30 and the latter for those from 13 to 15, prevented any competition for the same personnel. Perhaps the Govan experience with young folks was most in evidence in the Fellowship of Youth, which Hugh defined regularly at the beginning of each new winter session as having three specific components. First was the sharing in the Youth Service on Sunday evenings in the church at six o'clock. This service he planned with the young folk in mind. Second, immediately after the service there was a Fellowship

Meeting, which took the form of lively discussion in which free expression of views was encouraged, especially concerning the implications of Christianity for everyday life. Third and finally, the evening closed with Family Prayers, taken in turn by the members of the Fellowship. A further innovation introduced by Hugh was the Weeknight Meeting, held on Fridays at 7.30 in the evening. The programmes were of four kinds—social, special (films or discussions), musical and talks.

In human terms, probably the most significant aspect of his time in Leven was the creation in the manse of the first experience of stable and continuing home life which Hugh ever enjoyed, created by the warmth of Isabel's affection, and by their identity of shared vision and dedication to it. Here the family were all born—the older girl, Molly, and the twins, Colin and Ruth. They sustained in no uncertain fashion—to leap a few decades ahead—the clerical tradition which Hugh had clearly valued in his own interest in his clerical predecessors: for Molly was to marry John Harvey who became eventually minister of Govan Old and then Leader of the Iona Community; Ruth married Norman Shanks, a senior civil servant at St Andrew's House, who entered the ministry, and after a very successful term as Chaplain to the University of Edinburgh, was appointed Lecturer in Practical Theology and Christian Ethics in the University of Glasgow; while Colin, the other twin, also entered the ministry and, after a charge in Airdrie, became minister of Dedridge, within the Ecumenical Parish of Livingston. Four generations of ministers—and a fifth probably coming along with Ruth Harvey, now a candidate for the ministry—how many generations does it take to make a dynasty?

As the story has gone so far, apart from its beginning, one might be forgiven for thinking that the War had not touched St John's. Quite the contrary. The limiting and trying conditions imposed by restrictions and blackout hit the Church, but these were impediments to test the loyalty and spirit of the congregation, and as such they were transcended with typical Fifers' courage and humour. The lists of those who went off to the War, and who more sadly did not return, were statistics which no minister worth his salt would ever fail to respond to. Hugh was a pastor, and—what is fast becoming a disappearing phenomenon—a *visiting* pastor, and he was instant in his attendance upon news of a bereavement or a dear one reported missing. These occasions he carried in his heart, and it was a form of ministry for which Govan, with all its rigours and depression, had not fully prepared him. But he grew into it quickly.

Hugh, however, could not insulate himself from what was happening in the rest of the country and on the battlefields of the world, and the motivation which in 1939 had raised so acutely the question of his becoming an Army Chaplain returned in another form. This time—it was now March 1942—he decided to spend from May to September in service with the Church of Scotland Huts. The decision was taken in response to a need for younger men to staff the Huts, sited at points of heavy troop concentration or in lonely parts of the country near gun-posts or searchlight batteries; or they might have to man a mobile canteen, to go out to units with no social facilities. In the more established of the Huts, the minister would be responsible not only for the day-to-day organising of the usual canteen food provisions, and programmes of concerts, debates, discussion groups and so on, but also for offering the ordinances of the Church in the form of daily prayers, Sunday services and the ever necessary pastoral counselling.

But by September of 1942, Hugh was sending to each member of the congregation a letter, in which he confirmed that he would shortly be leaving them to go to be minister in North Leith. He did so with regret, because Isabel, the family and he himself had all received much kindness from the congregation. There was no question of any dissension, and no recrimination over Hugh's departure. Hugh interpreted the call to Leith, as he had done the call to St John's, Leven, as something which he had not sought, but to which he had been directed. There was something essentially unworldly in his attitude to the two situations, and there never arose anything in either of the two ministries to suggest that he had been mistaken in his interpretation.

CHAPTER 4

North Leith Parish Church
(1942–51)

D H Whiteford

Hugh Douglas came then to North Leith Parish Church after a short ministry at St John's, Leven, in November, 1942. The North Leith manse was just a few doors away from my father's manse in Summerside Place. We were therefore close neighbours, but we also shared a common Osborne ancestry going back several generations, and belonged to a huge cousinage not unusual among Scottish families.

North Leith was a busy, thickly populated parish, with a mix of industry, shops, bonded stores, ships chandlers, the old barracks in North Fort Street, schools and garages; at one end streets of good class residences and at the other old type tenements running down to the docks.

It was a well staffed Church with a membership of over 1500 and with a set of unique and priceless communion silver, and was renowned for its famous 1st Leith Battalion of the Boys' Brigade. There were also five other Churches of Scotland in close proximity, plus a Baptist Church and a United Free Church (Continuing). In the 1940s all were well supported, but by any standard we were grossly over-churched, and although the move of people up the Ferry Road to the new housing areas at Granton and Crewe Toll had begun, the families who moved still maintained their connections with North Leith and regarded themselves as 'Leithers'.

The late Revd J R S Wilson, whom Hugh succeeded, had been a popular expository preacher much in demand at Evangelical Conferences, and he had made up a congregation in the Evangelical tradition of his time. Hugh came from a very different background. As we have seen, he had been assistant to Dr George MacLeod at Govan Old where he had been part of a ministerial team exercising a pastoral and social ministry which had put the Church at the centre of parish life. The insights, ideals and methods which Hugh had seen vitalize Govan he brought with him to North Leith, in many ways a parish not unlike Govan.

I became part of the North Leith team in April 1943, between service in the RAF and joining the Army as a Chaplain at the end of December. These were busy months, with visiting of housebound old folk up and down tenement stairs, and of patients in hospitals all over Edinburgh; with the Youth Fellowship on Sunday evenings, the 'BB' on Friday nights, the summer BB camp at Upper Cloan near Auchterarder; and a month on my own when Hugh and Isabel were on holiday on Iona, when I was thrown in at the deep end and had to cope with eleven funerals! In war-time North Leith, one visited on foot or on bicycle or by tram; motor cars and petrol were unknown.

We met on Monday mornings, Hugh, Jean Grieve, the Church Sister and myself, when the week's work was discussed and apportioned. If I was given thirty visits to do by next Monday, they were done, not because I was afraid that I would be given a dressing down if I had not done them, but because Hugh would have done his stint, and his share was always greater than mine.

Because of our family relationship we had much in common; he was only some eight years older, and there was no generation gap. He talked about his own hopes and beliefs in Gospel, Church and Ministry with quiet conviction. In the few months I was his assistant, he taught me better than he knew, for I shared his convictions and I have never had cause to depart from them.

He took immense care with people; he listened to them; he had endless patience. He did his best for people, even for those who were sometimes trying to use him, and he suffered fools, although perhaps not gladly. He had the ability to speak to people of all kinds, he took them as they were: the old soul alone in a dingy Leith tenement, the parents who had lost a son on war service, the young girl who was dying of tuberculosis; and in his sermons, prayers and his conduct of Sunday by Sunday worship, he gave encouragement to all who faced and feared the hardness and uncertainty of life in those grim war years.

In Hugh's first pastoral letter to his people (December 1942) he wrote:

> This is the beginning of a new ministry, but not I hope of a solitary ministry. You share in it along with me. We are fellow workers, not only with each other, but with God. Anything that I can do by myself will be of little use unless you join with me and lend me your support.

This was to be the basis of Hugh's ministry in North Leith, and beyond North Leith, for it was a principle of ministry from which he never strayed.

Things began to change in North Leith Parish Church, new ventures were begun, new experiments tried, most of them highly successful. A Youth Fellowship on Sunday nights was started, to discuss and explore what young people believed, if they believed, and why they believed, in the war-torn world of their time. A Life Boy Team was begun with 24 youngsters on the roll; a Bible Study Group replaced the old Wednesday night Prayer Meeting. But the new venture which broke with the previous parish patterns was the introduction for the first time of Holy Week services. This experiment had been thoroughly discussed and approved by the Kirk Session, but Holy Week services raised all kinds of ecclesiastical 'bogies'. So Hugh wrote:

> If anyone asks the reason for such an experiment being made, the answer is simply this: the two central facts in the Christian Faith are the Cross and Resurrection of Jesus

Christ. The purpose of any services during Holy Week is that we may be brought to a closer realisation of the meaning of the Cross and may share more fully in the wonder of the Resurrection.

Sixty people came to the Monday night service, 150 came to the Good Friday service. What Hugh had attempted to do was fully understood, approved and supported.

Coming as he did from a distinguished missionary family, Hugh was always keenly aware of the needs of the Church overseas, and sought to make this world-wide dimension of the Church's life a reality for those who were never likely to journey beyond the boundaries of Scottish Church life. North Leith had supported an Indian pastor at Kizum near Darjeeling for many years, and continued to do so. In 1948, however, Revd John Summers became North Leith's 'own missionary', linking the congregation with the work of the Hope Waddell Training Institution, Calabar, Nigeria; and in 1950 Miss Katherine Ramsay went out from North Leith to work at Jalna, India, where Hugh's father and mother had been missionaries.

British India and its future exercised the minds of politicians and churchmen before and during the war years, and especially among those families who had close ties with India. When would India be granted independence? What form would this take? Would India divide or remain one? Church Committees, Woman's Guilds, and Youth Fellowships all debated such questions. In 1944, at one of the evening services in September, the preacher was Mr Appadurai Aaron, Warden of the Students' International Club, Glasgow. In preparation for this visit Hugh wrote in the magazine:

After the service there will be a meeting in the Hall at which Mr Aaron will speak on the problem of India and the British Empire. This is one of the pressing problems of the day: and it is hoped that members and friends will take the opportunity which is offered of hearing the views of one who knows the situation so well, and who approaches it from a Christian viewpoint.

It is a little cameo from the past. History moves relentlessly on. Looking back over forty years one wonders how much or how little of Mr Aaron's hopes for his native land were fulfilled in 1947 at Independence, for history never quite turns out as we hope it will.

1942–1945 were war years, years of food shortage, clothing coupons, black-out, travel restrictions, war casualties, and preparations for D-Day and the defeat of Nazi Germany. But life must go on in home parishes no matter what is taking place elsewhere. In those difficult years much was done in North Leith to build up the congregation. Parish visitations were undertaken, congregational socials held for new members, parcels were sent to those on Active Service, the Leith Docks Canteen was staffed, and the Woman's Guild, the Youth Fellowship, the Sunday Schools, the BB all thrived. People were cared for pastorally, the Faith was preached, the Gospel lived, the numbers attending Church increased, financial support improved. It was all the result of an extremely active, thoughtful, carefully planned ministry to which people at all levels of parish life readily responded. For North Leith, Hugh was the right minister at the right time.

In the February magazine 1945, Hugh wrote commending George MacLeod's latest book, *We Shall Rebuild* (Iona Community: Glasgow 1944), the story of the work of the Iona Community on the island and on the mainland. What he said is worth quoting, for it reveals much of his own conviction and idealism, and his hopes and plans for North Leith.

Those of our congregation who are already friends of the Iona Community will have received copies of it, and as paper control limits the number of copies available, it is hoped that they will lend their copies to others to read. There is no doubt at all that this is a significant book. . . .

It is not to be expected that everyone will agree with what Dr MacLeod says, but it will not have escaped the notice of members of North Leith that recent experiments in our Church here, such as the service of Confirmation, the Communion services at Christmas and Easter, the Baptismal service with a family emphasis, and services during Holy Week, are all in line with the main trend of what the Iona Community is seeking to express. The parish visitation last September by which over fifty children were brought into our Sunday Schools, was a small 'try-out' of the principles of a congregational mission to a parish which is always central to the Community's work. If you can get this book, read it. It will set you thinking whatever else it does.

During the past 40 years the principles for the parish ministry set out in *We Shall Rebuild* have come to be accepted in parish after parish throughout Scotland by generations of ministers hardly now aware of their origin—but in the North Leith of the 1940s these were new ideas. They had to be fought for and proved. And it was through ministers like Hugh Douglas who found their idealism and vision nurtured by the Iona Community, and its distinguished Founder, that they have entered into the accepted pattern of our parish ministry today.

The years 1942–1946 had been busy and demanding ones for Hugh in which the foundation upon which he hoped to build in North Leith had been purposefully laid. It was fortunate that this basic work had been so thoroughly done, for what lay ahead in the years from 1946 to 1950 was to test the resilience, determination, faith and conviction of both minister and people in ways which they could not possibly have foreseen.

Nothing much had been done to the church building since 1879. Bomb damage had been sustained in 1941, but the church was still in use; only the windows had been blown in, or so it was believed. But the time had come, it was thought, to reconstruct the interior of the church more in line with contemporary liturgical and artistic principles. Plans were drawn up by Mr Ian G Lindsay, Architect, which involved the re-positioning of pulpit, organ, communion table, and a re-arranging of the choir area. The estimated cost was £6,000, a very considerable sum for a congregation to raise in those days. A Restoration Appeal was confidently launched.

Then 'Murphy's Law' began to operate: all that could go wrong did go wrong. It was discoverd that the roof of the church had been moved by the 1941 bombing and was in a highly dangerous condition; rot was discovered in the main beams of the galleries and in the South wall; and the hall roof was found to be in a dangerous state. So the congregation had to move to the hall for Sunday worship, put the hall roof right as a matter of urgency, and begin the task of raising a sum now far more than £6,000 for the immediate restoration of the church.

Throughout 1947, 1948, 1949 and into 1950 the slow work of reconstruction went on, and the steady work of raising the necessary funds went on. People gave, and gave again. Would the total sum required ever by reached? Was it beyond them? Bazaars were held, sales of work were organized, Church organizations all did their bit; donations came from well wishers far beyond North Leith; the Baird Trust helped. By the end of 1949 hopes were raised that the end was in sight, and that Easter 1950 would see the restoration completed. But the church was not quite ready by Easter; Restoration Day was 13th May, just before Pentecost, when the church was re-dedicated, Dr George MacLeod being the preacher on this historic day. Experts in church architecture have hailed what was accomplished at North Leith as one of the finest examples of the restoration of a Georgian church anywhere.

In his farewell sermon, looking back over his nine years as minister of North Leith, Hugh said:

I remember very clearly the days when we were in the throes of restoration . . . we did not have much money . . . there was considerable doubt even among the most loyal supporters of the scheme . . . and as work went on things seemed to be getting worse. On several occasions I went into the church at night . . . the water was dripping through the roof, the fungus was growing from the walls, everywhere there was dirt, dilapidation, scaffolding . . . a smell of dampness and rot. But I had a strong feeling that there were others who were with us in these days . . . the men who had ministered here before me . . . and all the others who had worshipped here and loved this place. You can call it imagination if you like, but to me it was a glimpse of the reality of our fellowship with the saints . . . and it gave me strength.

But does not God speak to us through our imagination making us vividly and compellingly aware of the truth we sometimes most need to know?

It must have been obvious to those who had to fill vacancies elsewhere in the Scotland of the time that the minister of North Leith was a likely candidate well worth considering; nor is the timing of such vacancies in the hands of those who will be called to fill them. Hugh left North Leith with real regret; many friends had to be left behind. But in the ministry he believed one goes where one is meant to go. It was the way he had come to North Leith, and it was the only way in which he could ever leave it. The call to Dundee Parish Church (St Mary's) was a new challenge and could not be refused. He said:

There are, I believe, certain things which we have all been able to learn here . . . parts of the Everlasting Gospel, which will certainly abide with me, and will also, I hope and pray, remain with you all.

CHAPTER 5

Dundee Parish Church (St Mary's) (1951–77)

Colin R Martin

There was a certain sense of inevitability in the Call to Hugh Douglas to be minister of Dundee Parish Church (St Mary's) in 1951. St Mary's was a prestigious charge with a high expectation of those who became its ministers. In their vacancy they were looking for a man of proven calibre and acknowledged gifts, a man of academic stature and intellectual ability, a good pulpit communicator with a caring pastoral interest. In Hugh Douglas, they unquestionably found such a man. The various threads of his experience in the ministry had formed a pattern which was to prove invaluable to himself, and which was equally to bring considerable benefits to the congregation and to the wider community in Dundee. Govan, Leven and North Leith had all been very different—different in challenge, different in demand, different in contribution— but together they formed a foundation of considerable strength for what was destined to be a deeply-appreciated 26 years of ministry in Dundee. Hugh was just about that magical age of forty, when 'life begins'—and in a sense, St Mary's was to be a new life for him.

St Mary's, Dundee has a very long history. A church dedicated to St Mary stood more or less on the centre city site now occupied by the present building from the twelfth century. That particular church, founded by David, Earl of Huntingdon, was probably small; and in a span of rather less than 200 years it suffered frequent and substantial damage from English invading forces. By the end of the fourteenth century, plans were put in hand to rebuild on the same site, and over the next one hundred years a Gothic church of great dignity and richness was completed, becoming one of the largest churches in Scotland at the time. Of that great structure, only St Mary's Tower, popularly known in Dundee as the Old Steeple, remains. This imposing single church was eventually put to the torch by English soldiers in 1548, and was never rebuilt as one church. The re-building which did take place almost immediately was of the Choir of the former building—the East end—and after the Reformation this became known as St Mary's or the East Church, the Parish Church of Dundee. Various developments of the adjoining areas took place later. The former South Transept was rebuilt in 1588, the North Transept in 1759, and the former Nave, attached to St Mary's Tower, in 1789. Thus the original St Mary's site was now occupied by four separate churches. Fire was once again to destroy the complex. On 3 January 1841, an overheated flue in the South Church began a conflagration which destroyed St Mary's, the South Church and the Cross Church, leaving only the Steeple Church and the Tower standing. The Town Council decided on a plan of rebuilding which would replace the three destroyed churches with two new ones. In 1844 the present St Mary's was completed. It is a church of considerable beauty, both externally and internally—a fitting place to continue to be known as Dundee Parish Church (St Mary's). These brief historical comments come from an excellent pamphlet on St Mary's which Hugh himself wrote around 1970.

The congregation Hugh was called to serve there represented a broad cross-section of the people of Dundee. By virtue of its physical position in the city centre, and of its ecclesiastical position as the Parish Church of Dundee, St Mary's hosted many official services; but in the regular Sunday-by-Sunday worship, there was gathered a congregation of considerable diversity from all parts of the city. Making this scattered congregation into a cohesive and established fellowship was a particular concern of Hugh's from the start of his ministry in

Dundee. Along with the work at St Mary's there was the Mission work at the Blackscroft, a particularly happy and devoted congregation on which many a St Mary's assistant (including myself) was destined to cut his ministerial teeth. Indeed, it says much for the Christian virtue and patience of the Blackscroft members that they accepted their role in the training of student assistants and probationers with a kindly stoicism—and, I suppose, the saving awareness that Hugh would always repair the more obvious evangelical damage! While the minister at St Mary's had no official responsibilities within the Town Council and the administration, St Mary's was the scene of the annual Kirking of the Council, and informal but strong ties were maintained with the City Fathers. Hugh was also invited to be Chaplain to Dundee High School, a post which he took very seriously and to which he gave great commitment. Contact with tertiary education involved Hugh, both personally and as minister of St Mary's, with University College, Dundee, later Queen's College of the University of St Andrews, and subsequently Dundee University. The academic respect in which he was held was recognised by both universities with the award of the degree of Doctor of Divinity from St Andrews in 1958, and the degree of Doctor of Laws from Dundee in 1971, coinciding with the end of Hugh's Moderatorial year.

Other chapters in this book make specific reference to many of the interests which were part of these 26 St Mary's years. There were 'one-off' situations like the celebrations for the 400th Anniversary of the Reformation in Scotland, when Hugh convened the organizing committee; or like the Moderatorial year in 1970–71. There was the development of consuming personal interests like marriage counselling, television work and the writing of *Coping with Life* (Arthur James: London, 1964, 2nd edition, 1988). There were appointments which recognized his growing stature in the national Church, such as his appointment to be a Chaplain to the Queen in 1959, and the appointment as Dean of the Chapel Royal in 1974. In a sense, given the calibre, the energy and the commitment of the man, these things were also almost inevitable. Hugh was a 'natural' for committees, boards and other appointments which needed authoritative leadership and unstinting commitment. He never struck me as an arrogant man, although I know that there were those who mistook a certain degree of reserve for aloofness. But he had undoubtedly a 'presence' compounded of the fact that he had physically a substantial impact, and also an aura of quiet self-confidence. I don't think I would characterize it as 'charisma' in the accepted modern sense of that term—but you couldn't ignore him! And people *didn't* ignore him, as is witnessed by the demands that were made on him in many fields.

But these St Mary's years were basically and primarily years of committed, unstinted, enthusiastic and fulfilling *parish* ministry. Leaving aside all the special services for particular bodies and groups, all the official occasions and formal demands, Hugh gave the St Mary's congregation leadership in worship which was intellectually satisfying and evangelically stimulating. The church itself fostered an atmosphere of dignity and beauty—the beauty of holiness—and the content of the services Hugh led Sunday by Sunday made further contribution to that atmosphere.

He was meticulous in his preparation. Despite the variety of demands on his time in the preparation of addresses, articles, broadcast scripts for all kinds of occasions, the priority of preparation for Sunday was paramount. Not for Hugh the regular last-minute rush of burning the midnight oil on Saturday. His aim was to have the various components of worship for Sunday safely gathered before Friday. Time in the study on Saturday night was part of his routine, but it was then a matter of ensuring that nothing had been left to chance rather than seeking some last-minute inspiration to cover the fact that everything had been left to chance. I would call Hugh a particularly good communicator rather than a gifted orator. Unlike some of his contemporaries—not least in Dundee at that time—he was not given to histrionics or theatrical presentations. He preached and got his message across with clarity of argument and a lack of affectation. There was a patent sincerity in prayer and preaching which was never contrived, yet always obvious.

In his pastoral work at St Mary's, Hugh was diligent and dedicated. He knew his folk, and he responded to their various needs. St Mary's was largely a gathered congregation, and the homes of members were widely scattered throughout the city. Priority visiting of the sick and infirm, the elderly and the shut-in members was a substantial burden, and involved careful planning to avoid unnnecessary running hither and yon, and criss-crossing trips which simply wasted valuable time. It was in the organization of his visiting pattern that Hugh demonstrated another particular strength. He kept his records very carefully. A card-index system was maintained rigorously, meaning that information was immediately to hand about each household. But that was very much a fall-back situation for others, for Hugh had an excellent memory and a speedy recall of circumstances and situations which had involved him personally and pastorally with individuals and families. Because he had that essential pastoral gift of being ready to listen before expressing an opinion or offering advice and counsel, his visits were appreciated. Large collections of letters sent to him, particularly at the time of his eventual retiral from St Mary's, are eloquent testimony to the compassion and concern he had shown to so many in their times of pain and pleasure, joy and sorrow; and the help, comfort and encouragement he had provided.

As was the case for so many others over the North Leith and St Mary's ministries, my personal contact with Hugh began when I was invited to become an assistant. In those distant days, Hugh had a kind of understanding with St Mary's College, St Andrews, which provided final year students who spent one year as student assistants, followed by one year as probationers. My personal arrival at St Mary's, Dundee, for my first duties as student assistant was less than auspicious. Commanded to present myself for Sunday morning worship duty, I went, as instructed by Hugh, to the back entrance to the church. As I went in, I was greeted by an impressive gowned figure I later came to know with respect and affection as John Sinclair, former member of the Dundee Catholic Apostolic congregation and for many years Church Officer at St Mary's. 'I've been waiting for you', he announced, and firmly led me into the Sanctuary, seated me in the back pew inside the side door, and said, 'Wait there'. And I waited, and waited, and nothing happened! People began to arrive for the service, and still I waited. Then in desperation I went back out the door, found John, and asked, 'How long do I have to wait?' 'Until your wife comes in with the baby', was the reply. I had been mistaken for the father of a child to be baptised that morning! My apologies for late arrival caused considerable amusement when eventually, flustered and shaken, I reached the vestry. I am happy to say that it didn't blight my assistantship, but it did provide Hugh with an often-repeated story at my expense.

There has always to be an anxiety that the distant past may be either idealized or dramatized. Rose-tinted glasses tend to colour our memories in a haze of nostalgic longing for the youth that is gone. But I say without hesitation and with complete honesty that what I saw and later emulated, what I was taught and what I learned during my two years with Hugh Douglas at St Mary's formed the basis on which my practical ministry was built. There was absolutely no way in which I could begin to imitate Hugh, and I never wished nor attempted to do that. But Hugh led me to see that the cure of souls in the parish ministry is the greatest challenge and the greatest privilege a person may have. And he led me to appreciate that it is absolutely essential to be a good organizer and good administrator in order to facilitate the preaching of the Gospel and the pastoral care of the people for whom the parish minister has responsibility. Everything Hugh did was *orderly*—not to the exclusion of all spontaneity, but rather allowing spontaneity a chance because the predictable was properly catered for. How often, in my own charges, have I thanked God for what I learned then.

As a 'Bishop' [Probationer-assistants often call the parish

minister, under whom they are working, their 'Bishop'—*Ed.*],
Hugh was demanding, but appreciative of effort. He was
critical, but always encouraging. He was approachable and
friendly, but required an acknowledgement of who was
'Boss'. There was no sense of the assistant either only being
allowed to do certain things, or being *landed* with certain
things. There was participation in the whole life of the
congregation—an expectation that opportunities would be
taken to gain experience on a wide front. There was plenty of
stimulation of effort, and an awareness that effort expended
met with positive response. Having returned to St Mary's
College from the RAF, I suppose I saw in these early days
some kind of equation in my relationship with Hugh and my
relationship as a Junior Officer with my CO. For me, it
worked. I learned a lot that I have striven to remember, and
saw little that I was anxious to forget.

My time at St Mary's was early in Hugh's ministry there.
Many of the things that came to fruition later were either just
ideas or were in embryo. (Hugh himself describes some of
these in his 1966 article, *The Work of a Central City Parish*,
reprinted here in Part II, Chapter 9.) The passage of years
brought awareness of new needs in both congregational life
and parish responsibility. Some of the attempts to facilitate
deeper fellowship in a scattered membership live on at St
Mary's, for instance in the Wednesday Club for couples.
'Hunger Lunches' sought to bring increased awareness of the
needs of the disadvantaged and underprivileged—and the idea
really was that you felt hunger, rather than eating bread and
cheese for lunch and making up for it with a gargantuan
dinner! Saturday night open air meetings in Caird Square
allowed for discussion of many kinds of topic—religious, moral
and social—although they seemed in my day inevitably to attract
one inebriated individual who always wanted to know, 'Who
was Cain's wife then?'—a question posed in the tones of one
who was about to destroy all credibility of Faith and Church.
Patterns of intensive counselling for those intending marriage
were initiated. A question and answer type of approach to the

senior classes through the School Chaplaincy at Dundee High was appreciated by pupils and staff. Some of it may not have been innovation, but there was no lack of application.

Lest all this seem like some eulogy of perfection, let me enter some caveats. Hugh did not find it easy to deal with smaller children in worship—and he admitted it. Perhaps it was because his own family were reaching maturity in his early St Mary's years, and perhaps indeed things became somewhat easier when he had his own grandchildren to cope with; but there was certainly a bit of an Achilles heel in terms of children's addresses; and I don't think Sunday School picnics were necessarily his favourite form of social activity. Against that, he had an excellent rapport with older teenagers. I think perhaps he found it easier when there was a specific degree of intellectual understanding. Again, while he was a man who enjoyed humour, Hugh could hardly have been described as a humorous man. It wasn't just stuffiness, but that reserve which indicates a certain shyness—and that might sound odd to those who knew Hugh less well. And while he was compassionate towards sinners, he was intolerant of fools. He set high standards for himself, and expected others to match them. He was never wittingly nasty, but he could be sharp when he believed it justified.

It would be as ungracious as it would be incomplete to end consideration of this major period of Hugh's ministry without making reference to the manse of Dundee, in the two locations it occupied while he was at St Mary's. Under the hospitable management of Isabel, the manse was a pleasant family home, and also the centre of much fellowship for the fairly constant stream of guests, long and short term. Babysitting was an extra-mural activity for assistants in the early days—although they were rather substantial babies! Isabel recalls with delight how, after my departure for Argentina, a member of the congregation asked her, 'And how is Colin getting on?' 'Very well', she replied. 'He's making new friends and getting involved in lots of activities'. 'I was sure he would', opined the lady. 'I do believe', said Isabel, 'that Colin has actually grown a few inches taller since he went away'. The look of incredulity with which that statement was greeted suddenly made Isabel realize that while she was talking of Colin, her steadily-elongating son who had gone off to boarding-school, the lady was talking of Colin, the decidedly past-the-growing-stage assistant who had gone off to foreign parts. Because he took his ministry so seriously, Hugh probably had less time at home than he should have had, but that made the relaxation and the shared love of home all the sweeter and more appreciated. And when a coronary drew his attention rather sharply to the dangers of over-enthusiasm and too many irons in the fire, the manse regime contributed largely to his recovery. Many have cause to remember with gratitude the Douglas manse hospitality.

How then to assess these 26 years at Dundee Parish Church (St Mary's)? It is always difficult to use the word 'successful' about a parish ministry, and yet successes there were—successes which illustrated the reality of a loved and loving congregation in worship, fellowship and mutual affection. There was fulfilment, the fulfilment which resulted from work well done and well appreciated. There was the right to a certain sense of satisfaction that the challenges identified at the time of the Call, and those which had surfaced later, had been accepted and tackled with vigour, enthusiasm and devotion. And, I'm sure, there was also that niggling self-criticism which wondered if more could have been or should have been done. To St Mary's, Hugh brought a host of good qualities: a recognition of deep responsibility, a heavy demand on himself, a determination to show 'zeal for the Glory of God', and a commitment which never wavered. He brought to St Mary's a ministry already 'run in', and St Mary's 'fine-tuned' it; and their reward was the benefit of 26 years of largely trouble-free 'motoring'. He retired in 1977, much admired, much honoured, much loved, and much missed.

Let the final assessment come from an essay written by his grandson David, then aged twelve, just after Hugh died. There is happy hyperbole at the beginning, astute appreciation in the middle, and at the end that childlike simplicity which often presents a truly considered opinion based on subjective judgment but offering acceptable objective fact:

My Grandfather was Moderator of Scotland, Chaplain to the Queen, and possibly the person who has had the most influence on my life. ... I admired him for being so generous and kind. ... He never lost his temper once when I was in his company. ... He was kind to everyone he met. He had no enemies whatsoever. Everyone liked him, respected him. ... When he actually came out of his shell, he was the best person to be with. ... On the night of his death, the world practically tumbled down around me. ... I knew for certain that I was saying goodbye to the best man that I had ever met.

CHAPTER 6

The Dundee Ministry
as seen from the Manse
Isabel C Douglas

I don't remember any period in any of our manses when Hugh did not work to an obvious routine, even if this was liable to be broken from time to time. I remember the detail of this most clearly when thinking of life in our Dundee manse, for that represents twenty-six years of our married life.

He was in the study by nine o'clock. He began with his own devotions and then worked at his desk, first clearing correspondence and after that making notes for any forthcoming speech or sermon, or simply reading. At twelve he normally went down to the office to work with the Church Secretary and sign letters before lunch. After lunch he was visiting in the parish, either in hospitals or private homes, until he came in at six o'clock for the TV News and the evening meal at quarter past six. After supper, if there was no meeting, he would visit homes in the parish in which there were people who were out at work in the daytime. He came home and walked the dog, thus getting his own exercise, which was essential.

This routine was, of course, sometimes interrupted by committees in Edinburgh or Dundee, by Presbytery meetings or meetings of various Trusts in Dundee. Hugh felt it was important to attend these Trust meetings and be familiar with their aims and objects. Sometimes disbursement of annuities was involved and had to be meticulously considered. At this time Hugh was active in the wider work of the Church, involving meetings in Edinburgh. For instance, he might tell me in the morning that he was off to a meeting in Edinburgh, would be back in the early afternoon, but would be going straight from the train into the parish and would be home for the evening meal.

Mondays were days off and we took these whenever possible, unless there was a funeral or something else that was urgent. We often went to Rosemount where Hugh played golf with a friend, Roy Hogg, minister of the High Kirk. I walked or read and met them for lunch at the Club House. If the weather was bad and we were in the manse, it was not so easy to make it a day off, but this became much more possible after a member who worked in the Post Office suggested to the Session Clerk, I think, that the telephone should be diverted on a Monday to the assistant's flat. This made a great deal of difference, for we could stay at home and enjoy reading. It was arranged that the assistant should telephone the manse at 10 o'clock in the evening with any urgent messages which had come in.

This assured a good start for the staff meeting on Tuesday morning. Visits of the past week were reported and visits for the ensuing week allocated. The pattern was usually that the assistant minister did all the hospital visits one week and Hugh the home visits, and they changed over the next week. Hugh also had a number of home visits by appointment.

Hugh had a Vestry Hour on Thursday evenings. When he first started Vestry evenings hardly anybody came, and he began to take the typewriter down with him to write his sermons from the notes he had gathered. Gradually this changed and the typewriter was no longer taken down. People began to use the Vestry Hour and eventually it became a very long 'hour', to Hugh's great satisfaction. Sometimes he came back well after 9 o'clock and felt free to watch television for the rest of the evening.

He liked everything to be ready for Sunday by Saturday lunch time. He spent Saturday afternoon watching sport on TV, especially rugby, and spent about an hour before the evening meal doing a complete run-over of Sunday services. Very often he preached at both services.

Holidays were, of course, quite different. We had a whole month in the summer and usually took a cottage on a croft on Iona. Hugh played golf and taught the children to swim and row. We had excursions over Mull. Each of the family was allocated a week in which to have a friend staying and we usually had a couple of our own friends for the last week. Correspondence was sent on and Hugh made good use of his dictaphone on wet days and sent a batch of letters down to the office for typing. He also used his holiday to work out some of his TV programmes. For instance, Ronnie Falconer (the Revd Dr Ronald Falconer, head of Religious Broadcasting with the BBC in Scotland) came up for a few days when the series *Coping with Life* was in the making. He and Hugh worked in our bedroom and when I went up with the morning coffee, I would find our bed littered with papers. The holidays must have been a great success because the girls brought their fiancés to Iona and later their own children. We enjoyed attending Evening Prayers and Sunday Services at the Abbey and having visits to the croft from all the friends and contacts who were also on the island. As well as the summer holiday on Iona (or at Arisaig), we often had a winter week at Crieff Hydro, where special terms were available to ministers through the Meikle Bequest, and also a break in the Spring.

Once we were home again, it was not always easy for Hugh to find time for family outings, but the family did see a lot of their father on holiday and there were the odd Saturday afternoons when the whole family, including the assistant, would go into one of the Angus glens or somewhere similar for a picnic. Also, I think it is important to remember that on special occasions such as weddings or other events involving the family, a minister can usually arrange to be free, given enough notice, and can take time off in a way many in other jobs cannot.

Hugh was absorbed in his work and often it was his own fault that he did too much. He was a very quick worker and got through a lot. He knew his congregations well and I would say the pastoral work was what he enjoyed most. He was able to be of real help in times of stress or calamity or disaster and people did not hesitate to approach him on these occasions. He seemed to enjoy preparing sermons and I am told he was able to do this more quickly than many ministers. I imagine he least enjoyed the administrative work which he knew had to be done, and attending Edinburgh committees and Presbytery meetings. He had good secretarial help and was always very fortunate in his assistants, who were often at the manse and were much appreciated by the Session and the congregation. We also had a very responsible and hard working Session and excellent Session Clerks who took on a lot of responsibility.

It always seemed to me that Hugh paid special attention to people as individuals. For instance, no matter how many young people were being confirmed, each got an individual blessing and a different text from Scripture. He usually wrote an annual letter during the Christmas season to girls in the congregation whose weddings he had conducted and who had gone abroad. After his death I had a letter from one of our girls in Norway who received his Christmas letter almost simultaneously with the news of his death. I also had a letter from an old lady living alone in Glastonbury who saw the announcement of his death in her morning paper and her post delivered his Christmas letter the same day. She had, years back, been helped by a broadcast talk of Hugh's at the time of her husband's death and wrote him through the BBC to express thanks; and from there a regular correspondence had continued. This attention to individual people showed itself too in his long correspondence with a young man in prison, which continued in each direction even when we were in Australia for some months.

In Hugh's retirement years he much enjoyed being Associate Minister to Bill Henney at Hope Park Church, St Andrews, helping with pastoral care and preaching. There was an excellent rapport between them and I think he was very much aware of the congregation's appreciation of his ministry. I now greatly benefit from the congregation's warm friendship.

My own Church work in Dundee was mainly concerned

with the Woman's Guild at branch, presbyterial and national level, and with the Young Mothers Group. I was involved with many others in the St Mary's Stewardship Campaign and was Convener of the Hostesses Committee. Recently I came across the photograph of 1,200 of us sitting down to a 'knife and fork meal' together in the Caird Hall. There was something unforgettable about it. The Boys' Brigade acted as ushers, standing on the steps as cars arrived, and helping the 'maimed and the halt and the blind' up the steps and to their seats. One old soul had had an operation for cancer of the nose, which had been successful. But Hugh could not persuade her to go out amongst people because her nose was bandaged. Eventually he persuaded her to come to the Caird Hall. It was her first time out. Such people and others added richness to the sense of fellowship experienced by us all that night and helped to prepare us for the Campaign.

At one point after a visit to an Australian congregation we started a Club for young couples rather than just Young Mothers. We felt this could survive longer if it only met once a month, and this proved to be so, because I gather it is still meeting. We also started a weekly Hunger Lunch in the St Mary's hall and our people were helped in running it by adjacent congregations. It was so central that it was a success from the start. People came in from their work. The idea was to have only soup and cheese and to feel hungry by evening, thus giving us a tiny experience of what it must be like to be truly hungry. A large sum was handed over every year from this project to Christian Aid. So it reminded us of the needs of the Third World and it fostered inter-church relations. Some winters we had Bible Study with other denominations. Also, in Marriage Guidance Hugh and I worked together, Hugh as the Founder Chairman of the Dundee branch and I as a counsellor.

I was of course glad to have as many people as possible to the manse. One of my greatest pleasures was, after a spell of working up to some big event, when it was safely over, to have a party at the manse for the committee involved and their spouses. We all enjoyed these celebrations. The groups worked very hard, often for several weeks, and it was good to have an opportunity for a 'post-mortem' and a buffet supper, often using two rooms at the manse with some people sitting on the floor.

After the family grew up, I had my own interests in the work of the community, the Church at national level, the BBC Scottish Council and the Thalidomide Trust. I was frequently asked if I did not resent my husband spending so much time on his work, and I do think that having my own interests enabled me to avoid that problem. We were in full sympathy with each other's occupations. And the Moderatorial year, naturally, was a highlight in our married life. We went everywhere together, travelling in great luxury, receiving so much kindess and caring hospitality, covering the life and work of the Church in so many differing circumstances and geographical conditions—a year to be remembered.

CHAPTER 7

The Retirement Years

James A Whyte

On 30 June 1977 Hugh Douglas retired from the charge of Dundee Parish Church (St Mary's). The Douglases had already fixed on St Andrews as the place for their retirement and had bought the house at Broomlea, Windmill Road. He described the choice in one of his talks to ministers on *Coping with Retirement* which are printed below in Part II, Chapter 11. St Andrews is, however, very close to Dundee, and with characteristic tact and sensitivity they decided to put a little more distance between themselves and Dundee during the vacancy in St Mary's, and until Hugh's successor could settle in. An invitation to fill a vacancy in St Andrew's Church, Brisbane, Australia for six months provided all the distance from Dundee that one could have desired. Hugh had already been the centenary preacher in St Andrew's Church fifteen years previously, so they were going to renew many old friendships as well as make new ones. In the talks on *Coping with Retirement*, he recognized that for himself this had been a happy way of dealing with the 'emotional trauma' of retirement and of easing into the new state.

Not that it was an idle time. In taking leave of them, at the Communion service on 11 December 1977, the Session Clerk spoke of Hugh's 'amazing energy and selfless dedication', of how Hugh and Isabel had come to be loved, and of how in a critical time 'you have brought us together in a way we could never have imagined'. Hugh's last sermon, on the Last Supper, showed his delicacy in handling an emotional situation, taking human experience and pointing it to the gospel. (Another form of this sermon is printed in Part II, Chapter 2.) Tactfully avoiding any reference to their imminent parting, he used his own experience as a child taking leave of missionary parents to illustrate the parting of Jesus from his disciples, and the glad reunion to show the doctrine of the Real Presence.

By the time the Douglases returned, Hope Park Church in St Andrews was facing a vacancy which it was foreseen might be protracted. The Kirk Session decided to appoint a *locum tenens*, and Hugh Douglas's name was immediately suggested. He was approached with some diffidence to see if he would consider undertaking the regular conduct of the services, and perhaps a little pastoral work. His willingness was immediate and unconditional, and it was not long before there was a bond of affection between the congregation and Hugh and Isabel Douglas. They both felt at home in Hope Park and decided to become members of the congregation, even before the new minister had been called. When, after a vacancy of ten months, the Revd William Henney was inducted, he came to a congregation well-prepared for his coming.

Again, with characteristic tact, Hugh removed himself in order to let the new minister settle in undisturbed. The distance was not so great on this occasion. St Leonard's Parish Church, just up the road, had become vacant, and once more a locum tenancy called. Isabel now divided her time between the two—Hope Park in the morning and St Leonard's in the evening. And when the St Leonard's vacancy was over, the Douglases settled in to membership of Hope Park, and to an accustomed place in the second back pew. The congregation felt as though they themselves had been honoured when, in 1981, Dr Douglas received the signal honour of being made a Knight Commander of the Royal Victorian Order at the time of his retirement as Dean of the Chapel Royal. There was great disappointment when it was learned that they would not be able to address the new Knight as 'Sir Hugh', since protocol determined that ordained ministers should not use the title.

Hugh was invited to be associated with the Kirk Session, and began to take the occasional service. In February 1982, after he had recovered from another heart attack, the minister and Kirk Session invited him to become part-time Associate Minister, and Hugh began his latest ecclesiastical appointment, which was to last until his death. The association proved a happy one for all concerned. Bill Henney described it as 'an enriching experience. . . . He and I hit it off at once. We were different in styles of ministry. But the mix was right. We understood each other and could laugh at the same things as well as be moved by the same things'. Hugh's style of preaching, quiet and almost conversational, was in contrast to the vigorous style of the minister himself; but if the style was different, the message was the same, and the two complemented one another admirably. On one occasion Bill Henney said to Isabel, 'I supply the push, Hugh supplies the intellect'. Too modest about his own considerable intellect, but aptly expressing the relationship.

The congregation was happy with its two ministers, one in a blue cassock and one in the red worn by Queen's Chaplains, sharing the services together. They were happy also to know that their minister had good support in the ever increasing demands of a growing congregation. Perhaps they were less aware of the value of Hugh's ability not only to share the preaching and the pastoral work, but also to be a pastor to his minister. Bill Henney recalls:

> He was the best listener I had met in the ministry. We had weekly meetings to work out services and duties. But these meetings became, for me, an important sounding for some of my own hopes and anxieties in ministry. Hugh would be waiting, teapot at the ready; relaxed chat and laughter; and then listening patiently and helpfully; occasionally interjecting some sound advice, with some reminiscence from his own wide experience.

He was also the unobtrusive pastor of the manse family:

Hugh was the nearest we had come till then of feeling we had our own family minister. He took a real interest in my wife and family. I took some ease in the knowledge that they had a minister and friend to whom they could turn.

Hugh was comfortable in St Andrews and these were happy as well as fruitful years. A warm friendship with Bill Henney, with the opportunity to serve a congregation which he loved and which loved him, was as deeply satisfying to him as it was support and encouragement to them. Bill Henney has said, 'I think that, with all his honours, he was essentially a parish minister'. He enjoyed the opportunities for preaching and for meeting people. He even enjoyed being told what he was to preach about: 'I would plan services in advance and invite Hugh to preach on particular themes. This both amused and challenged him, since some of the themes were ones he had never preached on before. He enjoyed the stimulus of preparing new material'. He enjoyed his relationship with 'The Boss', as Hugh called Bill Henney. This was mutual. 'He would refer to me as "The Boss". We both enjoyed that little joke. But behind it was his ready willingness to recognize me as his minister and his acknowledgment of the role of any parish minister'.

Life in St Andrews was not, of course, confined to Hope Park. There was always golf, and friendships in the Royal and Ancient Club, and the pleasure of taking visitors there. There were many friendships in the town, and many activities to enjoy. His calm and peaceable wisdom was appreciated and used by the Presbytery in difficult pastoral cases and visitations. He gave himself quietly, but without stint, though all the time there was the knowledge that some day one more heart attack would be his last.

That day came in the New Year of 1986, when on 2 January he suffered another heart attack and was in intensive care in hospital in Dundee. There was time for family and friends, and for his colleagues and minister, to visit. It was even thought that he might rally. But on 4 January he died. Bill Henney was one of the last to see him. 'The last time I saw Hugh was the day before he died. He was tired, but tried to be as courteous as ever. I sat at his bedside quietly and prayerfully. It was strange, but I felt that he was blessing me'.

He left instructions for his funeral to be in Hope Park Church, an occasion which none of the many who crowded the church to its capacity will ever forget. There was the courage of Isabel welcoming friends at the church door, and the gathering of those from far and near who had been touched by the many sides of his life: Moderators, Royal Chaplains, former assistants, and a multitude of those who had blessed him for his preaching and his pastoral care. The service was calm and triumphant—a celebration of God's gifts to Hugh Douglas and to us through him. When the interment was over we gathered again in the church hall, and laughter rang out over the tea-cups as former assistants, parishioners and friends swapped stories and affectionate reminiscences of Hugh.

On the Sunday following, the congregation of Hope Park was still in a state of shock, and their grief was almost palpable. The sermon I preached was on 'Laughter and Tears', and it ended:

> Much in my mind, and perhaps in yours, as I have talked of laughter and tears has been Hugh Douglas, and the service and gathering on Thursday. Tears there have been and will be—though that service, so calm and so uplifting, put one in mind of Milton:
>
> > *Nothing is here for tears, nothing to wail*
> > *Or knock the breast; no weakness, no contempt,*
> > *Dispraise or blame: nothing but well and fair*
> > *And what may quiet us in a death so noble.*
> >
> > ('Samson Agonistes')
>
> But Hugh would have found that pretentious. More remarkable was that meeting of friends afterwards, the happiness of shared memories, the sense that already we were sharing with him in the laughter of heaven.

PART II

Aspects of the Ministry

CHAPTER 1

Preacher

Introduced by Alan Main

To all of us who were privileged to 'sit under him', Hugh Douglas was an outstandingly gifted preacher of this age, widely acknowledged in Scotland and beyond as a true master of the homiletic craft, in whom the talents of a natural communicator were always wedded to a total seriousness and singleness of purpose. The secret of the understanding of what lay behind his accomplishment was, I believe, in reality simple and yet profound. For me, shining all through his homiletic work, the evidence is clear and unassailable from frequent scriptural allusion of a commitment both personal and professional, which stemmed right from the ordination vow which every minister takes at the outset of ministry: 'Do you believe the Word of God, contained in the Scriptures of the Old and New Testaments, to be the supreme rule of faith and life?' Hugh did, and in the Word of God written, and the Word of God incarnate, he found his inspiration and motivation, which sustained him through a life-time of preaching.

On so many occasions he loved to return to those marvellous verses of the fourth chapter of the Letter to the Hebrews:

> The word of God is alive and active. It cuts more keenly than any two edged-sword, piercing as far as the place where life and spirit, joints and marrow, divide. It sifts the purposes and thoughts of the heart. There is nothing in

creation that can hide from him; everything lies naked and exposed to the eyes of the One with whom we have to reckon.

(Hebrews 4:12–13, NEB)

This was for Hugh Douglas, as for so many of us, the foundation stone—and the ordination vow his commission to be not just a proclaimer but an ambassador. It is a high doctrine of preaching. In his *Coping with Life* television series, Hugh amplified the statement of his position and he did it quite unambigously.

> Preaching is not spiritual entertainment. It is not a kind of religious pep talk. It is certainly not a substitute for tranquillisers. It should never be allowed to produce an attitude of semi-idolatry for the man who preaches. It is the proclaiming of the Word which rebukes, heals, confronts, inspires, and challenges.

Though such an able speaker himself, Dr Douglas understood very well the difference between public oratory and preaching:

> Public oratory deals principally with human affairs. . . . Preaching is concerned with man, but with man in his relationship with God and his neighbours. . . . It was this preaching, the proclamation of the Good News, that was used by God for creating the Church, and the written New Testament sprang directly from the proclamation. Thus preaching is never meant to be seen as either a formal exercise or as a display of oratory. It is or should be a living dynamic thing . . . a vital channel between God and man.[1]

Reflecting on the purpose of preaching with my students at Christ's College, he declared that 'our task as preachers is twofold . . . to build up and strengthen the faithful to live the

Christian life in a secular society . . . but it is also to enable them, as members of the Body of Christ, along with ourselves, to proclaim the Good News of the Gospel to all the multitudes who wander like sheep without a shepherd'.[2] For him there was no courting of adulation and no misuse of his formidable preaching gifts for any cheap effect; and whenever recognition came, it was met by a convincing humility of self-regard.

How then did he prepare himself, this man who still confessed to feeling nervous before a service after forty years of preaching? The primary clue here lay in the attention which he paid to his private devotional life. He developed a very deep and thorough biblical awareness, which, when allied to his genuine scholarship, meant that he took the greatest of care over the context and background of any text from which he intended to preach. 'If we are to become preachers, we must first become interpreters' was a favourite maxim, and from C H Dodd he quoted the advice which is so clearly evidenced in his homiletic work:

> The ideal interpreter would be one who has entered into that strange first century world, has felt its whole strangeness, has sojourned in it until he has lived himself into it, thinking and feeling as one of those to whom the Gospel first came; and who will then return to our world and give to the truth he has discerned a body out of the stuff of our thought.[3]

Hugh Douglas was also an avid reader of all sorts of writing: biography, autobiography, the classics, theology, ancient and modern history, novels, poetry, current affairs. His sermons are studded with references drawn from a rich variety of sources, erudite but never beyond the capacity of the listener to grasp; and the principle which he followed was that 'it should be part of our preparation that we should search for nuggets of truth in the works of abler, more learned and more talented communicators or preachers than we can ever hope to be. . . . What a benefit it can be to have a spark from someone else to kindle one's own flame!'

It was his rule to start his preparation early in the week and, while recognising occasional necessity, he was firmly opposed to last minute efforts. This perhaps mirrored the ordered style of the man but, more importantly, it permitted him to put into practice a genuine insight, which I have also discerned in the writing of other masters of the craft of preaching. If one begins early there can take place an unconscious simmering on the back burner of the mind, as the theme is sifted through the week's work. This was very important, for Dr Douglas had a keen pastoral eye, stressing the necessary inter-connectedness of homiletics and pastoral care; and an ongoing relationship with his congregation, as the people to whom the Word was to be addressed—witness, not words alone, from the minister, and that vibrant kind of witness which understood well the difficulties of the world in which the worshippers had to live when they went from the church.

One further quotation will take us on to a different but related point:

> When we are preaching, it is the kind of people that we are that will make more of an impression, for good or ill, than our words or the manner in which we deliver them. So let us seek to talk about what we know ourselves to be true. Let us explain what we ourselves believe. Let us speak from our own experience. . . . Our concern should be to keep as far as possible our own integrity in being channels of the Word.[4]

The point is this: that all preachers preach first of all to themselves and out of their own individual faith and understanding of the centralities of the Gospel. For Hugh Douglas, and again it mirrors the multi-faceted nature of the man, this led his output in a rich variety of directions, but principally towards his abiding interests in exposition, ethics, apologetics and personal devotion. He had no time for the party banners

of theological predilection under which Christian people seek
so often to stand; yet I believe he would have been glad to
have been called evangelical, not in any narrow pietistic sense,
but with a solid grasp of the world and the society in which
the Word was to be cast. He was a slave to no one homiletical
style, but allowed the subject, theme, passage or verse to
dictate the development and shape of the sermon that was to
grow out of it.

His writing (and he always wrote out his script in full,
though seldom taking it into the pulpit with him) demonstrated the beautiful clarity of ordered thought, and his facility
in the use of flowing imagery and language always aided the
hearer's understanding since it was so carefully chosen and
crafted. Like his Lord, Hugh Douglas delighted in drawing
many of his illustrations from the world of nature and
ordinary things, as in the following passage on the ebb and
flow of the fortunes of Church and faith:

> The Church is never dead. Just as there are seasons of the
> year, so can the life of the Church show changes. There
> can be the times of luxuriant growth, as in summer, then
> the slow decline when the autumn leaves begin to fall,
> succeeded by the cold, hard days of winter, when
> everything seems dead. But, even when the branches are
> bare and dry, the buds are already forming so that once
> again—as always—there will be the glorious re-birth of the
> springtime. So it is with the Church.

Listening to or reading his sermons, one is aware of a true
craftsman at work, painting fine word pictures, whether of the
challenge or of the consolation of the faith, because he knew
that such images would best speak to the hearts and minds of
men and women and would remain most surely in their
minds. If, out of all Hugh Douglas's preaching, one were to
select but two notes to which he returned time and again, they
would, for me, be those of hope and expectation. In this, too,
he would have been addressing himself, his hearers, and all

who would don the preacher's mantle. 'The human instrument of the Word can be pitifully inadequate', he wrote, 'but still the Word keeps breaking through. . . . God has to work through human material, in the preacher and in the congregation. Both have a responsibility to give God his chance'.

The first of Dr Douglas's sermons which I have chosen for this chapter is an exposition of John 20:1–18 and is entitled 'Easter Day'. It is constructed in a narrative style and is a graphic re-telling of the story with a stage by stage interpretation. The beginning is striking, transporting the listener straight into the mind of the grieving Mary, with terse telegraphic prose and broadening the picture out to what is the heart of the problem for all humankind—the frailty of human life, the seeming finality of loss in death—and the power of the experience of the resurrection hope. This is a sermon of compelling simplicity, flow, and directness of style and presentation, and without an ounce of verbosity or any kind of padding.

My second choice is a sermon entitled 'Three Dreams', and in it Dr Douglas weaves together a dream about government, a dream about guidance, and a dream about violence and peace. It is a beautifully constructed piece of work, packed with high class material which is drawn from a whole variety of sources, evidence of his own very considerable erudition but always clearly comprehensible and arrestingly illustrated. The subject is never lost but is held to throughout and is brought to a fine concise conclusion.

My third choice would be Hugh's sermon 'Storm in the Mediterranean'. In this address he focuses his hearers' thoughts first on a list of human desiderata, skill, money, influence and power, against which he sets the question of faith, so often regarded as an optional extra. Then he allows the story of the storm and the shipwreck in Acts 27 to re-tell itself, interpreting the salient points along the way. The transition back to ourselves and our present world is accomplished in a skilful and natural way and the sermon finds its climax and focus in the words of the Communion Service.

For my final choice I simply could not pass by the last sermon that Dr Douglas preached. It is a reflective piece, addressing itself at Christmastide to the question of what difference the Christmas story can make in today's secular world. In certain ways for me this sermon is typical of Hugh. The Word powerfully spoken out of his observation of simple things—an 'Any Questions' radio programme, and the view from the manse window—and his being led to reflect again on the Word of God which he so loved. Poignant, too, at the end of his long and productive preaching life, to see him return to a key theme, the difference which the faith can make; seeing the world as it is, with all its faults and failings, yet always wanting to restate its potential, with God. In essence, perhaps an *apologia pro vita sua* and delivered in the thoughtful ordered style which was essentially his. He would, I think, have been pleased with it.

Notes

1 Quoted from Dr Douglas's lectures on Preaching and Worship given at Christ's College, Aberdeen in 1980.
2 ibid.
3 From the Inaugural Lecture as Norris Hulse Professor of Divinity, University of Cambridge, quoted by John A T Robinson in his Foreword to Dodd, C H: *The Founder of Christianity*, Collins: London, 1971.
4 Quoted from Dr Douglas's lectures on Preaching and Worship, Aberdeen 1980.

*　　*　　*

EASTER DAY

A sermon first preached in St Mary's, Dundee, on Easter Day 1975.

> Early on the Sunday morning, while it was still dark, Mary of Magdala came to the tomb. She saw that the stone had been moved away from the entrance. . . .
>
> (John 20:1–18, NEB)

There are four stages in this marvellous story of the first Easter morning, when Mary of Magdala came to the tomb to perform the last rites for the body of Jesus. The first stage began when she saw that the stone had been moved away from the entrance.

Speculation

It must have been an awesome and frightening experience for Mary in the darkness before the dawn. She came with no expectation other than that of finding a dead body. There was no 'sure and certain hope of the resurrection to eternal life' in her religious tradition. At the best, the dead were thought of as existing in a shadowy and joyless underworld. Death remained as the terminal boundary to life, and nothing worthwhile came after it.

So Mary must have come to the garden with nothing else to console her than that she might pay loving reverence to the dead body of Jesus. And now even that was denied her. Her mood could only have been one of dismay and speculation, wondering what had happened, what could possibly have been done with the body.

Death still brings dismay and speculation to many people. They miss the beloved physical presence. They have no sure and certain hope of what lies beyond the grave. They grieve for the departed, but especially they grieve for themselves, and there is no light in the darkness of their mourning, just as Mary was surrounded by darkness in the garden. She dared not look in the tomb, for fear of what she might see; and she ran to bring Peter and John.

Knowledge and discovery

There is a striking picture of Peter and John hastening to the tomb. Peter is the older man, so that he is lagging behind, but on the faces of both men there is a strained and anxious look. They are still at the stage of speculation.

John reached the tomb first; he peered in and saw the linen wrappings which had covered the body, but did not go in— and you can understand why. But Peter had a stronger and more robust attitude. He went in and examined the scene— and John's account in the Gospel bears all the marks of having been based on the evidence of an eye witness. The body was no longer there. But the wrappings, and the spices contained in them, were not unrolled and spread about the tomb. They were lying flat, just in the shape of the body they had covered. Even the napkin round the head was lying flat and separate from the body clothes.

At this stage they began to know what had happened. Whether they really understood the full consequences of the facts we cannot say. They were like any men, whether scientists or explorers, who had made a new discovery. They knew what they had discovered, but they could not tell where it was going to lead them. The body had gone and the linen wrappings were undisturbed. That was the extent of their knowledge. Like the discoverers of the Pacific in the sonnet by John Keats, they 'look'd at each other with a wild surmise'.

This is how some may still feel about life after death and about the resurrection story. They know that the early church only came into being because the disciples believed that Jesus had risen from the dead. They know that no one has been able to disprove the resurrection. They know the facts. But knowledge by itself is not enough. It is unsatisfactory only to have a theory. There has to be something more. There has to be another stage.

Experience

Peter and John had told Mary what they had seen in the tomb, but their knowledge made no difference to her. She was still lost in her sorrow, still desolate, still weeping. But she took one faltering step towards action. She looked into the tomb to see for herself. And then things began to happen.

It seemed to her that two angels asked her why she was weeping. And as she repeated her plaint that persons unknown had taken away the body of Jesus, she turned round and saw Jesus standing there and did not know that it was Jesus. As we read this most moving part of the Easter story, we see that what now happened to Mary was that she began to experience for herself the truth of the resurrection, namely that death does not mean the end of personal relationships. She was still in touch with Jesus.

It is through experience that we can find that knowledge is indeed the truth. Most of us dread the death of dear ones because it means, we think, the end of our personal relationship with them. Nor is it enough to tell us that time is a great healer. But how often it happens that one hears bereaved persons saying that they are aware of the presence of their loved ones who have died. This should not be dismissed as mere wish fulfilment. It is the experience of the Christian hope and the Christian belief that bodies are mortal but persons are immortal.

And this belief is based on what happened that first Easter morning. 'When thou hadst overcome the sharpness of death, thou didst open the kingdom of heaven to all believers'. This was the great shout of joy which sounded from the lips of Christians all round the ancient world.

> Jesus lives! thy terrors now
> Can, O Death, no more appal us.   (CH3:605)

That is why while Christmas warms our hearts in the cold darkness of winter, it is only Easter which can bring us the gladness and triumph which nothing can overcome.

Proclamation

When you compare the entrance of Mary to the garden with her departure from it, you see in brief compass the whole story of Jesus' work on earth. Here was a woman whose life had been wasted but whom Jesus had restored. After being raised to the height of joy, she had been brought to the depth of desolation and sorrow by his death. But now everything had come alive again for her and Jesus himself had commissioned her to spread the good news. 'Go to my brothers', he said, 'and tell them. . . .' So Mary went with great joy to the disciples with her news. 'I have seen the Lord!' she said, and gave them his message.

I am confident that all of us can do the same, if only the truth of Easter dawns on our hearts today. As the old legend tells us, when the Lord Jesus returned to heaven and Gabriel asked him if he had made no other plans for his work to continue than that his weak and wavering disciples should carry it on, the Lord replied, 'I have made no other plans, because I trust them'. So it is that today he trusts us to tell others by our words, and to show by the evidence of our lives, that he is risen, he is risen indeed!

THREE DREAMS

A Sermon preached to the St Andrews University Theological Society on 14 May 1973.

Today we are going to consider the three dreams described in our Scripture readings: 1 Kings 3:3–15; Acts 16:6–10; and Matthew 27:15–26.

In primitive societies, dreams were regularly regarded as messages from the gods. In the Bible it was also held that God could communicate with people through dreams. In our own time, in the post-Freudian era, the common interpretation of dreams is much more secular. We are accustomed to the general idea that in dreams it is the sub-conscious mind which is at work.

But I scarcely need to remind you that the various schools of psychology can differ widely from each other as to the interpretations of dreams. C G Jung gives an interesting example of this in his *Memories, Dreams, Reflections* [Collins and Routledge Kegan Paul: London, 1963], describing the beginning of the break which was to develop between himself and Sigmund Freud. They were in the U.S.A. together in 1909, and each day analysed each other's dreams. At that time Jung had what he believed to be a number of important dreams, and Freud could make nothing of them. Yet Jung, as the younger man, still looked up to Freud. What made him lose his respect, he says, was when Freud had a dream which he asked Jung to analyse.

Jung interpreted it as best he could, but added that much more could be said about it if Freud would supply some additional details from his private life. Jung goes on, 'Freud's response to these words was a curious look—a look of the utmost suspicion. Then he said, "But I cannot risk my authority". At that moment he lost it altogether. That sentence burned itself into my memory—and in it the end of our relationship was already foreshadowed. Freud was placing personal authority above truth' (p 154).

Jung then goes on to say that in turn he found that he had to tell Freud a lie in relation to one of his own dreams which Freud wished to interpret in a way which Jung felt was totally wrong. So, to keep the peace, Jung let Freud have his way— but the gulf between them grew greater.

Today there is still a reluctance to think of religion and dreams being connected, and most psychologists, for all that they differ so much from each other, would, I imagine, discount the Biblical attitude that God communicates with individuals through their dreams.

Be that as it may, Christians believe that God can influence the working of the human mind. And if that is possible at the conscious level, it is obviously equally possible at the subconscious level. So in the study of these three dreams let us be thinking, quite simply, of what God has to say to men and women.

A dream about government

Solomon's dream was about government, about the qualities which he asked God to give him as he faced the task of ruling his people.

First, of course, the very fact of his request showed that he regarded dependence upon God as of the greatest importance. He, as King of Israel, acknowledged his need of the King of Kings and Lord of Lords.

Second, he asked for an understanding mind.

And third, he asked that he might be able to discern between what was right and wrong.

Considering that kingship in those days meant despotism, tyranny and cruelty, these are remarkable requests. And they are still far from being practised by the governments of today after something like 3,000 years. Were I an elector at this time, I should be inclined to judge the suitability of the candidates by how they measured up to these principles.

Do they stand for dependence upon God? Do they recognize that there is need for more than loyalty to the policy of any one party? Do they regard the influence of God's commandments as the necessary foundation for society, so that it is not by might nor by power but by the Spirit of the Lord that we shall go forward?

Are they of a discerning and understanding mind? Do they recognize that issues must be decided not merely by a hard party line or by prejudice, but in relation to what is the truth? Are they ready to view the problems of all classes with sympathy and to decide their policy on the basis of justice to all?

And finally do they recognize that in politics as in every part of life there is a difference between what is right and what is wrong? Do they stand for integrity in their party as also in their own lives?

In his own day William Ewart Gladstone aroused violent opposition as well as devoted support, not least in relation to his policy for Ireland. There were many, indeed, who accused him of the basest motives in his efforts to do something for the prostitutes of the London streets. Yet in spite of every attack made upon him, his moral stature was unassailed in his own life time; and nearly a century later he stands out as one who continually sought to practise his own belief that anything which was morally wrong could not be politically right.

As a more recent biographer, Sir Philip Magnus, has written of him, 'Political life would have been meaningless to him without that purpose which attained its most outstanding public expression during three successive phases of his long career' [*Gladstone: A Biography*, John Murray: London 1954, p. xi]. These were his policy of setting the individual free from a multitude of obsolete restrictions; in arousing the British people to moral indignation over Turkish misrule in the Balkans; and in his crusade against English despotism in Ireland. The fact that his Home Rule bills ended in his humiliation and defeat in no way diminished his moral stature or his towering pre-eminence over all his contemporaries.

The present disillusion with and distrust of politicians simply emphasizes the urgent need for people of belief, principle and integrity in the political arena. It underlines the challenge for the Church to be actively concerned with politics, not in supporting any one party but in proclaiming that truth and justice must be upheld at all costs.

These are not merely dreams. They are principles of government which we need just as much today as did King Solomon 3,000 years ago.

A dream about guidance

The second dream is about the guidance of God and it is
described in four most interesting and important verses in the
16th chapter of the Book of Acts. Paul and Silas had been
travelling through what we now call Asia Minor, preaching
the Gospel. They had been hopeful of going north and east
along the shores of the Black Sea, but, we read, the Spirit of
Jesus prevented them and so they came to Troas on the shores
of the northern Aegean Sea, looking over from Asia Minor
towards Europe. There Paul had a dream in which he saw a
man of Macedonia standing and saying, 'Come over to
Macedonia and help us'. [This and the following quotations
are from the RSV.] You know what followed, namely that
Paul crossed over into Macedonia, believing that God had
called him; and so the Gospel came to Europe.

Who was the man of Macedonia? Obviously it must have
been someone known to Paul, but who? Paul would know
the man was from Macedonia, not by his dress (which would
not be different) but by personal acquaintance. It could well
have been Luke. Luke is the author of the Book of Acts, and
he indicates his own presence in a very modest way simply
by writing 'we' instead of 'they' to show that he was one of
the party. Thus in this passage at verse 6 we read, 'they went
through the region of Phrygia and Galatia'. There follows the
account of the dream and the man of Macedonia, and in the
next verse (10) we read, 'and when he had seen the vision,
immediately *we* sought to go on into Macedonia'. Luke had
joined the party at Troas, meeting Paul for the first time, and
the theory is that in his typically modest way he did not claim
the credit for inspiring Paul's decision—or at least for being
God's agent in doing so—but indicated in this subtle and
indirect fashion that he himself was the man from Macedonia,
because this is the first passage in which he writes of 'we'
instead of 'they'.

The point to be made is that God can and does work
through human beings and through the normal operation of
the human mind. Seen in this way, there is nothing crudely

miraculous about Paul's dream. He meets Luke at Troas at a critical stage in his journeying; Luke has come from Macedonia and as Paul slept he dreamt of Luke and saw the challenge of taking the Gospel to a new land. And, of course, he rightly saw this as the call of God.

Certainly God works in many ways, but do not let us forget that his guidance comes through events and through human beings. When John Reith was appointed to control the BBC as a young and unknown man, he noted in his diary that this was entirely due to God. His biographer points out that Reith made no mention of the fact that his employer, Sir William Bull, had warmly commended him for the new post. Thus he implies that Reith was wrong in attributing the appointment to God. What both Reith and his biographer appear to have forgotten is that God works through human beings, and that God could thus have worked through Sir William Bull's recommendation.

Surely the lesson for us is that we should look for God's guidance not just in striking or apparently miraculous ways (which we may never experience), but in all sorts of meetings with people, in events and in opportunities of our daily life. For in the words of Elizabeth Barrett Browning in 'Aurora Leigh':

> Earth's crammed with heaven
> And every common bush afire with God.

Belief in the Providence of God is fundamental to the Christian Faith, but it is not an easy doctrine to accept. It is so strongly challenged by all the signs of suffering, and of 'man's inhumanity to man' which 'makes countless thousands mourn'. Further, it is, perhaps, small comfort to those who are undergoing the hardships and tragedy of a particular historical process to be reminded that—

> God moves in a mysterious way
> His wonders to perform;

or that—

Behind a frowning providence
He hides a smiling face.   (CH3:147)

And yet I would submit that paradoxical as it may seem, belief in providence is all the more necessary when events are at their worst.

Human beings can and do learn from experience. The Great Plague in London was followed by the Great Fire. Disease-ridden hovels were destroyed and Sir Christopher Wren was there to plan a better city.

The loss of the American colonies in the reign of George III taught this country so to change her attitude to the question of overseas dominion that we were led to present the world with a new idea of empire.

The Second World War and the dissolution of the British Empire led on to an attempt to make something fresh out of the idea of Commonwealth.

Our present troubles in Ireland could—and one hopes and prays that they will—lead on to a better understanding of minority rights and to an attitude on the part of both Roman Catholics and Protestants, nationalists and unionists, which is based on tolerance.

But much will depend on human willingness to see the traces of Providence in history and to co-operate with God's providential working in the present. It is as if the Author and Creator of all things was composing a cosmic drama in which all men have their parts to play. But we are given our lines always in the existential present: we mishear them or wilfully misinterpret them. But the Author can take them—and our mistakes—and turn them into a greater theme. Looking back now, we can see how this has happened in the past. Looking forward we need to believe all the more strongly and to co-operate all the more faithfully.

A dream about peace and violence

It was the dream which Pilate's wife had at the very time that Jesus was on trial before him. She at once sent a message to

Pilate warning him that Jesus was a righteous man, that he should not be involved against Jesus, and that she had suffered much in her own mind at the thought of what was happening in relation to Jesus.

What could she have dreamt? We are told nothing more than this. But she must have known that Pilate was faced with the choice of releasing Barabbas—who stood for violence and brigandage—or Jesus who stood for peace. She must also have known that Pilate had been in trouble before over riots which had taken place when he was governor. And one can be sure that her anxiety was not so much for Jesus as for her husband and what was going to happen to him.

We know that Pilate took the easy way out and released Barabbas the man of violence, because he feared what might happen if he released Jesus, the man of peace. It was what any hard-headed governor might have done, weighing up the facts as he saw them. But in her dream his wife, with her deeper feminine intuition, saw that there was a goodness in Jesus which was entirely right; and so she pleaded in vain that her husband should let him be. Her intuition was correct; and today Barabbas and Pilate are known to us solely and entirely by their names being linked with Jesus, the man of peace.

The issue between peace and violence remains with us today, and it is aggression which seems to be predominant in our society. There is the violence with which immorality is justified and commended; the violence with which it is intruded through the airwaves into our homes; and there is the increase of actual violence in our society in gangs and muggings, in robbery and assault, in its association with our sport and even as in Ulster with our religion. It is as if the primitive instinct of aggression were being given even greater licence.

But there are deeper levels of intuition. And one hopes and prays that in spite of all the violence on the surface of our society the deeper instincts will increasingly come to the fore. Behind many violent and aggressive personalities there are frightened spirits, deprived of love, and frustrated by their very aggressiveness. Often they are violent in an attempt to justify themselves in the sight of their companions. And all their efforts lead to self-destruction.

The will to power is self-destructive. The man who seeks to save his life will lose it.

Have you ever thought of these words in terms of the age-long instinct of gambling? You can gamble in two ways. For yourself or for God.

The will to power gambles on self. This is as true of the individual as it is of a nation. Sadhu Sundar Singh, that great Indian Christian, was crossing a mountain range in a heavy snowstorm when he was joined by a Tibetan who was afraid of going alone. The cold was so intense that they had begun to despair of reaching their destination alive when they saw a man, who had slipped down a slope of snow, lying unconscious thirty feet below. The Sadhu asked his companion to help to carry the man to the village. The Tibetan told him he was a fool and hurried on by himself. Somehow the Sadhu just managed to get the man on to the path and struggled on with him on his shoulders. Some distance on he saw his former companion sitting by the wayside frozen dead. But the warmth of the Sadhu's exertions warmed the unconscious man so that he came to; and both reached the village alive. That is gambling for God.

But when men or nations gamble for self then they take the road to self-destruction. So it was with Hitler, when he claimed that the victory of his armies would settle the future of Europe for a thousand years. Only a year or two more were to pass before he himself was dead by his own hand, and the Third Reich was in ruins.

It is hard to remember this when the way of Jesus seems so weak and ineffective in face of violence. But when Jesus stood before Pilate he was betting his life there was a God.

You remember Studdert-Kennedy's poem 'He was a Gambler too', about the cross?

    And, sitting down, they watched Him there,
        The soldiers did;

There, while they played with dice,
  He made His Sacrifice,
And died upon the cross to rid
  God's world of sin.
He was a gambler, too, my Christ,
  He took His life and threw
  it for a world redeemed.
And ere His agony was done
  Before the westering sun went down,
Crowning that day with its crimson crown,
  He knew that He had won.

So let us pay heed to our dreams of peace and love. For it is the Pilates of this world who perish and it is the Barabbases whose own violence will destroy them. It is the righteous man, Jesus, the King of Love and the Prince of Peace, who lives on.

One Kingdom only is divine,
One banner triumphs still—
Its King a servant, and its sign
  a gibbet on a hill.
                           ('In hoc Signo')

STORM IN THE MEDITERRANEAN

A sermon first preached in St Mary's, Dundee, on a Communion Sunday in April 1967.

But the centurion paid more attention to the captain and to the owner of the ship than to what Paul said.
                           (Acts 27:11, NEB)

'I beg you to have something to eat; your lives depend on it'. . . . With these words, Paul took bread, gave thanks to God in front of them all, broke it, and began eating.
                   (Acts 27:34–35, NEB)

If you are buying a car—or even if you are only at the stage of studying the new models in magazines or brochures—you will see that many of them have 'optional extras'. That is to say, if you choose, you can have additional fitments over and above what are on the standard model—automatic transmission, power steering, even such unlikely items as cocktail cabinets and television sets. An optional extra is something you don't really need. You can have it if you want it—for more comfort or luxury.

Is then the Gospel an optional extra in life? Is it something we don't really need for the journey? Something for those who feel like it, who want a little extra comfort and cushioning, who have a leaning that way and are prepared to pay for the satisfaction of their tastes, however unusual those tastes may be? Perhaps a number of people would regard the Gospel in that way today.

And if you ask them, 'What is really necessary for journeying successfully through life?', they might very well say, 'You need a bit of power and influence—whether in a big way or in a small way. You need a bit of money to buy what you need and do what you want. You need a bit of skill—to be good at your job so that you can have these other things. Power—money—skill—with these you can go, make progress, be a success. But you don't need religion. That's an optional extra'.

This certainly seems to have been the attitude on the ship which was taking Paul as a prisoner on his last journey to Rome. You had *power* represented there in the person of the Roman centurion in charge of his prisoners—the power of the Roman Empire itself. You had *money* represented there in the person of the owner of the ship—perhaps an early Aristotle Onassis. It was a grain ship, taking corn from Egypt to feed the people of Italy. You had *skill* represented in the person of the captain of the ship. And obviously, when they were discussing the voyage, they thought that theirs were the only views which mattered. Anything that Paul had to say was the muttering of a religious eccentric. Religion was an optional extra, a fringe activity for those who felt that way.

But a fortnight later they felt very differently. They were in a desperate crisis. The ship had been blown off course by a terrible storm and it looked as if nothing could save them. In this situation power, money and even skill were at a discount. The centurion could do nothing with his power. The owner could do nothing with his money. And the sailors, the experts, those who should have been the saviours of the situation—why, they had given up hope and were preparing to get away in the ship's boat and leave the others to their fate.

It was at this point that Paul showed that religion was not an optional extra or a fringe activity. He took charge. In the grey dawn, with the gale howling and the waves thundering on the nearby coastline, he spoke to the 276 people on board that ship. He spoke words of faith, reminding them that their lives were in God's hands. He spoke words of commonsense, reminding them that they needed food to give them strength. And in front of them he did what was really an act of Communion: he took bread, gave thanks to God, broke it and began eating. In that moment the situation was saved. Morale was restored. People were no longer individuals crying, 'Every man for himself and the devil take the hindmost'; they stood together and, because of the leadership of a man of religious faith, they were all brought safely ashore. In the crisis it was faith that counted.

Perhaps this is a picture that can make us think, as we gather together on Communion Sunday. Perhaps it gives us an opportunity to examine motives—as in the old Scottish tradition we are expected to do—and ask just why we are here and what we regard as most important for our journeying through life. Perhaps we can get our priorities sorted out in the light of the challenge of the Christian faith.

We all agree that power, money and skill mean something to us all. Whatever our position, we like to feel that we have some power, some influence—even if it is limited to the four walls of an office, workshop or home.

In the same way we need money, and we find extra money very useful indeed to buy and to do what we want.

And, of course, we are glad if we can show that we are skilled and expert at our work, our trade, our profession.

But the point is that in the crises of life—and we all have these to face—we find that it is religious faith that matters most.

Take power. One thing that emerges from William Manchester's book *The Death of a President* is that behind the facade of power people are frightened human beings. The USA is the most powerful country in the world, and its President the most powerful man on earth. But one bullet from the gun of a crazed psychopath not only killed the President but cracked wide open the facade of power.

Take money. Yes, we all want money—but what does it amount to in the end? Think of the poor rich man who died just recently. He left eleven million pounds and he died of chronic alcoholic poisoning. And set against that the saying of a Scottish industrialist that 'character is the only thing we can make in this world which we can take with us into the next'.

Take skill. We can put men on the moon—but we can't keep the hungry millions on earth alive or give them a full life. We can produce computers which can tell us our Income Tax, play draughts, and express themselves in music—but we can't live in harmony with each other, as nations or as individuals.

Let's get our priorities right on this Communion Sunday and ask ourselves why we are here. Is religion an optional extra for us? Is it a fringe activity? Something to treat casually, like an occasional visit to the theatre, or dropping in once in a while to see an elderly friend? Or is it something for the very heart and centre of our being, to help us use our power, our money and our skill in the right way, and to make us able to stand firm in the evil day?

When Paul stood on the heaving deck of that ship off the shores of Malta and broke bread, he was showing both the bankruptcy of materialism and the true riches of the Christian faith. And, as we come to the Communion Table today, I think we can well forget the position we have—great or small—in the outside world; we can forget whether we came to church in a large expensive car or by bus or on foot; we can forget about our bank balances or overdrafts, our stocks and shares, our premium bonds, our dreams about winning the pools; we can forget about how clever we are at our jobs or our housekeeping—and we can face up to some simple and uncompromising questions:

Are we living the kind of life that lets us be real persons?
Are we using the gifts and talents which God has given us in the right way?
Are we in right and harmonious relationships with other people—at our work and in our homes?

If suddenly we were faced with a crisis and disaster in our lives, would we be able to say, 'The Lord is my Shepherd, I shall not want. . . . yea, though I walk through the valley of the shadow of death, I will fear no evil. . . .'? [Psalm 23:1, 4, AV].

Make no mistake about it. Religious faith can enable us to do this, if we cease deluding ourselves that it is merely a fringe activity. The Christian faith is for the wholeness and salvation of individual men and women, so that in all things they can be more than conquerors.

And more than this, the Gospel is for the salvation of the whole world. Without God, man is only a very clever and a very mischievous animal, who appears increasingly likely to band together in competing tribal groups to his own destruction. It is only when he can find the unity and fellowship of the whole human family that man will be able to survive shipwreck and disaster. It is only when he takes the bread of the world and shares it justly with his brothers that he will find strength to live. How else can he expect to do this except as a child of God, except by acknowledging God as his Father.

'Take bread and eat,' cried Paul. 'Your lives depend upon it.' The whole world is continually dependent upon bread. Some have far too little. Some have far too much. All are urgently concerned—primarily—with their own needs.

> The world is too much with us; late and soon,
> Getting and spending we lay waste our powers.
>
> (William Wordsworth)

But our lives as human beings depend upon the just sharing of the bread of the world. Who can show us how to do this but he who is the Bread from Heaven, who said, 'Take, eat: this is my Body which is broken for you' (1 Corinthians 11:24, AV)? The Gospel of this man is no optional extra. It is the Bread of Life, without which we shall die. He came that we should not perish, but that we should have everlasting—that is, abundant—life.

THE DIFFERENCE CHRISTMAS MAKES

Dr Douglas's last sermon, preached in Hope Park Church, St Andrews, on 29 December 1985, a few days before his death.

For in the tender compassion of our God the morning sun from heaven will rise upon us, to shine on those who live in darkness, under the cloud of death, to guide our feet into the way of peace.

(Luke 1:78–79, NEB)

In a recent 'Any Questions' programme one questioner asked if there was any point in emphasizing the Christian aspect of Christmas celebrations, when less than five per cent of the population in our country attended Church services.

On this Sunday after Christmas I too would ask a similar question, but with a different slant to it. It is: 'In our secular society, when so many look upon the Christmas Story as a kind of fairy tale, what difference can the Christian message make?'

I remember, one Christmas, looking out of our manse window above the River Tay. I saw three things which seemed to me to illustrate a secular materialistic view of life.

The sun was shining brightly, and from the purely non-Christian view, the sun is the source and origin of our planet and the life which it sustains. The earth broke off from the sun; and it is the sun which supplies the light, warmth and energy without which we should die. What difference does the Christmas Story make to facts like these?

I do not believe that there needs to be any conflict between our Christian belief and what the scientists tell us about the origin of our planet and of life upon it. From the Christian point of view, the more we know about the way in which the laws of nature work, the more we know about God. And again, from the Christian point of view, the Christmas Story has something to give which is of the greatest importance to a scientific and secular point of view.

The Christmas Story tells us that our universe is not a cold impersonal machine. In the words of our text, 'the morning sun will rise upon us because of the tender compassion of our God'. Behind the solar system, behind the infinity of space, there is a personal caring and compassion. At the heart of things there is Love. That makes a difference.

The Christmas Story tells us of the shining of a star where Jesus was born. Call it poetry or call it fact, but see that it speaks of a purpose and plan which are as real for all humans as they are for each individual soul. That makes a difference.

And the sun is the sun of which the prophet Malachi speaks (4:2): the Sun of righteousness, a prophecy fulfilled by the coming of Jesus. There is love, there is purpose—and there is goodness at the heart of things. And that makes a difference, to believe that evil is never going to win the day.

The second thing I noticed, as I looked from the manse window, was skein after skein of wild geese—hundreds of them—flying in their wedge-shaped formations towards their feeding grounds on the estuary of the Tay.

One of the wonders of the natural world is, of course, the remarkable phenomenon of bird migration. And again, from the purely secular point of view, this is merely another example of the way in which birds, like all other living creatures, have evolved from primitive forms of life. By this view man is just the same—the 'top' animal, the summit of the evolutionary process. He will go on evolving, and there is no need of God to help him to evolve.

So what difference does the Christmas Story make here? Well, it tells of a mother giving birth to a baby in a stable, beside the domestic animals, the ox and the ass. But man is more than an animal and the evolving world needs the teaching and example of the Jesus who was born in a stable.

For think of this sad and terrible fact. Here we are, nearing the end of the twentieth century, after all these aeons of evolution. Yes, man has evolved in a remarkable way, but how much moral progress has he made? Look at our twentieth century. It has seen a greater accumulation of mass murder and deliberate slaughter than any other century in recorded history. Look at our society. Violence is on the increase and is more widespread today than before. Honesty and fair dealing can no longer be taken for granted; and the integrity of our leading financial institutions is called in question. Think of the amount of wife battering, of baby battering and child abuse. Why, even the birds and the beasts do not sink as low as that. Human parents can be worse than animals in their treatment of their children. It is no use talking about the progress of man's evolution if the human race discards the teaching and example of its great religious leaders. And in this country that means that moral deterioration is bound to follow when increasing numbers reject the way of Jesus Christ who was born in the stable at Bethlehem. If there is to be any difference in man's moral progress, it will only come when we take the Christmas Story seriously as the sign of God breaking into the world in the Jesus who was

Born to raise the sons of earth,
Born to give them second birth.   (CH3:169)

The third thing I noticed as I looked from the manse window was a jet aeroplane flying at 30,000 feet or so, leaving its vapour trail behind it in the clear blue sky. And here was a sign of man's amazing technological achievements which make it possible for him to move from the earth into outer space. But of what real and lasting use are such achievements, if the world is still torn by strife, its natural resources being ruthlessly exploited, its environment being increasingly polluted and the threat of nuclear devastation hanging over it all the time? What possible difference can the Christmas Story make in such a situation?

It can give mankind a picture of what work is meant to be. It tells of shepherds who were doing their daily work when the glory of the Lord shone round about them. How far removed from that ideal is much of what men have to do as work today. But work ought to be fulfilling. It ought to be what men and women enjoy doing, not least if it is hard and demanding. And if the spirit of the Christmas Story is brought into daily work—and why should it not be?—what a difference it can make!

The Christmas Story tells of wise men—the scientists of their day—who were humble enough to look for God's guidance and were willing to learn from what he was going to reveal about himself in Jesus. We must all admire the skills of the scientists of our day. But the danger is that they should be tempted to usurp the role of God himself in creating and directing human life. The Christmas Story reminds us that before the majesty and power of God the wisest of us must remember to bow in awe and reverence.

And finally the Christmas Story tells us of angels whose song was 'Peace on earth to men who are God's friends'. Angels nowadays tend to be relegated to children's nativity plays. But to me at least they represent a power which the world sorely needs.

In our time there has been no more convinced atheist, no more trenchant critic of the Christian faith, than the late Bertrand Russell. But towards the end of his long life, not only did he become an indefatigable campaigner for peace on earth, but he also said this: 'What prevents the establishment of a humane society? It is the evil passion in human minds; and the solution is a very simple and old-fashioned thing, Christian love and compassion'.

The Christmas Story reminds us that such love and compassion do not come by themselves. They need the supernatural help of God. There can only be a brotherhood of mankind when it stems from and depends upon the fatherhood of God. And in relation to that fatherhood the angels' song is no mere fairy tale but one of the sure and certain signs of the difference which Christmas can make to this weary world.

CHAPTER 2

Leader of Worship

Introduced by David M Beckett

To a raw probationer emerging from university with a meagre stock of student sermons, each of which had taken weeks of reading and re-shaping to prepare, Hugh Douglas seemed both dauntingly competent and dauntingly fluent. Had he not been so sensitively encouraging in the workload he assigned to his assistants—a workload that gradually increased as experience and confidence developed—the effect of his own productivity might have been thoroughly demoralizing. For his was an integrated and well-rounded ministry, to an extent that makes it difficult even with hindsight to think of any single strand in isolation from the others. However full his diary, he always made time for a weekly session with his assistant to discuss visits, plan services, evaluate previous efforts—always with time for some wider discussion of ministry, for these were pastoral and not just administrative meetings. It was then that I learned to marvel at a programme that had room for committee work in Edinburgh, talks to church groups and secular clubs, civic and university functions and those regular television broadcasts—invariably followed, it seemed, by a deluge of correspondence—which extended Hugh's ministry far beyond the ranks of his own congregation. And always, astonishingly, he found time to sustain a full programme of pastoral visiting within the congregation also.

Yet from the whole spectrum of this integrated and prolific ministry, no part of it was more important to Hugh Douglas than the basic tasks of leading worship and preaching the Word Sunday after Sunday. His high public profile meant that he was much in demand as a visiting preacher. One of the few limitations he imposed on his service to the wider Church was to be parted from his own people's Sunday worship as seldom as possible. For all his eagerness that the Church should find new ways of serving the community and communicating the Gospel, he was never in any doubt that the Sunday worship of the parish church remained the very heartbeat of the Church's life.

The relationship between that Sunday worship and the pastoral side of the ministry was central to the services that Hugh led. Part of the secret of his humbling productivity was a discipline that rendered him incapable of wasting either time or experience. He managed to read widely (how? when?) and was well abreast of changes in secular thinking, of the new dilemmas posed by medical and technological advance. Observations on the insights that he gathered from his reading, as on things that struck him as significant in the course of his pastoral visiting, were carefully logged within the commonplace book he believed all ministers should keep. So, although there was hardly ever a direct reference in prayer or sermon to the visits he had made during the previous week, the congregation contributed more than they knew to the material which nourished them each Sunday; and Hugh for his part derived from his pastoral and literary contacts an awareness of how people in the pews were thinking, and the questions that baffled them, which made all his sermons easily intelligible and kept his prayers earthed in his people's concerns with a directness which was part of his special flair.

Looking back to material surviving from the early years of his ministry, one can detect the development of this directness and relevance in worship. Certainly there was a change of style in what Hugh wrote—a change most evident in public prayer. Services from North Leith days are in strongly traditional language, reflecting the measured dignified ethos of the 1940 *Book of Common Order* and incorporating many phrases from the King James (or Authorised) Version of the Bible. This opening of an intercessory prayer in 1943 leans heavily on the Litany in the *Book of Common Prayer*:

> O Lord God, King of heaven and earth, who dost rule over the whole family of mankind ... we beseech Thee that it may please Thee to give to all nations unity, peace and concord: to give us a heart to love and fear Thee and diligently to live after Thy commandments: to bring into the way of truth such as have erred and are deceived: to strengthen such as do stand: to comfort and help the weakhearted: to raise up them that fall: and finally to beat down Satan under our feet.

By contrast, this supplication, dated 1959, shows how much the language of Hugh's prayers had been simplified by then:

> Saviour and Redeemer, we need Thy help and guidance.
> Make us able to add something, however small, to the goodness of the world by what we do and what we are.
> When we meet joy and loveliness, let us see them as signs of Thee.
> When we meet difficulties, keep us serene and charitable and faithful.
> Show us opportunities of helping others.
> Strengthen us to contend for truth, if only by a word; and make our faith strong and fervent.

This refinement continued throughout Hugh's ministry—as in this supplication (undated) from one of his late services:

> Make us strong enough to bear the vision of the truth and to have done with all falsehood, pretence and hypocrisy; so that we may see things as they are, and fear no more.

To 'see things as they are' was a large part of what Hugh sought to help others to do. He himself does not seem to have encountered any great crisis of faith and he had no more interest in theological sophistry or precious liturgical niceties than most of his congregation. He did, though, have an abiding sense of seemliness and order in the church's worship, a conviction that services should display a logical and defensible rationale, an awareness of the symbolism that is always part of public worship and affects—for good or ill— a congregation's perception of worship's importance. His approach was broadly catholic, with room in it for praise and prayer from every part of the Church's heritage; and he valued good order, not from the arcane perspective of the liturgical purist, but because he believed it helped the congregation to relate to what was going on. Those students for the ministry who heard his lectures on Preaching and Worship delivered at Christ's College, Aberdeen in 1980 (extracts of which are reproduced below) must have been grateful for his clear and robust treatment of the practicalities as well as the neat humour with which he presented them.

Because the Christian cause and the honour of the Church mattered so much to Hugh, his material does not identify him with any party or faction. Manuscripts of sermons often include illustrations of pretentious or unwise practices in other places. Nearly always these have been edited out with marginal notes ('better not identify' . . . 'perhaps better omit') or modified to make sure they could not be interpreted as personal criticism. In Church courts or committees, or in private conversation, Hugh would argue his case cogently; but he did not regard it as any part of the minister's job to wash the Church's linen in the pulpit.

Whatever Hugh did, he prepared carefully. In 1965 he was asked to give a talk to his Youth Fellowship on 'Our Order of Service.' Many ministers would have been content to *ad lib* on such an informal occasion at the end of a busy Sunday. Hugh's notes reveal a talk constructed as carefully as any sermon and covering a wide range of topics: Pentecost, Justin Martyr, mediaeval worship, the eucharistic basis of Reformed services, the progression of praise items, the Christian Year, the sequence of prayers, the shape of the St Mary's service. That talk finished on a note that well sums up his life-long approach to this central task of the ministry: 'The whole point of worship is that it should be related to life. We come to be cleansed and renewed, and go out to do better in the new week.'

*   *   *

FROM LECTURES ON WORSHIP

Extracts from a Series of Lectures on Worship delivered at Christ's College, Aberdeen in 1980. These provide good insights into Hugh Douglas's approach to Worship and his aims in constructing Services.

The Sacred and the Secular in Worship

Liturgy comes from the Greek word *leitourgia*, which originally meant, particularly in Athens, a service rendered to the state or a duty imposed on wealthy and privileged people—a gracious type of super-tax. Thus a rich Athenian might have to perform certain 'liturgies' or 'folk-works', such as financing the production of plays at a drama festival, or paying for the costumes and paraphernalia of a public procession. It was a form of service to the community.

With the development of the Jewish and Christian religions, the word came to mean priestly ministrations, in the first instance among the Jews and then applied to eucharistic services and set forms of divine worship. But this stage had not been reached when the word is used in the New Testament. In Philippians chapter 2 verse 17 Paul is speaking of how he has given his life in running the race, and he says (NEB translation), 'But if my life-blood is to crown that sacrifice which is the offering up of your faith, I am glad of it, and I share my gladness with you all'. *Leitourgia* is here

translated as 'offering': and in his commentary Lightfoot
writes, 'Paul's language expresses the fundamental idea of the
Christian Church in which a universal priesthood has sup-
planted the exclusive ministrations of a select tribe or class.
The Philippians are the priests; their faith (or their good
works springing from their faith) is the sacrifice; St Paul's life-
blood the accompanying libation'. Note how 'liturgy' in its
New Testament meaning is identified with the whole of life.
. . . It meant religion in action, not merely within the Church,
but out in the world.

The reason why men like Ronald Gregor Smith and J G
Davies write of secular Christianity and the everyday God is
that they have sensed the danger of the liturgy of the Christian
Church becoming divorced from the life of ordinary people.
Ask the average non-Christian today what liturgy means to
him, and he will probably answer that it can only mean little
or nothing, because to understand the sacred mysteries is
obviously the prerogative of those who gather within the walls
of the churches where liturgies are performed. In the same
way address your question to the average Christian, and you
may receive differing answers. A Presbyterian might say that
he knows very little about any kind of liturgy and that he has
always thought of it in relation to Episcopalian or 'Popish'
forms of service. Both Episcopalian and Roman Catholic
Christians might think of liturgy in relation to their traditional
forms, and might comment on how it can become a source of
division within their respective Churches, whether through
loyalty to the Tridentine Mass in the Roman Catholic Church,
or through opposition to the *Alternative Service Book* among
the Anglicans.

Thus liturgy may become a matter for the experts who lay
down what are the proper forms of prayer, the correct
symbols, the appropriate colours, the established movements
and actions—all within the enclosed and exclusive circle of the
Church. In this connection I remember a church where the
minister was dedicated to establishing what he believed to be
the perfect liturgical service, according to the true traditions

of the Church of Scotland. As he drew nearer to his goal the congregation grew ever smaller, until a colleague was forced to conjecture that when the poor man had attained the perfect liturgy there might be no one left to share in it. Thus the separation between the sacred and the secular would have become complete.

There are some Christians in our day who believe that this separation is in fact so general in the organized Church that they have rebelled against the Church. Such a one was the late Revd Geoffrey Shaw, the founder of Gorbals Group in Glasgow which was based upon the East Harlem Protestant Parish in New York. He and the other members of the Group felt that the official Church was completely separated from and largely irrelevant to the people who lived in the Gorbals. Geoff Shaw and his friends therefore went to live in the Gorbals, so far as possible identifying themselves with the residents of that district and the conditions in which they had to live. Worship for the Group centred on a weekly celebration of the Lord's Supper set out on the kitchen table in one of the homes occupied by the members, who themselves comprised members of the Church of Scotland and other communions, including the Scottish Episcopal Church. And this worship was seen as entirely related to their respective vocations or jobs or forms of service, as also to what they were trying to do for the community in which they were living.

When Geoff Shaw became a town councillor in Glasgow, which was the initial step which he took on the road which led to his being elected as the first Convener of the Strathclyde Region, he attended a Kirkin' of the Council Service. Afterwards he was asked what he thought of the service. His answer came in one word—'Hilarious'. He was not seeking to be funny. This was the view of a rebellious Christian, a man who led a most self-sacrificial life and who literally drove himself to death in the service of his fellow men. In his view the Kirkin' Service was an empty form, unrelated to the lives of ordinary folk, in particular the underprivileged, Christ's poor and forgotten men and women.

I personally think that Geoff Shaw was wrong in writing off the organized Church, and in limiting his own view of the Church to the Gorbals Group and its like. But his life and his death remain as a challenge to more conventional Christians to consider much more deeply what they mean by the worship and the service of the Church. If liturgy becomes the private and mysterious province of the Church, then the likelihood is that in modern society service will increasingly become divorced from religion. It is not only that the State has taken over more and more of the service once rendered by the Church to the community, from the provision of hospitals and schools to the relief of the poor. It is also that many worthy persons who conscientiously seek to serve their fellow men seem to feel that the Church has nothing to say to them, and would, like Geoff Shaw, see little if any relevance in a Kirkin' Service.

But there is a great deal to be said for such services. For one thing, they are true to the Reformed principle of the lordship of Christ in the whole of life. It seems to me to be admirable that Town Councils and Incorporated Trades, the Red Cross and the St Andrew's Ambulance Association, the Armed Forces and the Police, the Boys' and Girls' Brigades, the Scouts and Guides, the Rotarians and the Soroptimists—and a host of other bodies—should still seek the blessing of God on their differing forms of service. They have good reason for doing so.

To serve the community constantly and efficiently is no easy task. It needs inspiration to prevent it from becoming dreary and burdensome. It requires a source of strength when spirit and body are weary and close to failing altogether. It is very hard to go on loving one's neighbour unless one begins by loving God with heart and soul and mind and strength. Thus the point of what Paul said about the love of Christ constraining him. It is this love, mediated through worship, both private and public, which enables ordinary people to do extraordinary things.

When Jesus spoke of loving one's neighbour he gave his teaching in the vivid form of the Parable of the Good Samaritan. We properly describe an act of worship in a church as divine service. But the act of helping an injured person lying by the roadside is even more truly described as divine service. The priest and the Levite in the parable represented liturgy in what might be called the sacred or vertical sense—the vertical line linking the holy God with man, in the worship of the Temple (or, *mutatis mutandis*, the Church). The Samaritan represented service (or liturgy) in the horizontal sense—the horizontal and secular line linking man with his neighbour.

Throughout his ministry, as in this Parable, Jesus sought to do away with the separation between the horizontal and vertical forms of service, between secular and sacred, between life and liturgy, between the world and worship. Thus he cried to his opponents, 'Alas for you, lawyers and Pharisees, hypocrites! You pay tithes of mint and dill and cummin; but you have overlooked the weightier demands of the Law, justice, mercy and good faith. It is these you should have practised without neglecting the others' (Matthew 23:23, NEB).

When you bring a vertical and a horizontal line together you fashion a cross. Jesus knew that he had to die on the cross if he was to show how alone life and liturgy could be united. Our Lord was crucified at the very point where the vertical and horizontal arms of the cross meet; the point of tension, the point where opposites are reconciled, the point of self-sacrificial love, as if to show that God so loved the WORLD (not the Church) that he gave his only-begotten Son, that whosoever believeth on him should not perish but should have everlasting life.

.... The aim and object of worship are to enable man to gain mastery over himself so that he may be saved from the dire consequences of his uncontrolled greed and lust for power. That is why liturgy must never be allowed to remain within the cloistered walls of a Church which is out of touch with the world. It was the Lord of the Church who died on the cross to show that life must be liturgy and liturgy must be life.

Fellowship and Mission in Worship

I am sure that one of the reasons why so many young people seem to find little to attract them in the worship of the Church is that they find no fellowship in it. I remember quite clearly how dull I found the services of the church to which my parents took me as a youngster. No doubt this was more my fault than that of the worthy and distinguished minister under whom we sat as a family. The fact remains that worship began to mean something for me when I started attending Sunday evening meetings in a private house, under the auspices of the Scottish Schoolboys' Club. There was little in the way of ordered worship. The atmosphere was very informal. The prayers and the talks were given by young men who often faltered and stumbled in what they were saying. But there was fellowship. There was sincerity. And I, along with many others, began to find that Jesus had something to say to us, that he began to be a living influence in our lives.

. . . . Again I remember when first I became vividly aware of what fellowship and mission could mean in a congregation. I was in my second year as a divinity student, and I had been asked to start work in Govan Old Parish Church in the autumn. I went down to see the set-up, on a lovely June evening. The first thing that interested me was that the church itself was open, and that indeed it remained open for prayer and meditation every day. This was a rarity in the Church of Scotland, most of whose churches remained closed for six days out of seven in those days. On this particular evening however, the church was not only open, it was being used. There was a steady stream of men and women coming and going from it. They were engaged in a Mission of Friendship to the parish area, in which some 10,000 people lived and round which you could walk in twenty minutes. This was the culmination of a two-year plan in which the congregation had been prepared, through fellowship, for mission. On the evening in question, volunteers came to pray in the church before going out, two by two, to do a specified number of visits in the parish. Many went out in fear and trembling, but all came back exalted and, in a measure, transformed, to give thanks for their experience of mission. This church was neither dull nor dying. It was alive and growing. Hundreds came into the fellowship. There was a class for first communicants numbering over two hundred, which ran for twelve weeks. There were many adult baptisms. The number of children coming to Sunday School so increased that two separate Sunday Schools had to be organized to cope with the demand—and so on.

Nor was the fellowship limited to the Sunday services. During the week a great variety of activity flourished in the neighbouring Pearce Institute, to which hundreds of people, young and old, came every week. Whether those who came attended church services or not—and inevitably many of them did not come to church—all that went on in so-called secular activities could be seen as being part of God's activity in the life of his children; and the fellowship in the canteen of the Institute, where bread was broken, was a counterpart of the breaking of bread in the Lord's Supper in the church.

. . . . My plea is that in your church and parish you should, under God, always seek to strengthen the worship and fellowship of your people so that you can lead them outwards in their task of mission. Do not look for sudden results. Be prepared to spend some considerable time in making your people ready. You may have to persuade your Kirk Session to go for part of a weekend to St Ninian's, Crieff, or to Carberry Tower for a retreat and conference to consider the whole question. You will find this a rewarding experience, with a good chance of success. You will then have to do something about the lapsed and the indifferent in the congregation itself. You will have to recruit volunteers who are prepared to help the elders in district visitation, so that in turn other and additional volunteers may be recruited for visitation of the parish. In all this you will be helped by the experience of other ministers, as also by the literature prepared by the Committees of the Church. What is essential is that the spirit of mission may grow and increase throughout our Church, especially among those like yourselves who are being called to the ministry in a difficult and challenging time, but one which is also rich in opportunity and bright with hope.

The Order and Conduct of Worship

There is a wide variety in the order of worship as found throughout the Church of Scotland. This is largely due to the differing traditions of the separated communions which were finally brought together in the Union of 1929. Thus when you are called to your first parish you may find an order of service different from that to which you have been accustomed, and which you may desire to alter.

Before you make any changes, it would be advisable to give some thought as to why this particular order of service is used. If it reflects some deeply rooted tradition in the life of the congregation, any change must be grounded on sound reasons and principles. It is therefore essential to have an adequate understanding of the history of Reformed worship in Scotland, a belief in the relevance to modern conditions of what you propose to do and a degree of patience and tact in explaining your purpose to the congregation.

. . . . The infrequent celebration of Communion was not the purpose of the Reformers. It was recognized by them that the Eucharist had been the basic service of the Christian Church from the earliest days. Calvin would have liked a weekly Communion, but was prevented by the civil magistrates from realizing his wish. Towards the end of his life he again protested against the practice of infrequent Communion, writing, 'I have been at pains again and again publicly to state that our custom is corrupt, in order that those who come after me may the more easily and freely correct it'. In spite of efforts to have monthly Communion, the old prejudice—indeed deriving from the Roman practice—in favour of infrequent Communions was so strong that he had to settle for quarterly celebrations.

Similarly in Scotland, John Knox was strongly sacramental in his attitude. His denunciations of the Mass were directed against its misuse, in the separation of the consecration and Communion. He too desired the Sacrament, in its primitive simplicity, to be more frequently celebrated—monthly, if possible. But the shortage of ministers in Scotland at the time made this difficult to achieve. In the following century the Westminster *Directory of Public Worship* enjoined that Communion should frequently be celebrated. And even although infrequent Communion remained the rule in the eighteenth and nineteenth centuries, the outline of the Eucharistic service remained as the norm of Sunday morning worship when there was no celebration.

It is the contention of the late Dr W D Maxwell that, largely due to Anglican influence, the authentic eucharistic outline was lost in the normal Sunday morning service of the Church of Scotland. This statement can be confirmed by comparing three service books, *Prayers for Divine Service* (1929), the *Book of Common Order* (1940) and the *Book of Common Order* (1979). The 1929 and 1940 books have essentially the same morning order of service, except for the position of the Lord's Prayer, which in 1929 comes at the end of the first prayer but in 1940 is placed after the second prayer of thanksgiving and intercession. The book of 1979, however, would gain Dr Maxwell's approbation, and reflects a growing tendency among a number of ministers to regard the morning service, when there is no celebration of Communion, as what has been traditionally called a 'dry mass', in other words the eucharistic order without the actual celebration.

.... Whichever outline is chosen, and this will depend upon the predilections of the minister or the tradition of the congregation, it is surely preferable to have some fixed order which is according to the use of the Church of Scotland than to have a hotch-potch which is dependent upon the whims of an individual minister. Either of the orders outlined is capable of adjustment in the event of special services; and neither is obligatory in the sense of being enforced by rules or canons of public worhsip. But when a seemly order of service has been used for some time, with due explanation where necessary, a congregation will not only grow accustomed to it but will be happy with it, because they know its rhythm and progression, and because they find it meaningful and devotionally helpful.

. . . . Formality is not in itself a virtue. It can be cold and unattractive. One welcomes the warmer approach which leads a minister to begin by extending a greeting to the congregation and to any visitors who may be present. Having established the family feeling he then proceeds to call the congregation to worship, and the service can proceed with simplicity and also, one hopes, with dignity. There is no need to introduce jocular asides at different stages—the place for these is in the children's address or the sermon, if indeed anywhere. There is no need to amplify the introduction to hymns by phrases such as 'Let us sing to the praise and glory of God in Hymn 525'. It is not even necessary to say 'Let us sing Hymn 525'— what else are you going to do with it? Avoid all unnecessary elaborations, all tautology.

As in the preaching of the sermon, so in the whole conduct of the service, avoid the parsonic voice. In the prayers do not strive for any unctuous or over-reverential tones. Again let simplicity, sincerity and earnestness prevail. If you move from prayer desk to lectern and then to pulpit, move naturally. Stand at or before the Communion Table to receive the offering; and even if there is no alms dish, stand, nevertheless, when the offering is being brought up the aisle to the Table, for it should represent the offering and dedication of the lives of the people.

The proper position from which to pronounce the Benediction is from in front of the Communion Table. Anyone who is a lay person or a licentiate should use the words 'be with us', and should not raise the hands in the act of blessing, keeping them folded as in prayer. It is after ordination to the ministry that it is correct to use the phrase 'be with you', when either both arms can be raised in the traditional Scottish manner, or the right arm, with the thumb and the two adjacent fingers also raised in token of the Trinity.

Should prayers be read or spoken extempore? In a church in which there are no set forms of prayer for daily or for weekly use, it is natural that there should be a continuing emphasis upon the value of extempore prayer. No matter how ordered a service may be, it is wholly in the tradition of the Church of Scotland that anyone who is conducting divine worship may feel moved by particular circumstances or by a leading of the Spirit to offer up prayers which well up spontaneously from the heart.

That having been established, one might say that any minister who is involved in the weekly conduct of worship would be well advised to prepare his prayers carefully, whether he reads them or not. Merely to leave one's prayers to the inspiration (or, sadly, lack of inspiration) of the moment could be characterized not so much as an excess of faith as either a deficiency in commonsense or even a tendency towards laziness. The fact is that those who criticize the use of a liturgy or of any read prayers may often fail to realize that they create a kind of liturgy of their own, even when they think that their prayers are completely extempore. And unless their minds are deeply nourished by knowledge of great devotional literature such as the Psalms, their language in prayer can be pedestrian and uninspiring. I remember hearing a relative of mine tell the story of how a worshipper had returned, with his sister, after a ten years' absence to the morning service in her Ayrshire church. The incumbent was a strong anti-ritualist who never dreamt of reading his prayers. After the service the visitor said to his sister, 'Well, Mary, I see that you are still sitting under "the droppings of the Gospel with great delight".' This singularly infelicitous phrase had become part of the unwritten liturgy of the minister, possibly without his being fully aware of it. An interesting addendum to the story is that this minister's son became one of the leading exponents of ordered worship in the Church of Scotland and, by the same token, of read prayers.

Anyone who begins a ministry by carefully preparing and writing his prayers can, over the years, build up a prayer book of his own, covering the whole course of the Christian Year. Such a collection of prayers can be of great value. It is probably not by any means wholly an individual's own work, for he may have drawn upon the great wealth of devotional material to weave into prayers of his own composition. Nor is it a fixed and unalterable liturgy. Rather can it be used as a basis, to be added to or enriched as the years go by, or changed and perhaps improved through increased knowledge and experience. What cannot be doubted is that the time spent in building up such a collection of prayers will never have been wasted. Nor does the possession and use of such prayers ever prevent for a moment the spontaneous use of extempore prayer when the occasion arises.

. . . . Whether published prayers are used verbatim or simply as a basis, the language of prayer should be simple and unadorned. The best writers of English have been noted for rarely using elaborate or polysyllabic language. There ought to be no striving for effect, either to be too obviously religious or too relentlessly contemporary. The *Book of Common Order* (1940) carried overtones of earlier years in the use of words like 'vouchsafe', which sound strangely in modern ears. On the other hand, I can remember phrases which have grated harshly, as in the case of one young man who prayed 'not only for those who are rich but also for the stinking rich'. The result of such extravagances is that one concentrates on the strangeness and forgets the purpose of the prayer.

Getting and Giving in Worship

. . . . In worship it is possible for us to become, by faith, more vividly aware of the way in which we are always surrounded by God's love and care. Worship should strengthen the relationship between the worshipper and God. But how best is this to be achieved?

It might be said that there are two main attitudes of mind which can be detected in worship. There is the receptive attitude, in which the individual is concerned with receiving or getting something of spiritual value through worship. And there is the attitude of offering, in which the worshipper is concerned to give what is due and worthy to God, through worship.

The receptive attitude is common in the Church of Scotland. One often hears it said by someone returning from a church service, 'There was nothing for me today. I got nothing from that service'. Presumably what is meant is that the worshipper did not like the choice of hymns, that the prayers were unhelpful, and that the sermon touched no responsive chord. In such a case the individual has come to church not to give but to get, not to offer but to receive. In this view the hymns should be such as appeal, the prayers should be suited to the individual's mood, and by the same token the hearer should approve of the sermon. Such an attitude is wholly understandable, and it is perhaps inevitable that it should always be a part of what a worshipper will feel. But is it not much too subjective? Is it not to make the attendance at worship too closely akin to the attendance at a lecture, a play or an entertainment, where those who go are expecting a performance to stimulate their minds or their emotions? It is certainly part of worship that the worshippers should find spiritual cleansing and inspiration through prayer; that they should receive—or at least look for—an answer to their problems and worries, their petitions and their requests; that they should be given encouragement to face their daily lives with greater faith and effectiveness. But worship is not all receiving, it is also offering. It is not wholly getting, it is also giving. It is not sitting to watch a performance, it is being a conscious participant in a meaningful activity.

It must be admitted that in the Church of Scotland the nature and the forms of our services tend to encourage the receptive attitude in worship. There is little active participation by the worshippers, apart of course from the silent participation of the faithful. The only vocal participation is in the singing of psalms and hymns, the repetition of the Lord's Prayer and the singing of a choral Amen in some cases after the Benediction. Might it not be that in consequence the worshipper tends to become like a sponge, soaking up the spiritual nourishment which is provided? Granted that this is an exaggeration, is there not a danger that the sense of offering in worship may be diminished, and that through concentration on the place of the sermon the objectivity of worship may be lessened? It is certainly the case that often the whole conduct of the service, apart from the singing, may be left entirely to the minister. When this is so it is all the more difficult for the members of the congregation not to regard the service as something of a solo performance. And surely that is not what the worship of the Church is meant to be.

. . . . It is surely important that the attitude of offering and giving should be encouraged. Nowhere can this be more truly recognized than in prayers and acts of thanksgiving. It is strange how thanksgiving can be overlooked or almost forgotten in some services. Compare the magnificent words of the *Te Deum*—'We praise thee, O God, we acknowledge thee to be the Lord. All the earth doth worship thee, the Father everlasting'—compare these in their splendid objectivity with, for example, the words of the hymn, 'Oh that will be glory for me, glory for me, glory for me', centred on the selfish thoughts and desires of the individual worshipper. We must avoid turning our worship and our prayers into a kind of querulous whining for satisfaction. Rather let us remember all that has been given us so generously, undeserving as we are, so that our worship can be an offering of praise and thanksgiving and we can dedicate ourselves, body, soul and spirit, which is our reasonable service.

This spirit of praise and thanksgiving can be expressed and also stimulated by the beauty of the church buildings in which our worship is offered. The bareness and simplicity of many kirks in Scotland lead to this aspect of worship being played down by some of our people. They are apt to concentrate on the eternal verities, conveyed in the preaching of the Word and through the austerity of prayer, unaided by what they might regard as unnecessary accretions. But beauty is one of God's greatest gifts, and why should it not be used as an integral part of the offering of worship?

. . . . Symbols are additional aids to worship. We have fought shy of symbols in the Scottish Church, again for the usual reasons and the fear of being 'ritualistic'. Be it noted, however, that we have not shunned symbols when they were incorporated in stained glass windows! There is no need for an elaboration or over-indulgence in symbols in our churches. But just as we need symbols and symbolic actions in our daily relationships with each other, so we can be helped in our offering of worship through these same means. The dove of the Holy Spirit, the sacred monogram, the Cross—all of these, along with others, can be used on pulpits, Communion Tables, pulpit falls and the like. Let them be tastefully picked out in suitable colours or in gold leaf, and their presence will be more easily seen and explained, for example, to children and young people.

Finally, remember how greatly our worship in church can be aided by observance of the Christian Year. It is not only that the Gospel truths can be consistently proclaimed in this way. The whole service can reflect the message, through hymns, readings and prayers. Advent comes with its atmosphere of waiting and expectation, leading us on to the warmth and loveliness of Christmas. Epiphany leads us to turn outwards to the non-Christian world. Lent brings us back to self-discipline and repentance. Holy Week unites us with Christians everywhere in the deepest devotion; and we pass from the dire sorrow of Good Friday to the triumph and joy of Easter day. This in turn leads us to the coming of the Holy Spirit at Whitsunday, the birthday of the Christian Church, and to the culmination of our faith in the worship of God who is Father, Son and Holy Spirit. What treasures of devotion are contained in the use of the Christian Year, and how impoverished would be our worship were we to leave them untouched!

A COMMUNION SERMON

Preached in St Mary's, Dundee, on 24 April 1977. (Auto-biographical anecdotes such as the two in this sermon were fairly rare in Hugh Douglas's preaching.)

> I tell you, never again shall I drink from the fruit of the vine until that day when I drink it new with you in the kingdom of my Father.
>
> (Matthew 26:29, NEB)

This was the last supper Jesus was to have with his disciples. These words show that he knew it—although no one else did.

We speak of the Lord's Supper, and that is what it has become in the experience and tradition of the Church. But as Leonardo da Vinci's famous painting will always remind us, it began as the Last Supper. It was the farewell meal which Jesus had with his disciples. It was the human Jesus, their friend and their leader, saying 'Goodbye' to them.

There is always sadness in farewell, and it can go very deep—the soldier going on active service for instance, or even saying goodbye to a youngster on his first journey to school. One can understand how Paul's friends from Ephesus wept bitterly as they escorted him to the ship that was to take him from their sight. I can still remember the aching sense of desolation I felt, over sixty years ago, as I stood on the deck of the Anchor liner that was taking me home from India to Scotland and saw my parents waving goodbye to me from the wharf at Bombay harbour. I knew that I would see them again in two years time; but when one is seven years old two years seems like an eternity.

For Jesus, then, this was a farewell supper. Later that night, we read, 'Horror and dismay came over him and he said to them, "My heart is ready to break with grief"' (Mark 14:34, NEB). It is in that context that we must try to understand what Jesus planned the Last Supper should mean for his disciples.

He was going to his death. He knew that they did not understand this.

He was setting out in faith on his last voyage.

What was he to do, what *could* he do for them?

What would any one of us do in parting? We would give a keepsake, a memento, a portrait or a photograph—something that our friends and dear ones could remember us by.

So Jesus took the Last Supper and gave it to his disciples as something by which they could remember him.

He took the bread and broke it. 'This is my body which is broken for you.'

He took the cup and gave it to them. 'This cup is the new testament in my blood which is shed for many. This do in remembrance of me.'

He knew that they would remember afterwards—after their desertion and flight; after the shame had passed. They would remember then what he had said. And they would realize that the awful death on the Cross, in its slow torture, its agony and horror, had been for their sakes and for the healing of their sins and for all people everywhere.

So the Last Supper is always a call to remembrance. As James Montgomery put it in his great hymn:

> According to thy gracious word,
>   In meek humility,

This will I do, my dying Lord,
I will remember thee.

Thy body, broken for my sake,
My bread from heaven shall be;
Thy testamental cup I take,
And thus remember thee.   (CH3:585)

So Paul could remind his converts at Ephesus of what he had
done and endured for them. So to others he could say, 'I bear
on my body the marks of the Lord Jesus'.

We have memorials to remind us of what others have done
for us, we have our war memorials. We have our keepsakes
and perhaps our photographs of our dear ones to whom we
owe so much. And when we remember how much others—
good men and women—have endured for the sake of their
fellow human beings, let us remember this Jesus who so often
has been the inspiration of such self-sacrificial love, the Jesus
whose body was broken and whose blood was shed, who died
that we might live as God means us to live. The Last Supper
is for remembrance.

But it is not only the Last Supper; it is the *Lord's Supper*.
It is not only the Supper of the human Jesus; it is the Supper
of the risen Lord. It is not only for remembrance of what was
done in the past; it is for realization of union with Jesus here
and now.

Jesus said, when he took the bread and wine, 'This is my
body. This is my blood'. In other words he was saying, 'This
is me, this is my real person—not just my death is what you
are to remember, you are to be aware of my presence'.

Let us not make the mistake of imagining that the Lord's
Supper is a kind of representation, like da Vinci's portrait of
the Last Supper. It is one thing to look on a portrait or a
photograph. It is another thing to know that the person of the
photograph is beside you.

When I was three years old my mother brought me home
to Scotland three months before my father was to follow us

at the beginning of his furlough. So that I would not forget him she had a photograph of my father on the mantelpiece in the bedroom. And each night when I said my prayers she would point to the photograph and remind me of my father.

One night I woke up and there, to my astonishment, my father was in the room. Before I had fully realized this I had pointed to the photograph and said, 'Why are you still up there?' And then the joy of the real presence of my father replaced the memory of the photograph.

The Last Supper becomes the Lord's Supper for us when the memory is replaced by the realization of the real presence of the Lord. When the disciples came to the tomb looking for the body of Jesus they were told, 'He is not here. He is risen'. So he is not in the memory of the Last Supper, wonderful and inspiring though the remembrance must always be. He is here in the bread and the wine as we receive them by faith. *This is Jesus.* He is the Lord who died indeed but who rose again and who is always present when two or three are gathered together in his name. This is the living Jesus and he is the Lord's Supper.

> Here, O my Lord, I see thee face to face;
> Here would I touch and handle things unseen,
> Here grasp with firmer hand the eternal grace,
> And all my weariness upon thee lean.   (CH3:573)

PRAYERS AT AN ADVENT SERVICE

Taken from a recording made in St Andrew's Church, Brisbane, Australia, 4 December 1979.

O God, before the worlds were created you were there. Through all ages you laid your plans, worked out your purpose, prepared everything for the coming of Jesus, the light of the world and the hope of men. Prepare our hearts for his coming to us now.

We know, our Father, that we are not worthy. We take our gifts for granted, we let our religion grow stale, we complain and grumble when we should be glad and thankful, and we do not look for opportunities of doing good. But we believe in you. We believe in the forgiveness of sin. We believe that Jesus makes all things new. So, cleanse, forgive and restore us now that we may go forward with peace in our hearts, a stronger determination to do our best for you.

You have set within us a longing for truth. May we never be content with false values or trivialities. With you are the words of eternal life. Keep our lips free from the words of bitterness and let us speak the words that cheer and comfort and make glad. We know from you that our treasure is in heaven. May we enjoy all our earthly treasure; but show us that it needs the deepening and enriching power of Jesus if it is to bring us nearer to you.

O God give us grace that we may cast away the works of darkness and put upon us the armour of light now in the time of this mortal life in which your Son Jesus came to visit us in great humility; that in the last day, when he shall come again in his glorious majesty to judge both the living and the dead, we may rise to life eternal; through the same Jesus Christ our Lord. AMEN.

We thank you, O God, for the glad tidings of the coming of Christ: for the prophets who foretold him, for the ages which looked forward to him, for the hope which remained constant in men's hearts. We thank you for his first coming, when he was made man for love of men—for love of us. We thank you for his second coming when he stands and knocks at the door of our hearts. We thank you that in the last days he will come again with majesty and love.

Hear our prayer, O God, for your Church. Let the light and truth of Christ shine among her members; and may all Christians hear the message of your love in the coming of Jesus, that they may be determined to serve and follow him in every sphere of life.

Be with this parish and congregation as they look forward to a new era under their new minister, keeping them alive to responsibilities, keen and active in membership, kind and helpful to each other—that our worship here may be the living centre and inspiration of all that we do.

We pray for the peace and prosperity of this country; and that at this time of election wise decisions may be taken. Bless and guide our Queen and all those who guide our affairs. Be with our own dear ones wherever they are, and especially with those who at this time are on holiday or in conference together.

We remember those who are in trouble: those who are burdened with care and anxiety, those who are unhappy and distressed, those who are sick, bereaved or in pain, and any whom we know ourselves and whom we name before you in the silence of our hearts. . . .

And now we thank you for the hope we have in Jesus that life goes on beyond the grave, that we can look forward to meeting again with those who have gone before us. Grant that when our time comes we may go without fear or doubt as those who are coming home to their Father; through Jesus Christ our Lord who has taught us when we pray to say: OUR FATHER. . . .

CHAPTER 3

Pastor

Introduced by William Henney

> Here is the most demanding and most rewarding side of
> pastoral ministry. More than any other profession, a
> minister is able to share in the joys, sorrows, problems and
> whole human experience of his people. A tremendous
> privilege!

These words come from a lecture Hugh Douglas gave on the
Pastoral Ministry. They were truly words from the heart. At
the heart of Hugh there was a deep awareness of pastoral care
for people and a remarkable gift in carrying out such ministry.
In each of his congregations that gift was much shared and
greatly appreciated. All sorts of people, old, young, Church
members, parishioners, were helped to lay hold on life just as
it was by Hugh's kindly wisdom and Christian counselling.

His ideas on pastoral ministry were much affected by a text
from the fourth chapter of Paul's Letter to the Philippians: 'I
have learned, in whatsoever state I am, therewith to be content' (Philippians 4:11, AV). For Hugh, that text was neither
negative nor indeed defeatist. It was the beginning of learning to
cope with life in all its joys and sorrows, successes and failures.

Alongside it, he liked to quote the prayer by Reinhold
Niebuhr:

> God grant me
> the serenity to accept the things I cannot change,
> the courage to change the things I can,
> and the wisdom to know the difference.

I was able to observe how he used his gifts of preacher and pastor both in relation to members of congregation and also to ministers. When he visited a home he brought a happy blend of dignity and humour and ability to put people at ease. One member put it very simply, yet truly, when she said: 'He has great presence but he is also at home with you'. When he entered a pulpit it all seemed so relaxed and people could relate to him. But there was also an expectancy from them. They knew there would be something for them that spoke to their lives, their problems, their joys and griefs. He seemed to preach almost impromptu. More than once a member would comment on his habit of announcing a text, then, removing his glasses he would look round, and begin to preach with scarcely a reference to any notes. But behind that apparent ease was much deliberate preparation and much drawing upon his knowledge of people and pastoral situations. He certainly got through to people. They remembered his words. He pointed them to God.

Ministers also learned from him. Sometimes we ask, 'Who ministers to ministers?' The students, assistants, fellow-ministers who worked with Hugh Douglas knew the strength of his pastoral concern for them. I personally counted it a very great blessing that he and I shared an associateship in ministry in the last years of his life. We would meet each Wednesday, usually in his study. He would first pour out some tea, share in some general chat and much laughter, and then ask about pastoral concerns.

Perhaps there would be some matter of illness. His own experience of a heart attack and hospitalization (see the transcript *It can't happen to me!* in chapter seven below) made him not only a sympathetic listener, but also a wise counsellor. Perhaps there was a marriage breakdown in some home. Again his deep interest in marriage guidance and experience in counselling was immensely helpful as I sought to help the family concerned. I was glad to heed a warning he had given in a lecture on Pastoral Ministry:

With the development of Marriage Guidance Councils which insist on strict standards of training from their counsellors, ministers should not take it for granted that they can rush into this sphere without some comparable knowledge and expertise.

In particular I was personally and deeply grateful to him at a time of a major pastoral issue requiring my clear response. He listened quietly, asked some questions, and then asked what response I intended to make. I told him, and he said, 'I'll support you'. Bless you, Hugh.

But then for Hugh Douglas, pastoral outreach had to be for all, whoever and whatever. For many years he had shared a correspondence with a man serving a long gaol sentence. The letters to and from Charles show the close interplay of faith and life. Charles would write of his deep gratitude for the friendship and understanding shown to him by Hugh, and of how his attitudes and life had changed dramatically over the years. He would ask his questions and Hugh would reply. Then Charles would send comments back until it seemed a complete course on faith and life had been covered! All sorts of subjects—Baptism, Biblical truth, moral standards, family relationships, local news—were examined. The Pastor and Preacher in Hugh Douglas came through strongly in this long correspondence undertaken in the midst of a very busy ministry. Charles has kept two hundred letters from Hugh.

Of course there were lots of laughs too in his relating to people. Gentle humour in the pulpit, laughter in homes, in his own home, on the golf course—life was a glad gift for Hugh Douglas. I recall how on Sunday mornings as we were getting ready to enter the sanctuary, my wife and children had to come through the vestry. Hugh would chat with them, smile delightedly with the children, and then enter the pulpit with that dignity and grace that people noted and respected in him.

It was this great ability both to speak words that made some sense of life for people, and to live out his words in his dealing with people that made him so loved. Of course all he said and

did was rooted and grounded in a strong faith in the God
whose love and grace are so richly revealed in Jesus Christ.
Truly God was and is 'God with us'. That Incarnation of Love
inspired Hugh Douglas to reach out to people. Not just in the
Church and not just to Church members. When he went out
into St Andrews on some quick shopping errand it usually
turned into some long series of pastoral encounters! In shops,
on the street, he would peer at and then recognize some face
and would exchange hearty greetings and stop to chat. He
never saw that as wasted time. Quite the reverse. He enjoyed
the meeting; and whoever had met him went on their way
happy to have done so, encouraged, helped.

Once when Hugh Douglas was seriously ill, a patient in the
next bed morosely assured him he would never work again.
Hugh often told that story with a delighted smile. He did
work again. Indeed the best years of his ministry were still to
come. The experience of his own helplessness helped him to
help many others trying to cope with life. The Pastor in him
grew. Thus Charles in one of his last letters paid the tribute
many would want to pay to him: 'Thank you, Hugh, for
everything you have done for me which has always been
good'.

'I have learned, in whatsoever state I am, therewith to be
content.' It was not surprising that Hugh Douglas kept
returning to that text. The contentment came from his fixed
trust in God, whatever the circumstances. It came through
clearly in his sermons and writings. It came through clearly
in his wise counsel and pastoral care.

*　　*　　*

PREACHING AND PASTORAL WORK

An extract from a lecture on 'Preaching to the Average Person' given to students at Christ's College, Aberdeen in 1980, as part of a series on Preaching and Worship.

So far we have invariably spoken of preaching to a congregation. Naturally so, one might say, to whom else? But a congregation is a gathering, an assembly, a fellowship, not a collection of isolated individuals gathered at random or met together by chance. Therefore preaching cannot be seen in a vacuum, separated from the pastoral work of the minister. A man is a preacher and a pastor when he is called to a congregation, and he should not neglect the one function at the expense of the other. . . .

It is difficult to understand why any man or woman should be reluctant to go about pastoral visitation regularly. For myself, I may indeed have had to push myself out to it when I felt under the weather or depressed, but I never failed to come back from it feeling cheered and encouraged by the fascinating variety of characters I had met, as also by the brave and cheerful spirit shown by so many of them in the face of adversity.

After all, it is only when we visit and come to know our members that we begin to see what kind of people they are and what involvements they have. Seeing them in church on a Sunday morning, trimly dressed and composed, we may feel that their lives follow a normal and uneventful course. Indeed when we visit for the first time everything may appear to go well for them. Equally, they may be waiting until they begin to know us better and trust us more. Some ministers find that it can take as much as five years before their people are ready to open their hearts. But you may be sure that Thoreau, the American writer, was not altogether exaggerating when he said that many people lead lives of quiet desperation. The friendly keeper of the general store at the street corner will tell you that she receives the most intimate confidences across the shop counter. The experienced general practitioner knows that when a young wife comes to ask for a prescription for sleeping pills it is often because of marital disharmony. And it is the minister who is out and about in his district visitation who comes to recognize the symptoms of tension and trouble, and whose help is sought increasingly.

You can be sure that ninety or more per cent of your congregation are constantly aware of some kind of personal trouble. It may be strained personal relationships. It may be family difficulties—with their in-laws or their teenage children. It may be disagreements with their neighbours. Or there may be business worries, redundancy or unemployment. And at some time or another every household will have to live under the shadow of illness or sorrow or bereavement.

Thus when you have been in your parish for some time and you see your congregation sitting in their pews, you see them differently. You understand why they keep coming to church; why they are anxious for you to take an interest in their children and young people; why Mrs Smith looked worried when you passed her in the street the other day; and why Mr Brown is sitting at the back of the church rather than in his usual seat nearer to the front. You will also realize why the Macgregor family have stayed away for several Sundays, and you will make a note to visit them as soon as you possibly can.

Such knowledge and understanding are bound to affect a minister's preaching. They will enlarge his sympathy and his compassion. They will make him turn to his Bible and to his personal devotional life. His sermons ought to have a wider range and a deeper meaning. As his hearers listen, they will feel that this is a man who even if he has not as yet gone through what they are enduring, is ready to stand beside them and assure them that there is help to be found. John Bunyan described a preacher as a man 'with the Law of Truth upon his lips, with the world behind his back, who stands as if he pleaded with men'. They will be the more ready to listen to his pleading and pay heed to his advice if they see him as one who instead of shutting himself up in the ivory tower of his manse study is prepared to step down beside them in whatever dark valley they may be passing through, so that he may lend a helping hand.

THOUGHTS ON PASTORAL MINISTRY

The first extract here is from a sermon on John 21:15–17 preached at the ordination of a minister in April 1975. The other two are from lectures Dr Douglas gave to gatherings of ministers on 'Pastor, People and Prayer' and on 'The Pastoral Ministry'.

Both Outgoing and Pastoral

When Peter had first been called, Jesus said he would be made a fisher of men. Now, in the new relationship, he was to be a shepherd of sheep. The new picture was not to supersede the old one, but to supplement it. The missionary outreach and the pastoral care were different aspects of the same task—and this is something which the Church must always remember.

The pastoral work has two aspects, in the words of Jesus. It involves feeding the lambs and tending the sheep.

There are those in the church—and they are not only the children—who need especial care because they are simple or innocent; open to hurt or in need of protection; lonely or aged; sick or in distress. A great and rewarding part of any minister's work is to ensure that such people are safe and secure in the fellowship and protection of the Church's fold.

But there are also those who are wise and able, skilled and independent. They need guidance in the things of the spirit, and they can only receive it from a minister who is humble enough to learn his craft by experience and by his growth to maturity under the great Shepherd and Guardian of his own soul.

We are living in a time when there is much criticism and questioning of the traditional structure of the Church. Too often those who are so critical are slow to come forward with any positive alternatives. Granted that the Church, as a living body, must always be open to the change and development brought by the Holy Spirit, nothing can alter its basic task of producing ministers who are both outgoing and pastoral, who are both fishers of men and shepherds of the flock, who are as adventurous in seeking the outsiders as they are diligent in caring for the flock.

Ministry to the Sick

There still remains with some of our people the idea that the minister only prays with the sick when they are seriously ill, or indeed in danger. But we all know how much prayer can mean and how valuable it can be in cases of illness. Serious or sudden illness can be such a frightening thing both for the sick person and for the family. The presence of faith creates an atmosphere not only where the too often forgotten factor of God's help comes into operation, but where the serenity is seen which can make all the difference between defeat and victory.

I wonder if you find that a sharing of experience can be helpful? Having had a coronary myself, I believe that it can be reassuring to talk from the background of knowing something about what such illness can be like and how it can be overcome.

There is a fairly general pattern of stages through which an ill person may pass.

First there is the initial shock, followed by panic or fear. There can come rather a desperate (or perhaps even a despairing) period of prayer. How important it is that from this the patient should go on to acceptance of the situation, to relaxation and to dependence.

Acceptance, for there is nothing else we can do. We might have prevented it earlier, but when illness has struck, we shall begin to get the better of it not by resentment but by acceptance.

Relaxation, instead of struggling. To be sure, we can fight for our lives, but we shall contend most effectively when we are relaxed, not when we are tensed with effort. Witness the outstanding athlete, the secret of whose successful contention lies in the degree of his relaxation.

Dependence. Illness can come as a humiliating experience, a blow to our pride. Thus we have to learn at once that dependence is another clue to recovery—dependence upon those who nurse and care for us, upon the medical skill which prescribes the treatment, and (for the Christian particularly) upon the love and healing power of God.

What of the cases where there is said to be no hope of recovery? One feels that there should be more co-operation, if possible, between doctor and minister. We all know of instances where we have had to go along, perhaps most reluctantly, with the doctor's decision not to tell the truth. It may not be possible to lay down any general rule, but one feels that too often doctors can underestimate the character and faith of their patients. Thus, starting with the initial untruth, one is left with an atmosphere of despairing deceit in which there can be the strain of play-acting, both by the patient and the family.

I have found it much better when, in a Christian context, the truth is told. I remember a member of my congregation who suffered from lung cancer with a secondary brain tumour. A small exploratory brain operation gave temporary relief—but the surgeon withheld the truth. Later, however, the patient extracted the truth from his GP. As a result he and his wife had no barriers between them. Each day had a special quality of its own, because the remaining days were so few. As an artist, the sick man found compensation, when his sleep pattern was destroyed, in his delight in seeing the dawn breaking. He took a particular joy in each one, simply because he knew that it might be his last on earth. I remember so well laughing and praying with him a few hours before he died; and there was a depth in our fellowship which could not possibly have been there had the barrier of deception stood between us.

Empathy and Sympathy

By empathy in the particular pastoral relationship of a minister with his people I also mean a sensitivity which, even if it is not part of the man's natural temperament, can surely be developed by experience. It involves the ability to stand where the other person stands and to see things from his or her point of view. This may be specially valuable in the case of those whom we call 'difficult' people. Often they are 'difficult' not only because of temperamental faults but because of the conditions they have had to bear or the way in which life has treated them. To regard them with empathy means that we can look at them with a degree of objectivity; and it is probably a good pastoral rule not to become too deeply or personally involved with 'difficult' people.

Indeed, my own view and practice has been to be careful about forming too close personal relationships with any individuals or families in a congregation. Inevitably one becomes more friendly with some than with others; but there is a difference between such natural friendships and being, to put it colloquially, 'bosom friends'. We have to remember that we are pastors to *all* our people; that we may be invited to share the close confidence of some of them; and that if we are seen to be in too intimate a personal relationship with certain people, then this may prevent others from opening their hearts to us in the way that they would like to. . . .

In our pastoral visitation we must always be ready to put our sympathy into practice, even in what may begin as a piece of routine district visitation. We never know what crisis or trouble may be brewing or may be in full swing behind the trim curtains and the freshly painted door. And if we are too pre-occupied with getting through the requisite number of visits, we may lose an opportunity through the very formality of our approach. I always remember a comment I heard about two ministers. One, my informant said, was always looking as if his mind was on the next visit he had to pay or the next person he had to see. The other always made one feel that one was the only person in the world with whom he wished to talk at that particular moment. We must avoid formality, and we must have sympathy.

This is especially true of our sick and hospital visitation. And here our sympathy may have to show itself in ways which may seem to be slightly unusual. The other day I was lunching with a well-known and extremely loyal member of the Church of Scotland, who was discussing a man who had been his own parish minister. He described how his wife had gone into hospital with a relatively minor complaint—a sore back, in fact. She was pleased when her minister came to see her, but considerably embarrassed when he took rather a long prayer with her. 'It was in the public ward,' said my informant, a staid and respectable Edinburgh lawyer, 'with everyone looking on. They must have thought that she was dying.' And this illustrates our problem. We must have enough sympathy with the person in question to decide what particular ministration is going to help them most; and this is not by any means always easy. In contrast with our upper-middle class friend, there are many people of all classes who will welcome and indeed expect a prayer in illness, bereavement or at a hospital bed. Rightly or wrongly, I have never had a rigid rule about such prayers, always trying to assess the mood and the atmosphere. Probably I have made many mistakes in my assessments, but at the same time such mistakes would, I feel, have been much more numerous had I adopted a system which had the danger of becoming formal or insensitive. . . .

Sympathy in such situations does not mean covering up unpleasant realities. It means seeing things, so far as one can, as the patient or the bereaved person sees them; feeling, if one can, the anxiety, the fear, the pain, the sorrow; being what one is called to be, the agent through whom the healing love and power of God may work. It may mean that the prayer should be shorter rather than longer and that it should above all be positive, true and hopeful.

LETTERS TO AND FROM PRISON

These are extracts from two of the letters in the long correspondence referred to in the introduction to this chapter. Dr Douglas's letter was written just a few months after Charles first wrote to him from prison. Charles's letter was written some five years later and is reproduced here with permission.

Dear Charles,

.... You say you would like to read books about religion. That gives a tremendous choice, but as a beginning I am sending on a book which was given to me by a good friend I made when I was preaching in Australia ten years ago. I think you will find it interesting, as it describes the way in which several different people became Christians, and what they were able to do. It is, I think, important to remember that men and women come to God in all sorts of different ways. The particular way in which they do this matters less than what they do with their lives after they have come to believe in God as their Father and in Jesus as their Saviour (or Liberator). It seems to me to be a fine idea that you should want to help people who have taken the wrong path, and I certainly agree that this is where your own experience could be valuable. This is a positive way of looking at your time in prison—as at your past life.

We don't get away from our past—it is part of us—but it can help us on rather than drag us down. Indeed it can be part of the plan which God has for us as individuals. If you think of the story about the prodigal son which Jesus told (recorded in St Luke chapter 15), you will agree that the prodigal would be much more likely to understand and help people who had made a mess of their lives than would the brother who had kept himself right but seemed to be more than a bit self-righteous. I am sure that it is a good thing for you to have a plan to help other people, and you can do this not only by talking at meetings but even more by the kind of way in which you live and do your job—which does not necessarily have to be a full time 'religious' one. I think you were a gardener. That is a good type of work—it keeps you in touch with God in nature. A good gardener can be a good Christian, and there are lots of ways in which he can show his Christianity, both at his work and in his spare time. The point I am trying to make is that if you have the idea, and ask for guidance and help in realising it, I believe that it will work out, and that it could work out in ways which you can't see at this precise moment.

Now as to what you say about the way in which you landed in jail. Obviously we cannot discuss this in correspondence, and I certainly do not want to be inquisitive and rake over what is in the past. Basically anything like this is a matter between each individual and God, who knows all the secrets of our hearts. I have no reason to doubt what you say in your letter. All I have to say is that we all need forgiveness and we all can find God's forgiveness if we are sincerely sorry for what we have done, confess it to God and ask for his help to do better in the future. This is not just 'religious' talk. It really is the truth for all of us if we are to come to terms with ourselves and start to grow into the kind of human beings that God means us to be. It is very important to remember that Jesus spent so much of his time with people who had 'missed the way' (the word used in the New Testament for 'sinners') and that when he died he was crucified between two criminals, one of whom asked him for help—and got it.

I am pleased to know that you are finding the Bible interesting. Yes, I believe that the Bible is true. Not in the sense that it is literally accurate in every word and syllable, but that it gives a true picture of how God communicates with man, above all in and through Jesus. After all, the people who wrote the Bible were capable of making mistakes, and the people they wrote about certainly made lots and lots of mistakes. But there is no other book like the Bible. It is unique, and it is the Word of God through which God can speak to us. Often, I am sure, you will find this as you are reading it. A verse or a passage lights up for you, and you find yourself saying, 'This is true, and it is for me'. Along with our prayers—the way in which we think of and speak to God—the reading of the Bible is a 'must' for all Christians. . . .

Dear Hugh,

. . . . I don't really know the answer why I wrote my first letter to you. But that letter must have been the turning point in my life, silly though it may seem. Slowly you guided me to take an interest in religion, which I thought at the time would not help my problem one little bit.

I started to read the Bible then, and other books on religion which I could get my hands on. And I must say I really took some stick from some of the other inmates, who would say, 'Surely you don't believe in that crap?' One day I had a right argument with an inmate about religion, who said that it was turning my head. It was then that I found that through writing to you in the first place, and taking a keen interest in religion, my inferiority complex was gone.

Now I don't need drink to build my confidence.

Through religion I have picked up the pieces of my shattered life and started afresh. I have never looked back since, but made progress in many ways. I can talk about most subjects freely, mix easily, I love to write letters (which at one time was a problem), my whole character has changed, and my outlook on life. Not one bit like my adolescent period.

For all these good things, all I had to do was to put my trust in God, and believe in Him, and work at it through His words in the Bible, 'I can do all things through Christ who strengthens me' (Philippians 4:13, AV). I see no reason now why I can't still make something of my life when I am set free from this place. . . .

OUR WHOLE LIVES FOR GOD

A sermon first preached in St Mary's, Dundee, on 1 May 1977.

I beseech you therefore, brethren, by the mercies of God, that ye present your bodies a living sacrifice, holy, acceptable unto God, which is your reasonable service.

(Romans 12:1, AV)

I should like to tell you about a Communion service which I had with a lady of eighty-four in her house last week. For many years I had taken Communion to her, as to other invalid and housebound members, after the Communion services in April and October. She knew this would be the last time I should do so before I retired, and she had gone to some pains to make it a special occasion.

I don't know when she was last able to come to church—certainly it was well over twenty-five years ago. But she knew a great deal about what was going on in the congregation and took the greatest possible interest in it. And she always made careful preparation for the Communion service. She had her little table spread with a clean white cloth, and on it a vase of flowers—fresh daffodils on this occasion—and the communion card which her elder had brought her. As far as possible, her room is like her church on Communion Sunday.

This always gave me the picture of what the Church of Jesus really is. The Church is wherever two or three are gathered together in his name. In the very early days, of course, there were no church buildings, and Christians had to meet wherever they could, very often in the houses of their fellow-Christians. It is people, and their faith, who make the Church, no matter where they are meeting. And time and again I have been as deeply aware of the reality of the Sacrament in such a room as I have been at the most crowded service of the Lord's Supper in church. I remember another old lady who always repeated the words of the Institution with me—so often had she heard them in church that they had become a very part of her life at home.

Surely, then, our homes should reflect the life and reality of the Church. I have always said that I wished more of our churches in Scotland were open during the week, but the reason that they came to be shut was that in the old days the home was the church during the week, not only with grace at meals but with family prayers every day. Even if we no longer have family prayers, let us not forget that, as in New Testament times, the Church can be in our homes—not least in the knowledge of the Church we have and the interest we show in it.

But on this particular occasion my friend had placed on the table not only the cloth and the flowers. She had placed ready, just beside where the bread and the wine were to stand, first a copy of the weekly *The People's Friend*; on top of that the New English Bible; and on top of the Bible her purse. That may seem an odd conjunction, but it had a deep significance for her.

First, *The People's Friend*. She had it there not because she thought it a specially holy periodical—although she never missed reading it—but because it contained a story by a friend of mine who is a regular contributor. In her confined condition friendship meant a lot to this old lady. She had specially asked me to meet before the service began her very oldest friend, whom I had never met. Similarly, she thought I would be interested to see a story written by a friend of mine.

The Bible, of course, was obvious. It had been her rod and staff all the years since she first went to Sunday School.

But what about her purse? Why should it be there? Simply because she was not only careful in the stewardship of her scanty resources, but she never failed to give, with remarkable generosity, her contributions for the work of Christ's Church and Kingdom.

Her friendship, her Bible, her possessions—they were all laid on the table beside the bread and the wine. And was that not wonderfully natural and right? In truth it was her whole life that was being dedicated to God. That is what the Communion is meant to do for us. It is that our whole lives should be brought under the love of God; that we should remember what it cost Jesus, who gave his own life in order that we might have life abundant; and that we should know that in the Communion we receive the grace, the help and strength that we need, to lead our Christian lives.

Finally, I must tell you what my old friend said to me before we had our Communion service. I thought she was a little more flushed than usual, and perhaps slightly nervous. Then I understood the reason: she said, 'All these years you have come and said prayers for me. Today, after you have taken the service and said your prayers, I am going to say a prayer for you'.

And so she did, very simply but with great sincerity. As you can understand, I was greatly moved. At the same time I felt this was a splendid illustration of the priesthood of all believers. Priests and ministers are not ordained to say prayers instead of, as well as on behalf of, their people. We should all be praying, as Christians, for each other, for ourselves and for the whole Church in the whole world.

Just one little old lady who was never out of her house. But how active a member of the Church of Jesus Christ! And how great an impact the Church would have, how alive and vigorous it would be, if there were many more such as she in its membership—to present their bodies a living sacrifice, holy, acceptable unto God, which is their reasonable service.

A PASTOR'S FAREWELL

Dr Douglas's sermon at his Valedictory Service in St Mary's, Dundee, on 26 June 1977.

> Meanwhile our eyes are fixed, not on the things that are seen, but on the things that are unseen; for what is seen passes away; what is unseen is eternal.
>
> (2 Corinthians 4:18, NEB)

A quarter of a century is a short time in the history of an ancient foundation like St Mary's, but it is the larger part of a ministry of forty years. And the fact that my wife and I have been with you for nearly twenty-six years makes us both deeply grateful, although we shall miss you all more than we can say. I have always believed that God guides us in his Providence and loving care. It was in that belief that I left North Leith in 1951, albeit with some hesitation; and it is in that belief that I am leaving St Mary's now, although I naturally find it hard to part from a congregation and a church who have won so deep and lasting a place in my affections. I shall always be grateful for the privilege I have had of sharing in your joys and your sorrows; for the work and the ploys and the fellowship we have enjoyed together; for the beauty of this building and the vitality of the worship; and for so many other things, like your loyalty and support, which will be happy and abiding memories.

Of course there must be some sadness of farewell. We should be hard-hearted indeed if there was no tugging at our heartstrings, no surging of emotions. But we shall not allow melancholy tears to predominate. 'Weeping may endure for a night, but joy cometh in the morning' (Psalm 30:5, AV). And in our lesson from Ezra we read how when the foundations of the ruined Temple in Jerusalem had been re-laid, it was impossible to distinguish the shout of joy from the weeping and the wailing. The older people wept for the days that were past. The others shouted with joy for the future of the rebuilt Temple.

And so today let the future dominate over the past. When the church here was destroyed by fire in 1841 there must have been weeping for the old building. But almost the first thing the Elders did for Dr MacLachlan, the minister, was to give him a new Bible for the new church that was to rise on the ruins of the old. The church was burnt on 3 January 1841, and the inscription on the Bible is dated 15 January 1841. There it lies on the Lectern as it has lain in the church since 1844. 'The grass withereth, the flower fadeth; but the word of our God shall stand for ever' (Isaiah 40:8, AV). One preacher of the Word goes, but another comes in his place. Thus I would ask you all to look ahead, to the younger man who will succeed me, whoever he may be. Be glad and hopeful for him. Be as tolerant of his mistakes as you have been of mine. Encourage him, support him and help him in the new challenges and opportunities which are opening out for you. Remember that the life of St Mary's goes on and that it lies in the future, not in the past.

Remember too that the real life of the Church is in the sphere of the things that are unseen rather than in that of the things that are seen. One of the things that I shall miss most, to be sure, is the sight of this building that I have come to love so dearly, and the pulpit which is dearer to me than any in broad Scotland. St Mary's is a lovely church and in these twenty-five years it has been cared for from roof slates to foundations: it has been maintained in its outer stonework and in the furnishing and adornment of its interior, at the cost of many thousands of pounds, so that it is a sanctuary which we love and of which we are justly proud.

But these things which we see and which delight our hearts are the expression of unseen things—of the faith and loyalty of all those who over the years have been generous to the Church because they loved the Church's Lord and Master, Jesus Christ. A building that is tended, loved and cared for as is St Mary's is a sign of a people who are in good heart.

And, of course, it is the people who matter more than the fabric. It is the living stones who are so much more important than the actual stones of the building.

Think of the Temple at Jerusalem which Ezra and his people were rebuilding. How many times it was destroyed! And yet the devotion of the Jewish people to their God and his House has been one of the wonders of the world.

St Mary's is one of the oldest foundations in Scotland, but the building here has been destroyed and rebuilt at least four times. This is a sign of the devotion of the members, throughout the centuries, to the unseen God, to the things that are not seen and eternal.

It is my earnest prayer that the same spirit may be seen in St Mary's as you face not only the challenge of an irreligious age but the difficulties of a vacancy. This is a time not to slacken your interest in the work and worship of St Mary's but to kindle and increase it. Support those who have to bear the heat and burden of the day, the key office-bearers, the vacancy committee, the staff and the assistant minister. Use your faith, be strong in hope. Show your love for St Mary's and for each other in the vitality of your fellowship.

Finally, my dear friends, let us all remember how this little life of ours is surrounded and upheld not so much by what is seen as by what is unseen. That is why Jesus told us not to be anxious about material things—God has supplied them by the unseen envelope of the biosphere which encircles this planet and makes life possible. Jesus came to show us that our treasure is not on earth but in heaven.

After all these years in Dundee I cannot go on one day's pastoral visitation but I pass the homes of dear friends who are no longer with us. Not a Sunday comes but that I can look in different parts of this church and remember the kind and loving people who used to sit there but are now with God. I remember years ago asking a lady why she no longer attended Church. She replied, 'It would be too trying. The church is full of ghosts'. Surely she was seeing it in quite the wrong way. The Church is built upon the foundation of the saints and believers who have gone before us. But we remember them with thanksgiving, not with mourning. They are just as much the Church as we are. We are the Church visible and militant, they are the Church invisible and triumphant. And they remind us, if we only have the sensitivity to hear their message, of what is the aim and purpose of our life here on earth.

It is to lay up treasure in heaven. It is to grow and mature in character. It is to develop more and more into real persons. It is to become ourselves, so that we shall be more ready to do the work which God has waiting for us when we pass through the gate of death.

That is why the things that are not seen are more real than any passing show of things, that is why they are eternal. What would life be without friendship? You can see your friends but the friendship that binds you to them is as invisible as it is real, just as is the love which binds you to your wife, your husband or your family—the love that death itself cannot destroy.

My wife and I would thank you all from the bottom of our hearts for the years here which have made these unseen things more real to us all. Even though I shall no longer be your minister you will always be our friends. Even when we do not see each other we shall be linked together by the unseen cord of God's love. The end of one ministry is the beginning of another—look at the plaque in the South vestibule bearing the names of the Vicars and Ministers of Dundee, and take heart! The Church lives on because of God's love in the risen Jesus. So let our eyes be fixed 'not on the things that are seen but on the things that are unseen; for what is seen passes away; what is unseen is eternal'.

CHAPTER 4

Minister to all Ages

Introduced by Martha Steedman

When the name of Dr Hugh Douglas is mentioned, people who knew him immediately speak of his relationship with them as individuals; he seemed to have that special gift of reaching out to all ages, and men, women and children felt he gave them his whole attention, whether listening or speaking to them.

It is clear from his ministry that he felt strongly about the importance of children coming to Church and was concerned about how they should be involved in Sunday services. He often stressed that worship is central in the life of the Church and that it was essential for children to see that worship mattered to their parents. It did not seem to him that children's addresses every Sunday morning were ideal for ensuring children's involvement, and he much preferred to hold regular family services and children's services at special times such as Harvest, Christmas and Easter. On such occasions he used intriguing objects very effectively: once in a Christmas Gift Service it was an ebony miniature of 'Talking Drums' from Ghana. Or he used vivid illustrations from history, the Old Testament, current affairs or football. But he made sure that he left them, and their parents, with not just a story but some important message about Jesus and the Gospel which they would remember.

As a parent himself, Hugh liked children to feel at home in church, to be familiar with the building and to know the minister personally. To learn about the Sacraments he thought children should be present at Communion as well as at Baptism, and so long as there was reverence, complete silence was not necessary, the most important factor being that the family were there together. If parents brought their children with them and there were strong links between Church and home, the children were better prepared to maintain their contact with the Church in later years when they were out in the world.

Through his links with schools, university students and youth work of all kinds, Hugh became very interested in the problems of adolescence and the difficulties of teenagers growing up in a secular society. His advice to the young was always positive, relevant and eminently practical. For example, in speaking to some sixth form leavers about relationships, he mentioned the possibility of misunderstanding with their parents, the joys and disappointments of new friendships and the need for caution when living in a permissive society. He stressed that real love between the sexes meant a deep, lasting relationship which could properly develop and mature only in marriage. Hugh's own belief came through strongly to them, and his sense of humour and his ability to understand their views and sympathize with their concerns made such talks of great value. He encouraged older people to try to give understanding and sympathy to the young, to enter into the problems and tempestuous needs of adolescents; and he stressed the role which parents had to play, particularly in listening, without giving criticism, condemnation or approval.

Hugh was frequently a great encouragement to those beginning to follow the Christian way. A member of a congregation where Hugh acted as *locum tenens* has said, 'I know of at least one teenager who at the time of our vacancy was very uncertain how she felt about the Church, and was thinking it held nothing for her. Dr Douglas in his preaching, his ways and his ideals helped her to make up her mind and choose to become a Church member'.

As he neared the end of his ministry Hugh's words often

had special significance for the elderly. Some of his talks to ministers on 'Coping with Retirement' (see Part II, Chapter 11) were brilliant and applicable to anyone facing retirement. The advice he gave them was full of commonsense and of realism about 'severe adjustments' to be made and physical and mental limitations to be accepted later on. But all through there was his vision of retirement as something that could be 'rewarding and exciting'. His last words in these talks spoke of retirement as starting 'another stage in this fascinating life which is our heritage as human beings'.

The way in which Hugh was involved in all the work of the Church and of the different groups in it, endeared him to his congregations. Mrs Isabel Dowie of Hope Park Church, St Andrews, where, after his retirement, Hugh was associated with the minister for a number of years until his death, has written:

> I think of [Hugh] coming into the church, a greeting, a word with those on duty and that look of expectancy and joy as he made his way to the vestry before a service. I remember him in many ways: in the pulpit preparing himself before preaching, preaching in which he made the teachings of Jesus so relevant to today's world and its many problems; the twinkle in his eye as he shared laughter with us; the interest in each one as he shook hands at the end of the service. . . .
>
> I remember one of the New Members' social evenings with people enjoying the lively dances and Dr Douglas sitting beside one of the Manse girls aged five. She was leaning against him, he was smiling down at her, she was smiling up at him; they were enjoying being together and enjoying watching what was going on. Dr Douglas was always happy when as a Church we came together in fellowship. I think too of the Woman's Guild meetings, of his pleasure at sharing in our evenings, his support and encouragement to the branch and to me personally as President. . . .

I remember one service when the minister came into church followed by Dr Douglas, and the visitor behind me said, 'The minister at the back is in a red cassock. Is he somebody special?' I didn't answer then but I will now. Yes, he was someone special.

* * *

FAITH IS FOR ALL AGES

Three sermons preached in St Mary's, Dundee, on successive Sundays in February 1969. They were preceded by a sermon from the same text on waiting upon God, particularly through private prayer and public worship.

Religion and Youth

They that wait upon the LORD shall renew their strength; they shall mount up with wings as eagles. . . .

(Isaiah 40:31, AV)

In this verse Isaiah gives three pictures of what 'waiting upon the Lord' can do for men and women: 'they shall mount up with wings as eagles; they shall run, and not be weary; and they shall walk, and not faint'. These pictures can well apply to different stages of our life: mounting up with wings as eagles can be a picture of youth, running without being weary is a picture of religious faith in middle age, and walking without growing faint is a description of old age sustained by faith.

Today our picture is of mounting up with wings as eagles. With some measure of daring for an elderly preacher let me look at it with you as describing religion and youth.

If you have seen the effortless soaring flight of a golden eagle, you know what an inspiring sight it can be, as the great bird mounts higher and higher. And in the same way youth can present an inspiring picture. It is when people are in their early twenties, for example, that they can be at the height of their physical and mental powers. It is the time for the highest achievements in sport, in athletics and in the absorption of academic knowledge. Nothing seems too venturesome or demanding to undertake; nothing seems too hard to master. Youth can soar above the greatest obstacles. All that youth lacks at this stage is sure leadership and guidance along with the maturity that comes from experience.

And that is why youth may sometimes come to grief. There is a legend of the eagle which soared so high that it was blinded by the sun and came crashing down to destruction. Sometimes the very gifts and abilities of young people may contribute to their downfall. Their idealism may lead them astray, when it is exploited and misused. Warm-hearted and impressionable as they are, they can become the tools of the smooth, the cynical, the selfish and the hard-hearted. So strong are the pressures they have to withstand that they need faith all the more urgently.

What price Jesus as a leader for young people today? There are three areas of experience in which I believe Jesus can make his claim and his challenge to young people, and where I believe that they can make their response.

Religious faith and life abundant

Many young people may fail to see that life abundant goes with Christianity, simply because they equate Christianity with the elderly and the lifeless. It is all the more urgent, therefore, for the truth about Jesus to be known and proclaimed. The truth is, of course, that he lived and died as a young man, that his teaching is that of a young man, and that his closest followers were probably all young men and young women. For example, Paul was a young man when he began his discipleship on the Damascus road, and this would be true of many of those who followed the Jesus who was to die when he was thirty-three.

It was the kind of person he was, with the kind of life he lived, that drew people to him. The significant fact is that a great many of the outcasts of society were attracted to him. Today they would be classed as the hippies, the drop-outs, the drifters, the drug addicts and the alcoholics. They were drawn to Jesus not because he shared their way of life and their addictions, but beause he offered them friendship and the kind of abundant life which they had failed to find.

I can remember a time, some forty years ago, when I was dubious about the claims made by Jesus. I was impressed by some of the arguments against Christianity and the criticisms of it which were fashionable. But the decisive factor in making up my mind to follow Jesus was this. The people—and especially a few whom I greatly admired—whom I knew who had the fullest, happiest and most joyous lives were not the critics of Jesus but his followers. The more I thought about it, the more I was sure that Jesus had something which could not be found in the same measure anywhere else, namely the gift of abundant life. The passage of the years since then has only confirmed me in my belief.

I am sure that young people today still find this to be true in spite of all the pressures which surround them. It is vital, however, that the older people show the signs of abundant life themselves. We have to present Jesus, not obscure him. Above all, we have to show that he calls us to carry not a cushion but a cross.

Religious faith as revolutionary

There is a great deal of talk about revolutionary movements today, particularly in the student world. If older people find this disturbing and perplexing, let them remember that in their own youthful, if quieter, days they too were very much in favour of change and very much against the stuffy attitudes of middle-age. Further, the facts are that most students today are reasonably law-abiding and are anxious to get on with their work. One suspects that most of the trouble is caused by a fairly small number of dedicated revolutionaries who simply wish to upset and destroy the present academic and social system.

It is here that youth will have to make up their minds. The revolutionary leaders are out to destroy, not to build up in any constructive way. Jesus, on the other hand, was and is a complete revolutionary, but with him revolution always leads to reconstruction on the right foundations. He does not destroy things. He makes them new.

Thus the older people must avoid turning the religion of Jesus into something which is cosy and comfortable and unadventurous. Every new generation sees the truth of Jesus from a different angle and seeks to apply it in a fresh way. This is right and healthy, so long as it is constructive revolution. In the long record of Christian civilization it is only when men have been true to the real spirit of Jesus that they have brought the right and lasting changes. This is what all of us must strive to do today.

Religious faith as self-sacrificial

There is an idea that anyone can be a Christian. This is true, in the sense that the appeal of Jesus is to any and to every human being. But it is untrue if it is understood in the sense that it is easy to be a Christian. It is not easy. It is very hard. The call of Jesus is to self-denial and to self-sacrifice. And that is why I believe that Christianity is urgently relevant to young people today.

This is a self-indulgent society in which we live. Youth is continually subjected to its pressures, perpetually urged by advertisements to buy lavishly and to treat themselves well in all sorts of enticing ways. And indeed our young people are probably the highest spending section of the community.

They also get more in grants and subventions than ever before.

But I believe that there can be a reaction against loose and self-indulgent behaviour. I believe that youth is idealistic at heart and that there are young people—more of them than we may imagine—who are ready to take a harder way because they believe it to be worthwhile. One can see how they are prepared to scorn delights and live laborious days for the sake of some worthy end. It may be sport, athletics, climbing or their chosen profession or career. More than this, however, there is a willingness to see that service is better than self. Probably there are more young people who are trying to do significant acts in aid of others than there ever have been before. I don't say that they are all orthodox Christians, for they are not. But I shall be surprised if many of them see their service as being unrelated to the way and teaching of Jesus. That is why I am hopeful, and why I believe, that our young people will in their own way respond to Jesus who said: 'I, if I be lifted up from the earth, will draw all men unto me' (John 12:32, AV). When they do respond, I know that they will mount up with wings as eagles.

Religion in the Middle Years

They that wait upon the LORD shall renew their strength. . . . they shall run and not be weary. . . .
(Isaiah 40:31, AV)

Today I want to speak about running and not being weary, about faith in the middle years of life.

We are familiar with the picture of life as a race. We never think of this race in terms of a sprint. Obviously it comes into the category of long distance running, which is the most testing of all athletic contests. All long distance runners know the test and strain of their races. They know that it takes qualities of heart and will to endure, and to pass through, the pain barrier. In a real sense, to be a long distance runner means that you must have resources of mind and spirit as well as a hard-trained body.

In the same way, the middle years of life are the times when we can be tried and tested severely. These are the years not only of physical and mental turbulence and change, but also of trial by circumstances of many different kinds. They are the years when we have to pass through the pain barrier and when our characters are really tested. In one sense this makes middle age a trying and difficult time. But in another sense it may be possible to capture a sense of exhilaration and achievement. After all, long distance runners do not run races merely to hurt themselves, but because they enjoy running. And our text implies that those who wait upon the Lord can enjoy the process of living, however testing it may be in the middle years.

Think of how we can be tested.

There is *the test of physical illness.* Middle age is the time when many people have to face this test. It can be a hard one to take. Just when they are, it would seem, at the height of their powers, busy and stretched in their work; when they feel they are achieving something useful and worthwhile in life— just then the blow falls. The shock is considerable. They feel that this can't happen to them. They are humiliated when they realize that in fact it *has* happened.

You and I can think of cases like this. But as we do, can we not also think of those who have gone on with the race of life, and who have not given in? Here is someone who has been left handicapped by polio, who accepts his limitations and who still does a fine job of work. Here is another who has suddenly lost his sight. He has had to adapt himself to a completely new situation in midstream, and yet he has done so. And there are many other examples. Examine them, and you will so often find that the secret of their endurance is their religious faith—that they have renewed their strength by waiting upon the Lord.

There is *the test of loss and sorrow.* How often it happens that the middle years bring these. We all have seen the happy homes where death has struck, just when people were looking forward to years of happy and constructive living together. I remember a family I knew in another city. The husband had died, leaving the widow with eight young children to bring up. I knew her in her middle years, and she was a fine example of one who continued to run and not be weary. Not only had she given her children a steadfast example and a good start in life. She had kept the faith when further blows came, when she saw one son die after injury through an accident; and later when a daughter had to go through a long and trying mental illness. What made one admire this widowed mother was just that she kept on cheerfully, no matter what pain barrier she had to come through. She was able to run and not be weary, and it was her religious faith which made her able to do so.

We could think too of *the test of family trouble and worry* which often comes on us in middle age. New strains can develop in our marriage, and our children can give us great anxiety in their teenage years and as they begin to strike out on their own. At these times we need the strong faith that comes through regular waiting upon God.

How do people manage to come through these tests? It is worth knowing, because one thing is certain: we are all going to be tested in some way. We cannot run the race of life without this, and if there is anything which can help us, it is worth finding out about it.

In the New Testament one can find much help and guidance in the letters—and the experience—of St Paul. He was a young man when he became a Christian on the Damascus road. But it was about twenty years later when he was in his middle years that he described his experience of life in these words written to the Christians at Corinth: 'Hard-pressed on every side, we are never hemmed in; bewildered, we are never at our wits' end; hunted, we are never abandoned to our fate; struck down, we are not left to die' (2 Corinthians 4:8–9, NEB). The words he uses here are all words used to describe the experience of soldiers. Life is a long race or life is a long battle—whichever picture you use, the message is the same. What is inspiring about St Paul's words is that they ring true. He is entirely realistic about what life can do to one, but he is also one who runs—or fights—without being weary. Listen to him. *Hard-pressed*—with difficulties, like enemies, surrounding us on every side. But *not hemmed in*—there is always a way out—or a way forward. *Bewildered*—of course we are; in face of the mystery and tragedy of life, who would not be? Why does this happen, and why, especially, to us? We are bewildered, but *not at our wits' end*. We may stay in Doubting Castle, but we are not—if we are Christians—slaves to Giant Despair. Faith opens the door. *Hunted*—it seems like it sometimes; dogged by Fate, we say, or bad luck following us all the time. But we are *never abandoned to our fate*. For the Christian, Fate never has the last word. It is God who has the last word, in his love and providence. *Struck down*—of course we are. But look at the faithful souls, the Christian long distance runners. They are not left to die. They are carrying on.

Here is realism; here is truth; and here is faith, waiting upon the Lord, so that a man or woman can run and not be weary. And here, I think is the secret of endurance. It is not just will-power. Rather is it that someone is humble enough to know that they need outside help, that they have to depend on God, so that when they are weak, then they may be made strong.

Further, Paul faces up to the fact that in middle age people begin to realize that they will not live for ever. They are mortal. He says: 'Wherever we go we carry death with us in our body, the death that Jesus died, that in this body also life may reveal itself, the life that Jesus lives' (2 Corinthians 4:10, NEB). We are mortal, life is hard, death is the end—but still we carry on, because we are in touch with the victor over death, Jesus who is himself triumphantly alive. So we run and are not weary.

Old Age Sustained by Faith

They that wait upon the LORD shall renew their strength.
. . . they shall walk and not faint.

(Isaiah 40:31, AV)

Our theme on these Sunday mornings has been that religion is for all ages—youth, middle age and old age. When Isaiah spoke of those who shall walk and not faint, I think he might well have had the old folk in mind. Those who must go at a slower pace, who can run no longer but who still carry on.

And what a wonderful example many of them can give us! It is a mistake to imagine that when people approach or pass beyond the span of three score years and ten they are decrepit or finished. It was only when Winston Churchill was in his sixties that he became Prime Minister, and he was nearing seventy when he led this country to victory in the war.

We can all think of outstanding examples of those who are old in years but young in spirit. In Church life I recall the intellectual stimulus given by Harry Emerson Fosdick in America, Nathaniel Micklem in England and George MacLeod in Scotland—and given by them when they were well on in their seventies. It is too easy to equate old age with a picture of senility and geriatric wards. Many of us can think of old people who put those of us who are younger to shame by their vitality and interest in living. They are the ones who walk and do not faint.

But are people like these the exceptions? Are they just those who have been endowed with a special intellectual or physical equipment and inheritance? I am sure that if Isaiah was speaking of old people, he was thinking not of the exceptions but of all those who, in old age, wait upon the Lord. Their religious faith makes a great difference to them.

Inevitably, advancing years bring their difficulties and their handicaps, both physical and mental. There are ailments, there are aches and pains, there are outward signs of ageing, and there is a general slowing down. What can religious faith do here?

It cannot stop the clock or prevent the changes. But so often it is a religious faith which helps people to accept the changes without mumping or moaning. Reinhold Niebuhr, the American theologian, once wrote a prayer which has become well known throughout the world. It runs: 'Grant us, O Lord, the serenity to accept the things we cannot change, the courage to change the things we can, and the wisdom to know the difference'. It is a good prayer, and its first clause applies effectively to those who are growing old. Old age is something they cannot change. And if we are to meet it in the right spirit, then we must accept it with serenity. Curiously, it is in accepting it that one can master it. It is when we recognize our limitations that we can work more effectively within them. We can go on walking without fainting. The outward man may perish, but the inward man is renewed.

There is another thing religious faith can do. I have often admired the way in which belief can help older people to find wisdom and maturity from their experience of life. Sometimes the impression can be given that old people are too querulous and critical, and I suppose that some can be like that. But when I think of those who have held strongly to their religious faith, the far deeper impression left with me is of sympathy and understanding with younger people, a faith refined and strengthened by experience, a kindliness in which there is no bitterness and a realistic optimism which is based on the kind of faith illustrated in the verse of the hymn:

> With mercy and with judgment
>   My web of time he wove:
> And aye the dews of sorrow
>   Were lustred by his love.   (CH3:694)

Because they believe in the Providence of God and have proved it in their own experience, they can walk and not faint.

The passage we read from the Second Letter to Timothy (2 Timothy 4:6–18, NEB) shows us Paul writing now as an old man to his young friend. So far as we know the words were written from Rome where Paul was held in custody awaiting his trial and, we believe, his execution. He wrote in complete awareness that he had not long to live, and for that reason his words are worth considering.

See how he looks on life. The last drops are being poured out on the altar as an offering to God. This is an attitude to note. People say, 'What do I get from life?', but what they should say is, 'What do I do with life?' Paul is saying that life is a gift from God. God trusts us with it, that we shall use it well. And we, in turn, offer our lives back to God. Now he is pouring out the last drops—of his life blood—on the altar. An inspiring attitude!

'I have run the great race, I have finished the course, I have kept faith.' There is no self-satisfaction here. It is just that he has kept going, he hasn't given in, and he has done his best. To keep faith in our lives is what matters—to be loyal and trustworthy in using these lives which God has given us. I suppose that where suicides really go wrong is that they fail to keep faith. They reject their trust, because despair has overwhelmed them, poor souls. But I think of others who are physically maimed and handicapped, and who never complain. They keep faith—and what an example they are to those who are more fortunate and yet more complaining!

'The prize awaits me,' said Paul. In the Olympic races the victor received a garland of wild olive leaves, but in the race of life of which Paul is speaking, it is the garland of righteousness, of eternal life. Is this a question of reward for good behaviour, a bribe to be good? It is a reward, but it is not a bribe. People live this Christian life—or ought to— because it is worthwhile in itself. It does carry a reward with it, the reward of sheer goodness. Nothing would make sense if there were no reward. If eternal life is real, then you find it here, and it goes on after death. This is the garland that does not fade away. This is why believing Christians can look beyond death, can see, with the eye of faith, life going on, can hope that they will meet again with those whom they have loved here.

I have noticed how often believing folk can, when they are old, think and speak of death quite calmly. It is because they believe that there is something after death, and nothing to fear. And so they are not worried. They keep right on to the end of the road, They walk and do not faint.

I do like the way in which Paul goes on in that passage with the most practical and everyday matters. He talks about his friends and his enemies, about those who have remained loyal and those who have let him down. He mentions his first trial when he was deserted by his friends but won a favourable verdict. He mentions his cloak, his books, and his notebooks that he wants to be sent on from Troas. He is pouring out the last drops of his life, but he is still interested in every detail.

There was a French editor who was carried in a tumbril through the streets of Paris to the guillotine. He is reported to have said, 'It is too bad to cut off my head, I want to see how all this is going to work out'. This is the spirit of those who, right to the end, walk and do not faint. Even when they feel that the words of the poet may be true, as they look on the world in all its troubles:

> I tell you naught for your comfort,
> Yea, naught for your desire,
> Save that the sky grows darker yet,
> And the sea rises higher.
> > (G K Chesterton: 'Ballad of the White Horse')

Even then, they look at the world with eyes of faith, because they believe that it is God's world and that he is working his purpose out, as year succeeds to year.

PICTURES OF LOVE FROM NATURE

A Family Service Sermon preached in St Mary's, Dundee, on 7 September 1975.

> O Jerusalem, Jerusalem. . . . How often have I longed to gather your children, as a hen gathers her brood under her wings; but you would not let me.
>
> (Luke 13:34, NEB)

When Jesus was teaching people truths about God and about men he very often used pictures from the world of nature. He spoke about a farmer sowing his seed, about birds and flowers, about harvest fields, about shepherds and their sheep. All these pictures told stories about God and his dealings with man. In our text he used the picture of a hen gathering her chickens under her wings to protect them from danger. And he illustrated in this way his own love for Jerusalem and its people, for he foresaw the danger they would have to face from their enemies. But while chickens ran to the shelter of their mother's wings, the people of Jerusalem would have nothing to do with Jesus. And in Chapter 19 Luke tells us that Jesus wept over them because he loved them and was sad at what was going to happen to them. Remember that Jesus loved people with the love which God the Father of us all has for everyone. And at our Family Service let us think about the love which we can find in our own families and the love of God our Father.

Love protects

Jesus used the picture of a hen protecting her chickens, and this is something you can see all kinds of birds and animals doing for their young.

Near the house in which we stay for our holiday in Iona there is a bay called Port Ban. This means the White Bay, and

The young Hugh Douglas in Bombay, India.

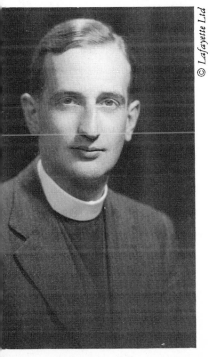

Hugh during his days at Govan, 1934-1939.

Hugh on holiday with George MacLeod (right).

Hugh and Isabel in holiday on Iona.

Leaving Brisbane Airport, Australia, 1962.

Teaching the children to row!

Granddaughter Jane welcomes Hugh and Isabel back from South Africa.

The Moderator visits granddaughter Suzie at school in Gorbals, Glasgow.

The Queen Mother visits Dundee.

A Stewardship Supper for members of Dundee Parish Church (St Mary's) in Caird Hall.

Receiving his CBE: Hugh and family outside Buckingham Palace.

Hugh Douglas, Moderator of the General Assembly of the Church of Scotland, 1970.

The Christian Family Training courses in Ghana, 1964.

Receiving his KCVO: Hugh, Isabel and daughters Molly and Ruth outside the Palace of Holyrood.

indeed it has lovely white sand. One day I went down to bathe there. The tide was far out so I thought I would walk along the rocks so that I could dive into deeper water instead of walking out a long way through the shallows. As I was walking over the rocks I saw a herring gull sitting ahead of me. As I came nearer it gave what must have been its warning cry—a repeated harsh *kyow*, *kyow*, *kyow*. And the next moment another gull appeared over the rocks and swooped right down at my head, passing a few feet above. Obviously there was a nest with baby gulls not far away, and there were the parents protecting them and warning me off. We saw the same thing a day or two later when we went to see a colony of fulmars nesting on a cliff further along the coast. There was always an adult bird swooping over us, keeping a wakeful eye on our movements.

I wonder if we sometimes forget how we were cared for and protected when we were small. We read about battered babies from time to time, but mercifully these poor children are the exception. Think of all the love and care which is poured out to protect babies and little children from illness and danger. This is what love means, and we often take it for granted. And this is the way in which God loves and protects us all. Why, our very bodies are made in such a way that they protect us every day from all kinds of infections, and we have been given ears to hear, eyes to see, tongues to taste and fingers to feel—all the senses which help us to walk safely through the world. Love protects.

Love provides

Another day we went for a picnic on the island of Mull to a bay called Knockvologan. As we were having our picnic four gulls came and settled on the sand a few feet away. Obviously they were looking for scraps of food. They were all herring gulls. One was a big male and the others were a mother and her two babies. The mother had a lame leg, but this did not stop her from looking after her children. And she had quite a job, because the big male gull was a greedy bird.

We tried to throw our scraps to the babies, but although they could fly they did not pick up the food. This was because the mother was still feeding them herself. She would snap up a bit of bread and cheese and fly off a few yards. The babies would come up to her chirping and crying, pushing their beaks up to hers. Then she would bring up from her throat the food she had swallowed so that they could eat it. The only trouble was that the nasty big gull had a habit of suddenly swooping down and snatching away the morsel of food before the baby nearest at hand could get it. So the mother had a busy time providing for her children.

And the same is true for most mothers. They have to plan the running of the home, the buying of the clothes, the cooking of the meals and all the rest of it. Of course the fathers have something to do as well. In fact one of the good things today is to see how many fathers and mothers work together as partners in running the home—yes, and in doing the housework and even cooking the meals. This is what a home should be—a place where love provides for all the family.

God has provided for all his family in this world. There is plenty for everyone. But sadly there are people and nations like the nasty greedy gull, wanting the best for themselves. That is why so many children in India and Africa and other countries have too little to eat. In our own country today we can be so concerned to keep up our standard of living—which often means the luxuries we enjoy—that we can forget the poor and the hungry. But if love provides and if we love God, then we have to love our needy brothers and sisters and do something to provide for them.

Love trains

One day we were walking along the shore road past a field with a gate. In the field were a man and a girl and a black bull calf. The man and the girl were trying to get the calf through the gate on to the road and the calf wasn't having any. He was having a fine time. He would be brought up to the gate and would seem to be just on the point of being pushed through, when he would toss his head, kick up his heels, and with a jump and a swerve be racing about the field again. Just as we passed we heard the wife of the calf's owner say, 'We'll need to get his mother to him'. And she walked up the road to where a big brown cow was grazing peacefully. I don't know what she said to the cow—perhaps it was something in Gaelic—but in a moment there was the cow lolloping along at a spanking pace, through the gate and into the field. And in two ticks she was out again with the bull calf trotting obediently at her heels. Love trains and disciplines.

If we always had our own way and got everything that we wanted, it would be very bad for us. It is because good parents love their children that they train them, and it may be that the children grumble and complain. But we all have to learn the meaning of life, and it is better to pay attention to the advice of those who have had experience than to learn the hard way. Hardly a day passes in summer but we read of accidents, some of them fatal, on the roads, on the hills, in the sea. Many of them happen because people have not been trained properly in the use of cars and roads, in swimming and boating, in climbing and walking. There are far too many accidents in living, because it is the fashion to do your own thing, to suit oneself, and to pay no attention to good advice.

God, who loves us, will never force us to do what he knows is best for us. But this does not mean that he forgets to train us. He has made the world in such a way that if we do not live by his law of love, then we have to take the consequences; we learn the hard way, and the hard way is not always or by any means the best way. Better far to look to Jesus who has shown us the right way and who assures us that by walking in it we are obedient to God our Father and learn the lessons which he wants us to know.

CHAPTER 5

Teacher and Trainer in the Faith

Introduced by Gordon G Stewart

As a teacher and trainer in the Christian Faith, Hugh Douglas had two main objectives. First, he sought to build up and strengthen the faith of Christians so that they could witness more effectively in a predominantly secular society. Second, he desired to enable them to proclaim the good news of the Gospel to those who had never heard it. These objectives sharply focused all that he believed in and did in his ministry. Whether in his training of assistants or of congregational office-bearers and leaders of the congregation, his fundamental belief that there were things to be learned that they might thereafter be lived, permeated his teaching.

In the years 1959–63 I experienced this, initially as student assistant and, for the following three years, as assistant in Dundee Parish Church (St Mary's). Fundamental to all that was taught and learned in these years was Hugh Douglas's desire to hand on his experience of the things that mattered in the life of a parish minister. Such were not only the professional and practical skills which he believed to be essential for specific tasks, but also the ongoing questionings of someone committed to the belief that a Christian is always on a journey of knowledge and discovery. Although as assistant I did not preach often, my understanding of preaching and worship were built up in the worship itself as he conducted it and in personal conversation and discussion. For him, the task of the preacher was 'to build up the faithful and with them to proclaim the good news to the outsiders';

whilst the purpose of such preaching was 'to awaken in our hearers a divine discontent, so that they will not be satisfied until they find rest for their restless hearts in God who has made them for himself, and discover fulfilment and abundance in his service'.[1] The preacher was 'the channel through which can come the message of healing and reconciliation'. With Hugh Douglas, assistants learned this by listening, rather than by doing.

Such could not be said for the assistant's youth work and pastoral experience. In these the assistant was given great freedom; but always there was accountability. In youth work this meant the regular and sometimes uncomfortable questioning of assumptions about the ignorance of the un-Churched and the knowledge of the Churched in any discussions about God, creation and the meaning and purpose of life. Always Hugh Douglas sought to build up the knowledge of both groups by making sure that belief in God and commitment to Jesus Christ were seen to make life more meaningful and worthwhile. So, in Christian education programmes for adolescents, the exploring of the basic truths of Christianity was balanced by the questioning of contemporary attitudes and life-styles.

> A Church which has its windows shut and its doors closed so that the disturbing noises of the outside world will not destroy its peace—that is a Church which is likely to stifle itself with the odour of sanctity. We must move, both in thought and in action, where our Lord Jesus spent so much of his time, out in the world, with all its temptations and degradation and yet with its rich and fascinating flow of life.[2]

These words of Hugh Douglas sum up his view of the Church's responsibility in the educating of its own young people and those 'outside'.

If assistants were almost totally responsible for youth work, all pastoral work was shared; nowhere were Hugh Douglas's gifts as an educator and trainer more in evidence and greater in influence. Behind all the systems for, and details about, the visiting of the sick and the housebound, the taking of Vestry Hour (when members of the congregation and others came to see the minister about all kinds of matters) and the routine visiting of members in their homes, there were Hugh Douglas's definite views about this educating process in the assistant's training. 'It is above all essential that before he is faced with the full responsibility of his own congregation he should have had every chance of testing himself and his beliefs in the wide field of human nature.'[3] (Nowadays, of course, 'he' could equally well be 'she', since many women are ministers.)

Central to this process was his belief that it is the minister's task 'so to come to know the truth and reality of Jesus that we can appropriate them for ourselves, and then convey the lessons we have learned to the souls of those who have called us to be their shepherds and pastors'.[4]

In observing Hugh Douglas seek to achieve this there was much to be seen and learned: for example, how graciousness and firmness could reduce potential argument and resolve difficult situations; how discipline and moral courage ensured that 'nettles were grasped' immediately whenever members made complaints, or aired grievances, or expressed disenchantment or disappointment about some aspect of the congregation's life; how deep compassion for the underprivileged, the disadvantaged and the inarticulate were essential for any minister seeking to bring Christ's love and justice to all members of a congregation and to all who lived in its parish area. Such teaching was not only expressed in words of theoretical instruction and in examples of practical action, it was 'earthed' in personal experience. Explaining one's beliefs and speaking from one's experience were the fundamentals needed for any teaching ministry. Assistants soon learned through his example that only humility could ever prevent such personal references from sounding arrogant.

Explaining one's beliefs and speaking from one's experience were also the criteria used in teaching and training the congregation in general and the office-bearers in particular. The ferment in contemporary thinking in the 1960s, as secular thought became increasingly dominated by humanism and as some leading theologians appeared to be rejecting much of traditional belief, was met by a positively firm but intellectually fair teaching ministry Sunday by Sunday; and the considerable upheaval in current moral values and standards of personal ethics and behaviour were faced in teaching sermons in which there was no equivocation—'As a Christian, I have to accept the teaching of Jesus as having an absolute claim on my loyalty'. Throughout the Christian Year, the great truths of the Gospel were set before the congregation with clarity and conviction, no matter how unfashionable or uncomfortable the words might be. Others might be seeking to demolish traditional understandings of Christianity and the Church, but Hugh Douglas's natural teaching ability sought to build up faith for those on the Christian journey of life. So, over the years, series of sermons were preached on biblical subjects: for example, what is the Bible? the Old Testament Prophets, the Four Gospels, the Miracles of Jesus, the Beatitudes, the Gospel Armour (Ephesians 6). Other series, always biblically based, were preached on issues in contemporary thinking: for example, Formalism, Humanism, Secularism. Never far from his teaching were the great issues of 'life' and 'death' themselves.

In the specific training of members, these aspects of Hugh Douglas's teaching ministry were much in evidence. Groups of office-bearers were gathered together to consider their duties and responsibilities; First Communicants were led to new understandings of Christian faith and life in a thorough and masterly exposition of the Apostles Creed and its relevance for contemporary Christians; groups were helped to understand the duties and responsibilities of being Christ's followers as true stewards of God's grace and God's gifts. Yet again, for Hugh Douglas, Christian education was concerned with more than matters of the mind, for such were reckoned to be of no consequence unless they affected how life was lived.

Nowhere was this better illustrated than in two vastly different congregational events held in the early 1960s. First, the whole congregation was involved in one of the first Christian Stewardship Campaigns to be held in the Church of Scotland. A large number of the 1800 members were involved in the planning and visiting, and over 1200 members enjoyed a most successful Stewardship meal in Dundee's Caird Hall. Christian liberality increased and, in Hugh Douglas's own words, 'There was a new spirit in the congregation and several new forms of service emerged'. Second, more than eighty of the congregation, aged from nineteen months to seventy-five years, took over the whole of Carberry Tower and its then newly-opened annexe for a weekend. In discussing, and seeking to live out, the opportunities and responsibilities of being part of Christ's family the participants mixed happily together. In Hugh Douglas's view, 'it was a resounding success'; and the training of that weekend became the initiative for training in the life of the congregation.

Apart from that love and devotion which he had for Jesus Christ, Hugh Douglas's greatest inspiration as a teacher and a trainer came from his belief in, and love for, the Church. Assistants were left in no doubt as to their responsibilities in the life of the Church. The fact that many of his thirty or so assistants have over the years contributed significantly to the leadership of the Church of Scotland at General Assembly, Presbytery and congregational levels is witness to his inspirational skills as a teacher and a trainer. To assistants and members alike he would say enthusiastically, yet humbly—'It is for us to persevere in the Church, knowing that it contains the truth about human nature, the truth about right relationships and the truth about God's plan for redeeming his rebellious children so that they may live in harmony with each other'. Daily he gave himself to the building up of the understanding of such a faith. Year after year he devoted himself to the teaching and training of others so that they in turn might joyfully and conscientiously proclaim it.

Notes

1 Quoted from Dr Douglas's lectures on Preaching and Worship given at Christ's College, Aberdeen in 1980.
2 ibid.
3 ibid.
4 ibid.

*   *   *

THE REALITY OF THE HOLY SPIRIT

A sermon preached in Hope Park Church, St Andrews, on Whitsunday 1982. The Scripture readings were: 1 Kings 19:8–16; Acts 2:1–17; and John 14:15–27.

They travelled through the Phrygian and Galatian region, because they were prevented by the Holy Spirit from delivering the message in the province of Asia; and when they approached the Mysian border they tried to enter Bithynia; but the Spirit of Jesus would not allow them. . . .

(Acts 16:6–8, NEB)

When we think of Pentecost we naturally remember the spectacular events in Jerusalem, when the Holy Spirit came with power upon the apostles and the early Christians. That was a wonderful occasion and there can be no doubt as to its reality: it was the birthday of the young Church.

But perhaps in identifying the Holy Spirit with the first Whitsunday we may tend to separate ourselves from the reality of the Spirit, simply because we have no experience of similar ecstasy and enthusiasm. That is why I ask you to turn to an occasion quite a few years later and to a region far away from Jerusalem. Paul and Silas, with Timothy, were in the wild, inhospitable and mountainous regions of what we should now call north-west Turkey. Paul wanted to continue the missionary outreach he had begun some time earlier in what was then Galatia. He was anxious to preach the good news in the cities of the prosperous Roman province of Asia, a great and challenging enterprise. And then the Holy Spirit spoke—not with a mighty rushing wind or in tongues of fire, but (as in our Old Testament Lesson) in a still small voice. And the message was 'No' (verse 6). So they tried again, this time moving up towards the Black Sea coast; but once more 'the Spirit of Jesus would not allow them' (verse 7). A disappointment? Undoubtedly. But they went on seeking an opportunity, for they were sure this was the authentic guidance of the Spirit. And they were right. The verses that follow tell us that when they had changed direction and come to Troas on the Aegean Sea, Paul was given the vision of a man of Macedonia appealing to him to 'come across and help us'. So they crossed over to Europe and a greater mission began, one that changed the history of both the Church and the world—because the Spirit had said 'No'.

When the Holy Spirit says 'No' to what we want

My point is that in our ordinary lives as Christians we should be on the look-out for the message of the Holy Spirit, even when it seems to be negative.

Some of you may remember the name of Donald Fraser, one of the great missionaries of our Church in the early years of this century and grandfather of the present Solicitor General for Scotland. [Now Lord Fraser of Carmylie, Minister of State at the Scottish Office—Ed.] Donald Fraser spoke to some of us divinity students about how the Holy Spirit might guide us in our ministries. He told of how his fervent hope had been to go to China in the 1890s as a missionary. But the Foreign Mission Committee said 'No' and sent him to Africa. He said how hard it was for him to believe that the Holy Spirit had spoken through a Church Committee—and anyone who knows Church Committees can understand that!

But consider. He went to Livingstonia, following on and developing the work of Dr Laws in a splendid way in what is now Malawi. He trained evangelists, one of whom he sent across the border into what is now Zambia. This evangelist's name was Kaunda, and he was the father of Kenneth Kaunda, later President of Zambia. Whenever Kenneth Kaunda is in Edinburgh, he visits the little Donald Fraser Memorial Chapel at the Church Offices. The Holy Spirit said 'No' to Donald Fraser's desire to go to China, because he was destined to go to Africa.

In our own spheres, however different, there are times when our hopes and dreams seem to be negated, when we are frustrated and disappointed because the doors are shut. These are not the times to turn on our heel and go away in a rage. This 'No' may be the message of the Spirit for us. Other doors may open. Like Paul and Donald Fraser, we should go on seeking. There are times when the mist comes down on a mountain when someone is engaged in a climb. A climber does not give up. He finds shelter. He looks for something in his knapsack to eat and drink. He waits until the mist lifts and he can see his way ahead once more. Let us do the same when the Holy Spirit seems to say 'No' to what we want to do.

When the Holy Spirit says 'Yes' but we are reluctant

This would seem to happen regularly. The Bible is full of instances. In our Old Testament Lesson we heard God challenging his prophet: 'What doest thou here, Elijah?' Elijah was on the run because of opposition and danger. He was told by the Spirit to go back to the scene of conflict and get on with the job.

This can happen in our time. This is not an age in which the Church as an organization is greatly supported. It is quite a challenge, especially to young people, to 'Stand up for Jesus'. But how often there can be felt this quiet, unremitting pressure. Listen to Francis Thompson in his poem 'The Hound of Heaven':

I fled Him, down the nights and down the days. . . .
From those strong Feet that followed, followed after.
   But with unhurrying chase. . . .
   They beat—and a Voice beat
   More instant than the Feet—
'All things betray thee, who betrayest Me.'

This is the love that will not let us go—the Spirit saying 'Yes' when we are reluctant. God is always seeking us.

Is this indeed the Holy Spirit, the Comforter?

When we think of the comfort of the Spirit is this the meaning? Surely we are meant to look for peace and serenity. Yes, indeed, but not the peace given by tranquillizers, not the serenity which means an escape from reality. Here is a question for us all to answer: Is the comfort of the Spirit a sedative or a stimulus? In our hearts we can have little doubt as to what our answer should be.

The Greek word 'to comfort', *parakaleo*, is properly translated in modern times as 'to encourage'. The famous Bayeux Tapestry shows William the Conqueror and his troops landing on the shores of England, and woven into it is the legend: 'William comforteth his soldiers'. And William is shown as doing so by applying his sword to their posteriors! Our Spirit is not a sedative but a stimulus.

And this is true for people of all ages. I think of what a lady in her seventies once said to my wife. She was someone who had recently come through recurring illnesses, recovering only to be laid low again, and she said: 'We should not merely tolerate and bear what seem to be our disappointments and set-backs. We should turn them to positive good'. And indeed this is precisely what the Holy Spirit, the Comforter, enables us to do, by his encouragement. Let us remember the reality of the Holy Spirit on Whitsunday 1982.

Finally, since the General Assembly has called for a national act of repentance and return to the Word of God in view of the Falklands conflict, let us think of how the Holy Spirit may encourage us as a people in these critical days. Let us pray that out of these sad events good may come, in showing not only that unprovoked aggression must be restrained, but that victory may lead to justice, reconciliation and a lasting peace. If, as we all hope, the Falkland Islands are liberated, let us see to it that our political leaders are reminded of the words of the great Edmund Burke: 'Magnanimity in politics is not seldom the truest wisdom'. Above all let Christians remember that this is God's world, that over and above all questions of national sovereignty 'the earth is the Lord's and the fulness thereof; the world and they that dwell therein' (Psalm 24:1, AV).

So on this Whitsunday let us pray that the Spirit may guide warring nations to plan together what may be best not only for the Falkland Islands and their people but for the good of both hemispheres of Planet Earth.

HOW WE EXPERIENCE GOD'S KINGDOM

A sermon preached in Crathie Parish Church on 30 August 1981. Balmoral Castle is in the parish of Crathie and HM the Queen was in the congregation on that occasion.

The Pharisees asked Jesus, 'When will the Kingdom of God come?' He said, 'You cannot tell by observation when the Kingdom of God comes. There will be no saying, "Lord, here it is!" or "there it is"; for in fact the Kingdom of God is among you'.

(Luke 17:20–21, NEB)

If today you asked the question, 'When will the Kingdom of God come?', you would be given many different answers.

Some would pinpoint an exact date in the immediate future when a cataclysmic event will occur. Others would postpone it to a time infinitely far away. Still others would be sceptical of its realization in any era in this imperfect world.

But Jesus did not relegate the Kingdom of God to the future, whether immediate or remote. On this as on other occasions in his ministry he spoke of it as being capable of realisation in the present. What did he mean?

The phrase 'Kingdom of God' means the sovereignty of God, the reign of God. To believe in the Kingdom of God means that you believe that God is not dead but alive; that God has not resigned but reigns; that God has not abdicated but is still in control of his world. The Kingdom of God is not something which is going to happen; it *is* happening. It is not just for the future; it is here in the present.

Our text can be translated from the Greek in three different ways, each of which shows an aspect of how the reign or sovereignty of God can be experienced. It can be rendered as 'The Kingdom of God is within you' or 'The Kingdom of God is among you' or 'The Kingdom of God is within your grasp'.

The Kingdom of God is within you

This describes the response which you and I, as individuals, can make to God who is always seeking us. We can accept God's reign in our lives; we can decide to 'set our minds on God's Kingdom and his justice before everything else' (Matthew 6:33, NEB). This is how religion can come alive for the individual.

It can happen in many different ways. Our decision may be one of the heart, as when we are moved and stirred by some strong gospel appeal. God speaks to our hearts.

Or our decision may be one of the mind, as when G K Chesterton said that he was first convinced of the truth of Christianity by reading the arguments put forward by secularists and atheists against it. God speaks to our minds.

Or our decision may be one of the spirit. One of the best-selling autobiographies of our time was *Elected Silence* by Thomas Merton. In it he described how after a modern Rake's Progress in Cambridge University here and Columbia in New York which had brought him down to the depths, the Holy Spirit led him to the life of a Trappist monk. And so far from removing him from the world, his monastic life led him to help thousands of those who read of his spiritual pilgrimage. God speaks to our spirit.

In whatever way we come to the decision, the end result is the same. We put God first. We realize that the Kingdom of God is within us.

The Kingdom of God is among you

But Christianity is not merely the experience of the individual, a private matter for the believer. 'No man is an island'. Life is meeting. We are made for love and fellowship. Thus Jesus, after his lonely decision in the wilderness of the Temptation, chose a group of ordinary folk to be with him. This flowered into new birth as the fellowship of the Christian Church at Pentecost. The Kingdom of God is among you. It means that God must come into our relationships with each other.

We need God in our intimate personal relationships of friendship and love. There is always tension in such relationships. Tension can be bitter and divisive. But in another sense it is the necessary prelude to a deeper understanding and a creative growth. It is when God comes into our relationships that tensions can be resolved and reconciled. For when we begin to put God first, we learn to see the other person not as an object for our pleasure or satisfaction or dominance, but as a person who is to be loved just as much as we love ourselves.

Jesus came in order that such relationships should spread through the Church into the world. 'God was in Christ, reconciling the world unto himself' (2 Corinthians 5:19, AV). To be sure, individual Churches and a divided Christianity present an easy target for criticism. Nonetheless it is in and through the Church that the primacy of God in all human relationships is preserved. I well remember the time when, as an undergraduate, I was convinced that there was a stronger fellowship in the University Rugby XV than I could ever find in the Church. After fifty years I can see how little I knew then about the depths of fellowship, and how much I have learned from the fellowship of the Church all over the world. For the Kingdom of God is among us.

The Kingdom of God is within your grasp

The Kingdom of God can be the experience of the individual, and it can be the experience of the fellowship. But it must never be seen as being limited to special individuals or to exclusive fellowships. It is for everyone. And how urgent it is for the Church to proclaim that there are no barriers to prevent anyone from coming into God's Kingdom and accepting God's reign.

There are no *social* barriers. As a young minister in Glasgow in the Recession of the 1930s how often I heard it said, 'The Kirk is no' for the likes of me'—as if the Kirk was a 'reservation' for the middle and upper classes. There are no social, class or race barriers in the Kingdom of God.

There are no *intellectual* barriers. The Church, thank God, is not limited to those who have had higher education or who can talk in theological jargon. While one is delighted to see the alert minds harnessed in the service of Christianity, the truth remains that they can come no nearer to the understanding of God and union with him than can some humble and saintly old woman living in a tenement room. 'I thank thee Father,' said Jesus, 'for hiding these things from the learned and the wise and revealing them to the simple' (Matthew 11:25, NEB).

There are no *moral* barriers. The Kingdom is not merely for the so-called 'good' people, and certainly not for those who think that they are in the top grade, morally speaking.

Remember what Jesus was like: the friend of the tax-gatherers and sinners. Remember what he said: 'I am not come to call the righteous, but sinners to repentance' (Matthew 9:13, AV). And again, 'Why do you call me good? No one is good except God alone' (Luke 18:19, NEB).

The Church is not the collection of the self-righteous. It is the fellowship of those who confess their sins and who know that they can't go it alone.

And so for everyone the barriers can come down and the Kingdom can be within their grasp. But does it still seem far away? Remember Browning's 'Ah, but a man's reach should exceed his grasp, Or what's a heaven for?' ('Andrea del Sarto'). And remember that we are not alone. As someone has said, Jesus points us with one hand upwards to our goal. And how far off it can seem! But with the other hand Jesus draws us on, bringing the Kingdom within our grasp.

LIFE AFTER DEATH

A sermon preached in St Mary's, Dundee, on 10 November 1974.

'God is not God of the dead but of the living.'
(Mark 12:27, NEB)

Life is surrounded by mystery: and perhaps the greatest mystery of all is the question of what happens after death. It seems so final. Terminal is the word used of fatal illnesses, implying the end: the end of our term of life in this world.

But death is not final for the Christian believer. Death does not have the last word. Our belief does not rest upon the so-called proof offered by the Society for Psychical Research, by those who study ESP phenomena or by the activities of the Spiritualists. Christians do not reject any of these lines of enquiry, but they depend for their belief upon their own faith in God, in Jesus and in his teaching and his resurrection. They believe that it would make life here meaningless and purposeless if there were no life hereafter.

If this is so, then at once we have to face the teaching of Jesus about reward and punishment, about heaven and hell. Critics say that this teaching is based on bribery and fear, and scornfully talk of 'Pie in the sky when you die'. They forget that the teaching comes into Jesus's Parable of the Sheep and the Goats—the parable which deals most urgently with the feeding of the hungry in this world, the very challenge which faces us all today. Further, anyone who rejects belief in God is not likely to be attracted, let alone bribed, by thoughts of the Christian's reward in heaven.

Perhaps it will help us if we think of heaven and hell, reward and punishment, in terms of the kind of people we are. Obviously there are selfish people and unselfish people; there are people who live bad lives and there are people who live good lives. An old minister once said: 'Too many tombstone inscriptions presuppose the last judgement'. By that he meant that too often it is taken for granted that everyone goes straight to heaven. But supposing that there is a man who has lived entirely for himself, sweeping others out of his way, ruthless and cruel in achieving his own ends, caring nothing for those in need—after death will he be different, will he be forgiven by God, will he go to heaven? Jesus did not say so. In Matthew chapter 25 he said quite the opposite.

Can God forgive anyone who does not repent? Jesus never said so. That would make God condone wrongdoing, not forgive it. Jesus said that those who do not repent are punished. Indeed it cannot be otherwise, because they bring the punishment upon themselves. They do so in this life and we are told that it will be so hereafter. God cannot forgive them if they shut the door on him.

Now the picture of hell as a place of fire and destruction is only a picture, but it does represent a truth. Fire destroys, it turns wood into ashes. And evil destroys human beings; it makes them less than human, it turns wood into ashes. This is the punishment that self-centred lives bring upon themselves. (Even astro-physicists talk now of areas of destruction which they call 'black holes'—a physical picture of something like hell.)

But we still believe that no one is out of reach of God's love. The key to the door of hell is on the inside, as has been said. Thus there has grown up in Christian teaching the idea of purgatory in the life hereafter—a stage of learning, discipline, purification and progress.

To think about purgatory does not mean that one accepts the Roman Catholic teaching about purgatory, least of all the medieval idea that by indulgences, masses or the lighting of candles we can earn remission from purgatory for the souls of the departed. Rather can we think of it as C S Lewis has pictured it in *Letters to Malcolm: Chiefly on Prayer* (Geoffrey Bles: London 1964). He writes, 'I hope that when the tooth of life is drawn and I am "coming round", a voice will say, "Rinse your mouth out with this".' *This* will be purgatory—uncomfortable but cleansing, painful but a necessary stage in progress.

And so to heaven! What do we think of this? Again we are given pictures in the New Testament of golden streets and pearly gates. The details do not matter, but again the pictures contain a truth. A city is a place of infinite variety, containing all sorts and conditions of people. I think there is a grain of truth in the story of the man who didn't like harping and so felt out of it in heaven. It would indeed be exceedingly dull if we all had to do the same thing. But the picture of a city tells us that in our state of being in the hereafter there will be all the variety that we need.

And heaven is also a society—the communion of saints it is called, or the fellowship of believers if we feel shy of thinking of ourselves as saints. This conveys a most important truth, namely that life after death is never lonely. It is life together, it is life in a fellowship, it is life with and for others. It is a pity that to so many the idea of life after death is bound up with ghosts. Now I have never seen a ghost, but I have talked with those who are sure that they have done so. And I am prepared to believe that there may be such things as ghosts. But if they do exist, then I fear that they are appearances or memories of people for whom something has gone slightly wrong in life after death. Perhaps they are for a time earth-bound spirits; perhaps they are going through some kind of penance or purgatory. I don't know. I only believe that those who are really involved in the fellowship of believers, in the society of heaven, are far too busy and far too happy to spend their time footering about haunted houses, let alone conveying dispirited and uninspiring messages to those who frequent spiritualistic seances.

This brings me to the last point I wish to make, which is our belief in the resurrection of the body. It is sometimes thought that this means that the particles of bodies which have mouldered in the grave, been burned in cremation, been blown to bits in an explosion, must all be re-assembled at the last day. This is a misinterpretation of St Paul's splendid picture in 1st Corinthians Chapter 15 when he talks about the natural body which dies and the spiritual body which issues from it as the flower from the dying seed. I believe in the resurrection of the body in this sense, because I believe in the real person surviving death. If life goes on, then it is life which is fuller and more abundant than the best we have known here. And how can I express myself without a body?

So Christians believe in life after death. Death is terminal. But if life here is a school, then death is the end of the school term. It seems that the holidays are beginning when the term is over. In the words of C S Lewis about death: 'The dream is ended; this is the morning. All our life here is only the cover and the title page of our story. After death we begin chapter one of the story which no one on earth has read; which goes on for ever; in which every chapter is better than the one before'.

THE CHURCH AND ITS ELDERS

A sermon preached on the occasion of the Ordination of Elders in St Mary's, Dundee on 17 October 1965.

What we have seen and heard we declare to you, so that you and we together may share a common life, that life which we share with the Father and his Son Jesus Christ.
(1 John 1:3, NEB)

What are we doing when we ordain and admit elders in the Church of Scotland, when we solemnly set them apart by prayer?

Obviously we are seeing a welcome addition to the numbers of those who are entrusted with the leadership and maintenance of the Church as an organization. And equally obviously our view of the Eldership will be coloured by our view of the Church. If the Church is like any other human organization, then what we are doing today is not essentially different from appointing office-bearers or committee members in any club or society. There may be an added flavour of religion about it, but that will not make much difference if the Church is not really different from other human bodies. And further, if we study the statistics we shall not necessarily be encouraged by seeing that, while the total Church membership is declining, the number of office-bearers is increasing. On that basis, more and more people would be appointed to do less and less!

So if we are to understand the purpose of the Eldership we must understand the nature of the Church. We believe that it is more than just a human institution. But is there truth in the following definition which comes from America?

A Presbyterian Church is a fellowship of middle class people who enjoy being affiliated with an organization of good standing in the community, to which they can belong

175

with comfort and without heavy expenses, who believe in brotherhood within well-defined limits, and in social progress if it is not carried too far; most of whom cast a conservative vote, and who find real satisfaction in listening to good sermons and tolerable church music, and in being associated with respectable people of their own class.

Perhaps this might be regarded as an unfair description, more of a caricature than an accurate picture. But I suspect that there is enough truth in it to stimulate and challenge us to shake up our ideas about the Church and have a good look at them again. This may indeed be what the Church is allowed to become in the eyes of some, but it obviously is not the picture of the Church which we are given in the New Testament. To focus our vision and sharpen our understanding, let us turn to our text. These words are a description of the origin and nature of the Church.

'What we have seen and heard'

John is going right back to the historical fact of Jesus Christ. He is the origin of the Church's life, and John spoke of him as one who had been living flesh and blood. The tradition of the Church derived from him.

Now there is great value in tradition. It means a lot to me, as I am sure it does to you, that we are doing something today, in ordaining elders, which was first done in Scotland on this very spot in 1558. And the Reformers who did this were taking Scripture as their guide: they believed themselves to be in the tradition which went back in an unbroken line to the early Church and to Jesus Christ himself.

Ah yes, there is a great value in tradition. But in itself and by itself it can become dead and empty. If we depend upon the prestige of age when we think of our office, then there is no guarantee that there will be vitality in our exercise of that office. A nonentity can sit upon a monarch's throne, a fool can inherit an ancient peerage, and the fact that there have been elders in St Mary's since 1558 is no assurance that they will be effective in 1965.

But what keeps John's picture from being one of a merely empty tradition is that when he speaks of what he had seen and heard, he is not speaking just of the man Jesus. He is speaking of God breaking into human history in Jesus Christ, and he is speaking of a Jesus who is eternally alive.

God broke into history in Jesus in a new way. The Church is not just a human organization like any other society or club. If it had been, it would have died long ago. That it still lives in spite of all its weaknesses and errors is a sign that God brought it into being and God is with it.

And if the Church lives today, it is not because of the wisdom, the goodness, the strength of its members. It is not the Church of Scotland or of England or of Rome—it is the Church of Jesus Christ. It is because he lives that the Church is alive.

Thus the Church owes its origin to the real man Jesus in whom God broke into history. And the Church owes its continuing life to the living Jesus who is with it till the end of time.

'We declare to you'

If you believe something you have to share your belief with others. You have to proclaim it. You have to witness to your faith.

In our own time there has, I think, been something of a reaction against the proclamation of the Gospel. The Church has been criticized (and not without reason) as a talking shop; and indeed as a body which talks largely to itself. This world needs to be convinced by the actions of Christians that they really do mean what they say.

But we must remember that the Church would never have begun, let alone continued, without the proclamation of the Good News. To be sure, the first Christians went into action, but they would have thought it meaningless unless they had told people that what they did was in the name and for the sake of Jesus.

And so today do not let us be ashamed of the good news of Jesus. By all means let us express our faith in good works, but let us not hide our light under a meal-tub. We don't need to preach sermons. Without doing that we can make it perfectly clear that whatever we try to do, we do it as Christians, as followers of Jesus Christ. This is the only way in which others will hear about him.

Do people know why we are members or office-bearers in the Church? Without ever standing up to speak in public, we can make it perfectly clear that we are here because of Jesus Christ. And unless we do so we are failing in our duty.

*'So that you and we together may share in a common life . . .
which we share with the Father and his Son Jesus Christ'*

Sharing in a common life which we share with God through Christ—compare that with the earlier picture we considered of what it means to belong to a Presbyterian Church! Don't let us be content with anything less than the highest view of the Church.

When we talk about the fellowship of the Church, let us remember that it is more real and deeper than the fellowship of any club or society. It doesn't depend on being able to pay an entrance fee and annual subscription. It doesn't mean being proposed and seconded by other people. It is not limited to those who share a common hobby or interest, be it golf or flowers or bingo. There is something radically different about the fellowship of the Church.

It is the fellowship not merely of human beings, but of the Holy Spirit working in human beings.

It is not just a gathering of similar people but of all kinds of people; often of people who are different from and opposite to each other; people of every class, of every colour, of every temperament. What binds them in fellowship is no natural affinity. It is the love, the *agape* of First Corinthians chapter 13, which binds them to God and thus to each other.

Thus there is something about this common life which you can literally feel as different from and as richer than what you can find anywhere else. It is life as we are meant to have it—in all its tensions and reconciliations—because it derives from the very life of God himself which we can share in, through Jesus Christ.

And when elders are ordained in this fellowship, it is not because they are better than others who are not ordained, or are superior to their wives whom the Presbytery of Dundee think ineligible for the Eldership. [Before the Church of Scotland General Assembly passed an Act declaring women eligible for the Eldership, Presbyteries discussed and voted on the issue—Ed.] They are chosen as representatives of the fellowship to use their gifts in increasing its usefulness; to make this ancient office throb with life, because Jesus is alive; to show to others that they do what they do as servants and followers of Jesus Christ; and to share increasingly in the Christian life itself—the life which is full and abundant, the life which comes from abiding in Christ like the branches in the Vine, the life which flows eternally from God Himself, our Creator and our Father.

CHAPTER 6

Inspirer of Christian
Devotion and Service

Introduced by D H Alec Watson

There was a man. . . . with the dust and the fire of the world on his clothes, but carrying his shrine with him everywhere.

Lord Rosebery, in writing about Thomas Chalmers, might well have been describing Hugh Douglas. The 'dust and the fire of the world' not only come into his sermons, but were evident also in his pastoral ministry. It was his awareness of the dust and the fire of the world and the damage and the havoc which they can cause that made him acutely aware of the need to develop a relationship with God. And so he carried his shrine with him everywhere.

In one of his talks on the Devotional Life, Hugh had this to say:

Often one has 'put up a prayer' for wisdom as to how best to deal with the quirks of temperament or the bitterness of frustration. Equally there is the prayer before one reaches the hospital ward when someone is desperately ill—the prayer that one may be delivered from clumsiness and given enough sensitivity and compassion to be of some real assistance. And which of us in the Vestry before a Kirk Session meeting containing all kinds of threatening possibilities has not urgently prayed for help and guidance? Or again on a Sunday when one's preparation seems to have been woefully inadequate and the resultant sermon more dull and lifeless than usual, which of us has not sent up a cry for the Spirit to illumine the darkness of our understanding and lend inspiration to our words?

For Hugh the devotional life was an ongoing conversation with God in which he endeavoured to practise the presence of God. This sense of the presence of God he acknowledged had to be carefully cultivated by setting aside special times during the day to be alone with God. With typical honesty he acknowledged how difficult it was for him to find that time in the course of the day: 'It needs discipline, persistence, practice, until the barriers of self will and slackness are broken down and we are home to God'. As an aid to devotion he found the Church of Scotland's annual publication *Pray Today* helpful, 'not least because it reminds me of wider interests than my own and strengthens my sense of belonging to the fellowship of the Church'. He found the New Testament in Greek another valuable way of stimulating meaningful prayer.

From his own experience of wakefulness in bed at night he found time 'for self examination and self realisation. Time for remembering to be thankful. Time for remembering others and their needs. Time to think of the pattern of God's Providence working out in our lives. And time to remember our dependence upon him'. Sometimes too in those wakeful hours he planned themes for sermons and addresses. He once told a neurotic lady about this. To which she replied (unthinkingly), 'That will certainly help you to go to sleep!'

The importance with which he viewed prayer was very clear in the short service of intercession for sick people after the evening service in St Mary's. This was very much on the Iona model. People were mentioned by name and an up-to-date report given.

He felt very strongly about the dangers of drug dependence, seeing it as 'both a challenge and an opportunity to the Church to show that there is a constructive and feasible answer to what is one of the major problems of our time'. And he said:

'Prayer is not our escape like tranquillizers—it is a means whereby we are in touch with the reality of God and thus are enabled to face up to all that life brings'.

This concern to make people face up to the reality of God found expression in his preaching. It was James Black in his *The Mystery of Preaching* who wrote: 'But behind all preaching, during our preparation in the study or in the execution itself, there should be the shadow of a listening people. To forget that is the next crime to forgetting God'. Hugh forgot neither. In speaking to a Dundee In-Service Group on the Minister's Devotional Life, he had this to say (reflecting on his ministry): 'When it came to preparing and writing my sermons I could never settle down to this without some effort to find what the Word had to say to me and in quietness seeking to see how this related to the needs of the people whom I met during the week and to whom I should be preaching on the Sunday'.

The sermons selected for this chapter speak for themselves, illustrating in different ways how he tried to lead his people to make their own personal response to God and to let God work in their lives, striving with his help to be truly Christian men and women. The sermons also show his desire to mobilize the membership of the Church to be alive and active, in society as well as in the life of the Church, and to take seriously the responsibility of sharing the gifts entrusted to them. We can see too his concern to make the church building a sanctuary and a place of hospitality where God can be found, worshipped and adored and where people are at home with God and with each other.

What does not come through was his zeal in reaching out to those outwith the fellowship of the congregation of which he was minister. So it was with enthusiasm he identified himself and St Mary's Church with a Church Extension area, Douglas and Angus, on the periphery of Dundee to which I was appointed to work as an assistant to Hugh. There was also his commitment to a weekly stint in the City Square in Dundee where, with others, he presented the message of

God's love and made himself available to befriend and to answer questions about his faith. This prepared him for what was to follow on radio and television where his gifts as a communicator and an inspirer of faith came into their own.

Spacious and gracious are two words which I shall always associate with Hugh as an inspirer of Christian devotion and service. He always had space and time to give to those who called upon him for help, and it was always given with grace and courtesy and, lurking in the background ready to surface at any moment, a shy disarming smile putting you at ease; and the secret was the shrine which he carried with him everywhere.

*   *   *

WHEN OUR FAITH IS WEAKENED

A sermon preached in St Mary's, Dundee, on 28 January 1973

But when I thought how to understand this, it seemed to me a wearisome task, until I went into the sanctuary of God.
(Psalm 73:16–17, RSV)

You know how things sometimes seem to pile up and combine together to form a depressing picture? For a start, the weather does not help, nor does the incidence of flu and other illnesses. In addition, various events or public comments can combine to underline the difficulties of maintaining a positive belief and a hopeful attitude.

I experienced this recently. There was for example the opening of yet another High Court in Dundee last week. Time was when this was a rare occurrence, and when murder in Dundee was almost unheard of. Now a High Court seems to sit in Dundee every few months, while murders and other crimes of violence and passion are all too common. Some of us were discussing this just before the High Court opened, and the remark was made that basically the crime rate was due to the breakdown in morals—which is certainly a matter of deep concern to the Church. At just about the same time news came to our home of two events which illustrated the contemporary situation. Friends who had devoted their lives to Christian work wrote to say that their younger son and his wife had told them that they had lost belief and could no longer call themselves Christians. And we heard of yet another couple whose marriage had come apart because the vows taken at the Church service had been flagrantly broken. One wondered if the Church was on the way out.

It is not surprising that the cumulative effect of all this is to make one wonder, like Eli when things were going badly for Israel, if the Philistines were always going to be victorious and if the ark of the covenant was lost for ever. And then I remembered the Psalm from which our text is taken, and how it reflected a situation very similar to that which I have been describing. The Psalmist did not attempt to gloss over or to disguise the difficulties in the way of faith. He was not like those who imagine that if you pay no attention to unpleasant facts they will simply go away. He was a man who faced up to the testing of his faith and who won through to achieve a stronger faith than he had before. I recommend Psalm 73 as a tonic to your faith. It gets down to brass tacks. It deals with hard realities. And it gives some excellent spiritual advice. [The quotations below from Psalm 73 are from the RSV—Ed.]

This man believed in God, but he found it hard to do so. 'Truly God is good to the upright,' he says, 'to those who are pure in heart. But as for me my feet had almost stumbled, my steps had well nigh slipped'. And the reason for this was that the facts of life seemed to run counter to his belief. The wicked were getting away with it. They prospered. They grew sleek and fat and rich. What was more they scorned the righteous, jeering at them maliciously for their outworn ideas and puritanical behaviour. As a result they made a great impression on the gullible public, who began to cry that religion was useless and that God was powerless when the wicked were doing so well.

There is a great temptation today for Christians to feel like this. They tend to ask themselves why they should hold on to standards of behaviour which are so generally neglected. Why not compromise? Why not go with the crowd? Many who do so seem to be none the worse for it.

The Psalmist felt this temptation. He wrote: 'All in vain have I kept my heart clean and washed my hands in innocence. For all the day long I have been stricken, and chastened every morning'. He was an honest man. He knew the weight and the effect of the pressures—and I suspect that many of us do the same. He went through a real struggle, an authentic crisis of faith. He knew that if he gave in to his doubts he would be disloyal, untrue to the tradition in which he had been brought up. But he found it so difficult to understand. He wrote—and these are the crucial words which are our text: 'But when I thought how to understand this, it seemed to me a wearisome task, until I went into the sanctuary of God'. When it came to the bit, to the acid test, he stuck to the one essential thing—he went to worship in God's House; and then he began to see things clearly, because he became sure of God.

That is why the Church is necessary, not just because it is an organization, an institution, a social tradition. It is necessary because it witnesses, by its very existence, to the reality of God. When our faith is weakened, the odds are that this is because we are impressed by all the current difficulties, the critics and the opponents of the Church, the villains who seem to flourish by defying the moral law and the command-ments of God. What we are apt to forget is that God is there all the time. The thought of him gets driven from our minds. But it should not be so, and it need not be so: and the Church and its worship are there to remind us that God is alive. Indeed it is those who pin their hopes on evil who are like those in a dream. For evil is not the truth; it is the truth distorted; evil is not good, it is good gone wrong. It is the nightmare, it is the will o' the wisp, to follow which means that the way is lost and destruction threatens. It is the hollow delusion which ensnares those who have not grown to the maturity of goodness.

And this is brought out in a vivid way by the Psalmist. He says that when he was depressed and embittered it was because 'I was stupid and ignorant, I was like a beast toward thee'. He had lost his personal relationship with God. He was like an unthinking animal; and it took the experience of worship in God's House with his fellow-believers to bring this home to him, so that he could begin again to be certain that God was with him all the time, and in every experience of life.

Our trouble is that we tend to divorce God from our daily living, to imagine that he is remote and far off, available only for those who can scale the heights of spiritual experience. But this is not so. God is down to earth—in Jesus. He is not far away. How far away is God, then, you ask? Listen to the poet's reply:

> As far as love from friendship is, as reason is from Truth,
> As far as laughter is from Joy, and early years from youth,
> As far as love from shining eyes, as passion from a kiss,
> So far is God from God's green earth, so far that world
> from this.   (Source not traced)

And so across the gap of thousands of years a Hebrew poet and a twentieth century poet are at one in their experience of God. Listen again to the Psalmist, speaking of God and to God:

> Nevertheless I am continually with thee;
>   thou dost hold my right hand.
> Thou dost guide me with thy counsel,
>   And afterward thou wilt receive me to glory.

You and I can feel like that about God. Indeed if God is real at all, it is the only way we *can* feel about God—that he is with us, that he supports us, that he guides us, and that at the end he will take us home to himself. So we find zest and strength for living.

And be sure of this. Just as the Psalmist could not have come back to faith without the help of God's House, no more can we get along without the Church. While the Church is there, we do not give in. If principles are denied, we hold fast to them all the more. When morals are flouted, we do not compromise but keep our standards. If we see a spiritual infection spreading like an epidemic, we view it not as something to accept with resignation but as something we must resist. Where society is sick and diseased, we seek to bring health. Where others drift, we stay firm. When some give up the struggle, we go on fighting. And like the Psalmist we can say: 'For me it is good to be near God; I have made the LORD GOD my refuge, that I may tell of all thy works'.

WHAT HAPPENED TO DEMAS?

A sermon preached in St Mary's, Dundee, on 13 July 1958.

Demas hath forsaken me, having loved this present world.
(2 Timothy 4:10, AV)

On these last Sunday mornings we have been thinking of two companions and friends of St Paul, namely Barnabas and Timothy. I do not know if you have felt the same as I have, that when we study the kind of people his friends were, we also find ourselves discovering more about St Paul himself. It is a truism that you come to know a man by his friends, and I think that we can well follow this out in the case of St Paul, who probably strikes us as being a person so remote in time, and in some of his writings so hard to follow, that it is not easy to think of him as a person whom we know.

We should certainly think of him as being a friendly man, and as a man who depended very much indeed upon the help and comfort that his friends gave him. We know, of course, that he was in the habit of adding lists of names at the end of his letters, names of people whose greetings he was conveying or to whom he wished to be remembered. Someone once went to the trouble of counting up the number of friends whom Paul mentions, and calculated that he names sixty people in his letters, while Luke mentions twenty others in Acts as being associated with St Paul. This is a large number, considering the few documents which we have, and they can only have been a small fraction of the total number of friends whom he had. Surely this shows us very plainly that the early Church was knit together by friendship. St Paul's missionary journeys covered a wide area of the ancient world, but although the seas divided these little Churches from each other, it was friendship which kept them together; and it was Paul who so often provided the link of friendship between the Churches, through the wide circle of his own friends.

The Church of Jesus Christ ought always to be an essentially friendly place. This does not, of course, mean that we should seek to promote any false or artificial kind of friendship. Rather ought our friendship to flow naturally and graciously from all that we have in common with our fellow Christians. A Church is the House of God; Christians are the family of God; and if friendship is not obvious or is lacking in any Church, its members should not rest content until they recapture this essential and natural element of the Christian fellowship.

There is no doubt that Paul was a man who could not have survived without his friends. Do not think of him as a remote and unapproachable figure, independent of human help and companionship. Anyone like that is likely to be a power-drunk dictator or a psychological case; but Paul was entirely human in his sense of needing his friends to stand by him. Take, for example, his relationship with Titus. Writing to the

Corinthians, he says that although a great opportunity opened up before him in Troas, he had no rest in his spirit because Titus was not there to share in the challenge with him. Again, later in the same letter he says how much he was cheered by the good news which Titus had brought him from Corinth: 'So much the more overflowingly did I rejoice in Titus' joy, because his soul found rest in all of you' (2 Corinthians 7:13). How true this is of us all. If we have good fortune, it means so much more when our friends show their pleasure in it; and if we are in trouble, how greatly we are strengthened if we have friends to stand by us. It is a true saying that friendship doubles your joys and halves your sorrows.

So it was with Paul. He tells the Philippians how thrilled he was by their thoughtful kindness to him. He confesses how much he depends upon the prayers of his friends to support him. Although he had a quick temper, he was always ready to work for reconciliation, as we saw in what followed on his quarrel with Barnabas over John Mark; and we can take it that the Hymn of Love in 1 Corinthians chapter 13 expresses his ideal of friendship. And have you ever noticed the number of phrases which he uses to describe his friends, phrases which all begin with the word 'fellow'? His friends are his fellow-workers, fellow-partners, yoke-fellows, fellow-athletes, fellow-imitators of Christ, fellow-slaves of Christ, fellow-soldiers, and fellow-prisoners. He links them all together, inspiring them with his generous sharing of his life and experience, making them feel that they will go anywhere and do anything with a man who has such a welcome for them and makes them feel so much at one with himself.

Our text this morning refers to one of Paul's friends. There are only three short references to Demas in the whole of the New Testament, but, as William Barclay has suggested, from them we can perhaps picture something of the complete relationship and its progression; and the picture is all the more striking in view of what we have just noted about St Paul's need of friendship and his constant use of it. This is what we know of Demas:

In Philemon verse 24, Paul speaks of him as 'Demas, my fellow-labourer'.

In Colossians chapter 4 verse 14 (also written from Rome), he simply refers to him as 'Demas'.

In our text from 2 Timothy chapter 4 verse 10, he says, 'Demas hath forsaken me, having loved this present world'.

There is not a word about the background from which Demas came; there are no details about the kind of work which he did with Paul; all that we know of Demas is contained in thirteen words. But they are enough to give us a clear indication of the making of a Christian, followed by his deterioration.

There was a time when Demas was keen and enthusiastic. Paul trusted him, depended on him, gained strength from him. Demas had the Pauline title conferred upon him which was the greatest compliment which the Apostle could give: he was 'Demas, my fellow-labourer'. He was one of the team, pulling his weight, making his contribution, throwing himself into the work. You must imagine the situation in Rome, where Paul lived in a kind of free captivity. He was under guard and supervision by the imperial soldiers, and his position was far from being secure, since the threat of trial and sentence always hung over him. But he was free enough to carry on his work. From the house in which he stayed, messages and letters would continually be going out to the different Churches and groups of Christians; to it there would come the news of how the Faith was faring in all its different centres. Mark was there, restored to friendship, perhaps making his first rough notes for the Gospel which he was going to write. It would be a precarious position for all in Paul's group, but how active and joyous a time it would be! And Demas was in the thick of it.

But something must have happened to Demas. Perhaps it was the burden of having to stand up to the demands of discipleship. Perhaps he just did not have it in him to be a constant and loyal worker. Whatever the reason, he began to fall off. The most noticeable thing about Paul's relationship with him is the restraint which the Apostle uses. There is never a word of complaint or reproach. But when next he refers to Demas, in his letter to the Colossians, he has to be honest about him. He does not say: 'I am having trouble with Demas' or 'Demas is not doing so well as formerly'; he simply says: 'Demas greets you'. No longer can he call Demas a fellow-labourer. Demas is still there, but it looks very much as if he is no longer really one of the team.

It is people like Demas, at this particular stage in his history, who remain a constant problem in the Church. They are not away from the fellowship, but in no sense could they be said to be pulling their weight in it. Like Demas they have had their stage of first enthusiasm, but it has not lasted very long. Once the excitement has begun to wear off and the long steady pull of the Christian life has begun, they have been reluctant to stand up to it. To put it bluntly, they do not have what it takes. They do not cut themselves off from the fellowship, they still like to have their names on the roll of a Church, but however kindly one may feel towards them, by no possible stretch of imagination could they be called 'fellow-labourers'. Demas is still a worry and a headache in the twentieth century. There are thousands like him in the membership of our Churches in Scotland today, people who could be doing so much more for themselves and for the congregations to which they belong, but who are just letting things slide. They are still there, but there is not much more that you can say about them.

The trouble is that the process continues. It does not remain static, it gets worse. Once Demas began to get careless, timid or indifferent about his Christian faith, the rot set in and he was on the downward path. There is a sense of inevitability about the next reference which Paul makes to him: 'Demas hath forsaken me, having loved this present world'. There is so much that Paul could have said. He could have called Demas a traitor, a deserter, a coward, a slacker—but he does none of these things. Paul is lonely, old, anxious, seeing no other prospect before him but his martyrdom and death. Depending as he did so greatly on human friendship and support, he might well have branded Demas for all time as one who had thrown in his hand and let him down in a dastardly fashion. But he utters no word of reproach. He states the simple facts, and the impression one receives is that he is far more sorry for Demas than he is for himself. It is what Demas is missing, now and for all eternity, that is concerning him. Once the pull of heaven weakens, then inevitably the hold of the world strangles a human soul, and this had happened to Demas. 'He that is not with me,' said Jesus, 'is against me' (Matthew 12:30, AV). And again, 'You cannot serve God and Mammon' (Matthew 6:24, AV). If you do not make God your chief end in living, then you will make the values of the world your chief end in living. The temptation to which Demas yielded is still one of the most dangerous temptations for members of the Christian community today.

You see what happened. Demas weighed up the chances, and they were all against Christianity. Everything seemed to point to the fact that Paul was going to die and the Christian Church was going to become a dead letter. The world and its values seemed so strong. And the same is true today. All the forces of the world seem infinitely stronger than anything which the Church can marshal on its side. Demas, however, had forgotten God and he had forgotten Jesus. He gambled on the main chance, and he lost, once and for all. The same choice as faced him faces us all. It is whether we are going to take his way, or the way of Paul. If there had been a majority of people like Demas in the early Church, then indeed it might have dwindled away. But thank God, the majority were with Paul in his service of Christ and in his faith in God. You and I do not have an easy task when we set our faces to stand for Christ against the world's values, and to make God our chief end in living instead of any lesser but seemingly more attractive aim. But make no mistake about it. The power that controls the world was with Paul and not with Demas. Let poor Demas go into the mists of history. He and his like make no permanent impact upon the course of human life. Let our way be different, following the Christ who is the Way, the Truth and the Life.

THE MASTER CRAFTSMAN

A sermon preached in St Mary's, Dundee, on 27 May 1962.

Take away the dross from the silver, and there shall come forth a vessel for the finer.

(Proverbs 25:4, AV)

Take dross from silver, and the silver shines out pure.

(Dr Moffatt's translation)

Tonight we are going to think about how God makes men and women of us all; and I should like you to think of him as the Master Craftsman in this respect. This aspect of God's work was brought home to me when I once heard a well-known silversmith talking about the craft. It was on an occasion when a beautiful piece of silver was being presented to St Andrews University. It was a magnificent rose bowl; and its centre piece was a perfect little figure of St Andrew himself, standing beside the cross, which in Scotland we know as the saltire cross. After the presentation, Leslie Durbin the silversmith spoke to us about the way in which he had made the figure of St Andrew; and as he spoke I found myself thinking of the work of the Master Craftsman in our own lives.

The persuasiveness of God's love

Like myself, you may have thought that silver is hammered or beaten into shape. This is not so. It is true that hammers are used, but Leslie Durbin made it clear that we are not to think of this as being the exercise of brute force. Silver is a metal which has to be *moulded* and *persuaded* rather than *bludgeoned*. The silversmith deals with it very much as the potter deals with the clay, strongly but gently persuading it into the desired shape.

There is a notion—and it is a mistaken one—that Christianity is a hard and harsh religion; and so people have thought of God as a harsh task-master who bludgeons and forces us into following him. But there is no justification for that, either in the Bible or in our own experience. If we look into our own hearts we know that God has never forced us to believe in him. He does not hammer us into submission. He always leaves us completely free. We know ourselves how futile it is to try and compel others to do what we want them to do. If this way is tried with children, it produces results opposite to the ones desired. No, God does not deal with us in this way, but in one which is infinitely better and more powerful.

God persuades us. God shows us what is best for us to be and to do. As Paul put it, the love of God constrains us. God is always knocking at the door of our hearts, always seeking entry. But he will not break in the door. It is we who have to open to him. So it is that the beginning of his work in us is when we respond to the persuasive pressure of our Creator, who is the Master Craftsman. He is the One who cares for us, who cares so much that the dross should be taken away from our lives in order that the silver may shine out pure. Thus the beginning of our becoming God's men and women is when we ask him to take over, and to start his work in our lives.

God's patience in creating

It is so important that we should be aware of letting God begin this work. This is why emphasis is laid, and rightly laid, on moments of decision for Christ. But equally we should never imagine that any such decision means that God has done all that he has to do with us; that we are so completely Christian that we have not anything more to learn. Any single decision is only a beginning; and the truth is that we have to go on making new beginnings all our lives. This came home to me all the more, when I heard the silversmith speaking about the making of the figure of St Andrew.

A figure like this is not chiselled out of a block of silver, as a sculptor chisels a statue out of a solid block of marble. It is the result of a long patient process. First there is the drawing—in this case it was based on a painting of St Andrew by El Greco; then there is a plasticine model, which can easily be altered; from this a plaster cast is made; after that a cast in bronze, so that any imperfections may be seen in the hard metal; and only when all this has been done and tested for faults, is the final mould ready into which the pure silver is poured. It is a quest of the ideal, so far as humanly possible. It is trying, as it were, to take away the dross so that the silver may shine out pure. What patience and care it means!

This is the way in which God the Master Craftsman deals with us. Yes, indeed, the silversmith takes infinite pains in making a silver figure of St Andrew; but think of all the patience and care which Jesus spent on the making of Andrew, the disciple and the saint. He began with Andrew the rough and simple fisherman, because he saw the true metal in him. But there was dross to be taken away before the silver could shine out pure. Jesus was at work on Andrew during long days and months, and what patience he showed for the flaws in Andrew's character. Andrew did not understand Jesus, Andrew let Jesus down, Andrew went into hiding with the others after the Crucifixion. But Jesus never let Andrew go. He was always leading him on from his failures to something better, always replacing the imperfect Andrew with a finer Andrew. And so at last there was fashioned Andrew, apostle, missionary and martyr; the man who went to his death on a cross, but who asked that his cross might be a different shape from that of Jesus, because he did not think himself worthy of an upright cross like that of his Master. Andrew was the man whom God had made through Christ.

So does God work in us. Once let God into your life, and his patience is infinite, his love will not let you go. We all make mistakes in spite of our decisions and promises; we fail and we go on failing. But this does not mean that we have to give in. We must remember that God's hand is always upon us, that he is still at work, taking away the faults, making us better in spite of our backsliding, showing us how we can learn from our wrongdoing and become better. This is the making of the Christian man and woman, this is taking away the dross so that the silver may shine out pure, so that we may grow to the measure of the stature of the fulness of Christ.

The testing and the marks of Christ

But even when the silversmith has completed his silver figure, his work is not done. He has to submit it to the Worshipful Company of Goldsmiths for testing. If it does not come up to standard, the examiners are quite ruthless. They put a hammer through it because it is not good enough. Only if it passes the test is the silver stamped with the hallmarks. You will see them on any such piece of silver, the marks recording the maker, the place, the date and the standard of the silver.

Let us not forget that Christianity has its standards also, and that they are high. There are those who think they can get away with anything as Christians, but no sincere man or woman can do so. Rather do they realize that there are times when God examines their lives and says, as it were, 'This . . . or this . . . or that part of your life and your behaviour just will not do. It is not good enough. You are not coming up to standard. You will have to put away this way of thinking or that way of acting, and start all over again'. How splendid it would be if Christians saw their lives like this and kept their standards high! And why should they not? It is not that God expects us to be wonderful people, but he does expect us to do all that we can and to do our best; never to be content with the dross when there is silver to be shown.

It is when men and women realize this that they begin to show the hallmarks of Christianity in their lives. Do you remember St Paul saying, 'I bear in my body the marks of the Lord Jesus?' (Galatians 6:17, AV). It was said of Francis of Assisi that he was so close in spirit to the Master that he bore in his hands and feet the print of the nails, and in his side the mark of the spear, which Jesus had borne in his body on the Cross. We may never expect to bear marks like those, but every man and woman of the Faith can bear the hallmarks of Christ's service—in the words written about Sir Philip Sidney by Matthew Roydon:

A sweet, attractive kind of grace,
A full assurance given by looks,
Continual comfort in a face,
The lineaments of Gospel books.

So Christians can show to others that they have been with Jesus and carry the marks of his workmanship.

The purpose of it all

I remember how Leslie Durbin, the silversmith, ended what he had to say about the making of silver. He told us that some people asked him what was the use of his craft and what he thought it achieved. His answer was a simple one: that he sought to show the value of good craftsmanship, to create objects of beauty which would stand the test of time and which would grow more lovely with use. What he did not say himself, but what I have come to know, is that he is one who looks upon his striving for the ideal in his work as an expression of his Christianity.

There are always cynics who ask what is the use of striving for the ideal, and who will thus question the value of the Christian effort. There were cynics like this in France in the eighteenth century when men were making their first balloon ascents. 'What is the use of such an effort?' they asked, and Benjamin Franklin the great American, who was there, replied, 'Gentlemen, what is the use of a newborn babe?' As men girdle the globe through space, we see that Benjamin Franklin was right. It is always worth while to strive upwards, to take away the dross so that the silver may shine out pure.

So never be discouraged about the value of making a beginning or continuing with the Christian life. This is God's purpose in Creation, this is his aim in working in the world and in us as individuals. There is nothing more worth while than seeking, with God's help, to be a truly Christian man or woman.

Have you ever thought that the Christian life, the Christian way, can be like silver: and in this sense? The more silver is used and tended, the more brightly it shines, the better it becomes. It is the same with Christianity. It only seems tarnished and useless when it is not tried out and put into practice. But use it and it shines out gloriously. Use it, and go on using it, and it will never wear away. Use it, and the dross is taken away—God takes it away, and makes you the men and women that he wants you to be.

> His grace will to the end
> Stronger and brighter shine;
> Nor present things nor things to come
> Shall quench the spark divine.   (RCH:561)

PERSONAL RESPONSIBILITY

A sermon preached in St Andrew's Church, Brisbane, Australia, 1977, at a service when new Elders were to be commissioned and set apart according to the order of the Uniting Church in Australia. The sermon as printed here is taken from a recording of the service.

> When he caught sight of him (that is, the disciple whom Jesus loved), Peter asked, 'Lord, what will happen to him?' Jesus said, 'If it should be my will that he wait until I come, what is it to you? Follow me'.
>
> (John 21:21–22, NEB)

Our theme this morning is personal responsibility and this indeed was the theme of the occasion of which we read from St John's Gospel. It's an interesting situation if you can imagine it, because there was Peter who had been so quick and impulsive to recognize Jesus as the Christ, who had always been the first to proclaim his loyalty, and then who had gone through the agonizing experience of a threefold denial and cowardice and running away. He was like a soldier in Christ's army who had been cashiered for cowardice. And now, beside the lake, beyond his expectation, Christ was commissioning him once again, by the threefold commissioning wiping out the threefold denial. And yet there was for a moment a flash of the old Peter. He looked and saw John, the beloved disciple, and because Jesus had told Peter that he was going to have a hard time of it, he said to Jesus, 'What about this man, what's going to happen to him?', as if, perhaps, John was going to be favoured again. But Jesus came back at him and said, 'If I want this man to stay until I come again, what is it to you? Follow me'. That is, you have your personal responsibility.

Personal responsibility is the beginning of our Christian

lives, and it is the continuing power of them too, because all of us in some measure are aware of God's call to us. It isn't just that we make up our minds that God is real. It is that somehow, some time, we have felt this whisper coming to us, this urge to be responsible to God, to make a response to him through Jesus; though sometimes we don't think that we want to do it, we're very reluctant to shoulder the burden of personal responsibility. If we think that we're exceptions in this, don't let us imagine that this is true; because the greatest of religious leaders have felt like this. You remember when God's call came to Moses? Moses said, 'Lord, no! I can't do it, I stammer, I can't speak to the people, let alone lead them'. When Ezekiel felt the call of God, he fell flat on his face. When Isaiah saw the Lord high and lifted up in the Temple, he said, 'Leave me, Lord, I am a man of unclean lips and I dwell in the midst of a people of unclean lips'. All of them desperately reluctant, but God said to Moses, 'I will give you Aaron to talk to the people. Do your job'. He said to Ezekiel, 'Stand up and be a man'. He said to Isaiah, 'Look, I've cleansed your lips and you're fit to do my work'. It's always been like that. Peter, you remember, first said to Jesus, 'Lord, go away and leave me alone; I'm not good enough'; but Peter wouldn't be left by Jesus. At the beginning of the Reformation in Scotland in St Andrews the call of the local congregation came to John Knox; and when he heard it, he went to his room and shut himself up and wept like a child at the thought of the intolerable burden of cleansing a corrupt Church and freeing a captive people. So it was down nearer our own time with Francis Thompson, the poet, driven to the Embankment in London by drugs and degradation, and yet knowing, as he said in his magnificent poem 'The Hound of Heaven', that God would never leave him. God was always seeking him, following after.

God calls us in Jesus to our personal responsibilities and that is what faces each one of us always—our responsibility to God as individuals. And you know, once we've made up our minds that we're going to do something about it, we've got a responsibility further to the Church. It's very easy, especially when days are rather difficult for the Church, to fob off our responsibility, to blame somebody else, to blame the 'sinners', to blame the parish council, to blame the council of elders; and yet we can't pass the buck. If we are responsible to God through Christ, we're also responsible as members of the Church. If, for example, one of us doesn't come to church next Sunday, well, somebody else may be sitting in our seat but *our* place essentially will be empty. If there's a bit of work that we could do and we don't face up to the responsibility of doing it, somebody else may have an extra burden to carry; but the work which *we* could have done may be left undone. We are unique as individuals in the membership of the Church, and each of us has a particular part to play for which we are personally responsible. Jesus is saying to us, 'Don't think about the other man or other woman, that's nothing to do with you. Follow me. Be personally responsible'.

And you see it spreads out from the Church to society; as Christians we have a responsibility not only to talk about our Christian faith, not only to show others that we go to church but also to put the teaching of Jesus into practice. It's very easy to have large humanitarian ideals. In the eighteenth century the French philosopher Rousseau said that his heart bled for humanity, and that was a noble statement to make. But the same Rousseau let his children go to an orphan asylum. It's very easy to be humanely inclined, and there are all sorts of causes to which we can at least give our verbal support. But what about our own responsibilities in our family, to our wives, our husbands, our children? At a time when they say that two million people are living together without being married in America, we have a responsibility to maintain the strength and stability of home and family life. In Victorian England, Charles Dickens, a marvellous creative writer, had all of his readers weeping over the death of his child heroine little Nell; but his own son said that his father's dream children were always more real to him than the children of his own flesh and blood. In the same way Dickens idealized marriage in his autobiographical novel *David Copperfield*, and ruined his own marriage by his association with the actress Ellen Ternan.

Let us be personally responsible for what we claim to be as Christians. You see, it's not only our personal individual responsibility, our membership in the Church, our debt to society: the Church itself has a responsibility to the world. For the Church is very good at making public pronouncements about what people ought to do and how the nations ought to live in peace and harmony with each other. But is the Church always able to live in peace and harmony within itself? What about our separations as Churches from each other? What about the hard words we say about each other? If we are telling other people what to do, we have a responsibility to show them ourselves. We're all against apartheid, and I especially had my memories of a visit to South Africa revived vividly by the programme on ABC television last night. But, my word, while we condemn apartheid, are we not guilty of erecting barriers ourselves within the Church? Are there no barriers of social distinction? Are there no barriers of money distinction? Are there no barriers between age and youth? Are there no barriers of snobbery? Would we all welcome with open arms the disreputable, the drop-outs, the unpleasant, if they came in and sought consolation and peace and help in a sanctuary like this? Let us be personally responsible as a Church for seeing that, if we make our pronouncements, we live up to their spirit in the fellowship of the Church itself.

It's all very difficult, isn't it, to be personally responsible. It seems almost an intolerable burden. We're all perhaps tempted to say, 'Who is sufficient for these things?' But remember whom Jesus chose. Go back to Peter, think of him, hot-headed, impulsive, always ready to try but always so apt to fail. Why Jesus chose him as the rock on which he was going to found his Church. Jesus chooses the average imperfect man like Peter. He chooses average imperfect people like you and like me. He doesn't expect us always to succeed. He knows that we'll fail, although he never lets us away with our failures. But he doesn't look for us being perfect; he just wants us to do our best in the situation in which we find ourselves and to look to him for help. That's why he says, 'Don't think about other people. Remember your personal responsibility. Follow me'. And indeed it is as we try our best to do that, that we reach our fulfilment and our maturity as Christian men and women.

MISSED OPPORTUNITIES

A sermon preached in Hope Park Church, St Andrews, on 1 July 1984. The Scripture readings were Revelation 3:14–22 and Luke 4:16–32.

And he said, Verily I say unto you, No prophet is accepted in his own country.

(Luke 4:24, AV)

What a shock and disappointment for Jesus! Luke tells us that he had come in the power of the Spirit to Nazareth, his home town, after the victory over Temptation. It was the town of Mary and Joseph, the town of his boyhood, youth and manhood, the town he loved. And in the synagogue he had known all his life he sought to share with his friends the whole message of his ministry, the love overflowing which he had for the poor, the broken hearted, the prisoners, the afflicted and those whom life had bruised. He must have poured out his heart, because they were all amazed at his gracious words. How wonderful if they had responded with their wholehearted support!

But then the typical small town temper took over. 'Isn't this the carpenter, Joseph's son? Who does he think he is, making these claims for himself?' They were indifferent to great issues, they were narrow-minded, they could not see past their own prejudices, they were blind to the wide horizons.

Jesus upset them, he disturbed them and made them feel uncomfortable. And in an extraordinary outburst of enmity and hatred they drove him from the town and would even have thrown him to his death but for the power of his personality.

The eighteenth century

The people of Nazareth are not the only people to have missed seeing how Jesus from the beginning has identified himself with the poor, the helpless, the prisoners and the exploited. Jesus keeps coming to every age and every generation, and often it is that the majority fail to welcome and support him, because they find him too disturbing, although they can indeed give him lip service.

In 1967 my wife and I travelled along the coast of Ghana, once the Gold Coast, and saw the chain of trading forts set up by the European nations where Africans were bought as slaves to be shipped across the Atlantic. A fort with some of the worst conditions was the one at Cape Coast, once run by the British, and perhaps the fort from which a certain captain of a slave ship set sail. He was John Newton who wrote the hymn 'How sweet the name of Jesus sounds' when he was still a slave ship captain and did not see that Jesus was asking him to release the slaves. He missed that opportunity—but Jesus was not done with him.

John Newton became an Anglican priest, and one day a young MP came to seek his advice as to how best he could express his Christian faith—by becoming a clergyman or by staying in Parliament. 'Stay in Parliament,' said John Newton, 'and do Christ's work there.' The man was William Wilberforce whose efforts were to lead to the abolition of slavery in the British Empire.

But while Newton and Wilberforce heard the gracious words of Jesus, many in the Church did not, being deaf and blind like the majority of the bishops who opposed abolition, saying that the New Testament told slaves to be obedient to their masters. Such people missed their opportunity, because they did not want Jesus to disturb them.

The nineteenth century

And what of missed opportunities in the Industrial Revolution? In 1841 the Revd George Lewis wrote of the conditions in his parish in Dundee. It had good people living in appalling slums with the highest infant mortality rate in the United Kingdom. It had one church, one school, twenty one mills, eleven baker's shops and 109 public houses. Of the owners of the mills not one lived in the area of the parish.

Many of the industrialists who built the slums to house the people who worked in their mills and factories were pious, churchgoing people, who also built churches and institutes with the profits created for them by their badly-housed and poverty-stricken labour force. Many of them went from their west-end houses and west-end churches to work in mission halls. But the majority of them did not see that Jesus was asking them to do more than that, and to do away with the slums and the conditions which caused the rickets, the typhoid and the TB. They missed their opportunities because they were not willing to be shaken out of their normal, comfortable routine.

But like Newton and Wilberforce with the slaves, there were those who heard and saw what Jesus was calling for. There were, for example, Lord Shaftesbury and the Factory Acts he fought for; Charles Kingsley and F D Maurice, the Christian Socialists; Octavia Hill and her pioneer work in rehousing the slum population; William Booth who wrote *In Darkest England* and led the Salvation Army to fight the evils of the slums. Nor should we forget that the rise of the Labour Party stemmed from what Keir Hardie had learned and taught about Jesus in his Lanarkshire Sunday School. People like them saw the truth of the gracious words of Jesus which was hidden from their contemporaries as it had been from the people of Nazareth.

The twentieth century

Perhaps it is too easy for us to look back with hindsight on previous centuries and be critical of the way in which Jesus's own people—the Christian Church—were blind and deaf to his gracious words. It is more difficult and more challenging to identify the areas in which His Spirit is speaking to the Churches today. That is why it might well be worth while to consider our lesson from Revelation, in which we read what the Spirit said to Church of Laodicea.

That Church was too comfortable, too complacent, neither hot nor cold but lukewarm. 'And,' said the Spirit, 'because you are like that, you make me sick'. Strong words, but perhaps salutary.

For in this country today the Churches tend to be comfortable and suburban; and perhaps it would be good for us to listen to the words which stir us out of our easy complacency and make us uncomfortable. When, for example, David Sheppard former England cricketer and now Bishop of Liverpool, writes a book called *Bias to the Poor* and gives a Reith Lecture which criticises both the Government and the Church for being ignorant of and indifferent to the lot of those who live in the inner cities, I don't know about you, but I am inclined to believe that what he says is true, and that he is only echoing in modern terms what Jesus said to the people of Nazareth in AD 30.

I have the same restless feeling when I read of Roman Catholic priests standing up against oppressive governments, whether it be in Central and South America or in Central Europe. Or when I read about the massive peace demonstrations or the growing numbers who are protesting against the destruction of the natural environment and the disappearance of birds and butterflies and plants. I do not agree with all that the more radical groups are saying, but I fear, more than I fear them, the dangers of becoming fixed in a rut, of being unwilling to hear what I don't want to hear or to see what I don't want to see. I have my prejudices like anyone else, but I pray that they will not be so deep-rooted as to keep me from having a mind that is open and eyes which will be strong enough to face up to the truth. I still care enough about the message of Jesus today to try not to miss my opportunities as the people of Nazareth did.

The personal challenge

One last thought. Do not let us push off the challenge of Jesus as if it were made in a general way to the Churches and not to ourselves as individuals. Christianity begins with the individual and with his or her response to the approach which Jesus continues to make today as he did to his first disciples and followers. He cannot do his work in the world except through the individuals who respond to his appeal. 'Behold, I stand at the door and knock: if any man hear my voice, and open the door, I will come in to him, and will sup with him, and he with me' (Revelation 3:20, AV).

You will have heard the story about Holman Hunt's famous picture of Jesus, as Light of the World, standing and knocking at the door of the human heart. Someone asked the artist why he had painted no handle on the door. 'Ah,' he answered, 'the handle is on the inside'. It is only you and I who can open the door when we hear his knock.

> . . . of all sad words of tongue or pen
> The saddest are, 'It might have been'.   (Bret Harte)

Don't miss your opportunities!

> If Christ should count you worthy, and should deign
> One day to seek your door and be your guest,
> Pause! ere you draw the bolt and bid him rest,
> If in your old content you would remain. . . .
>
> He wakes desires you never may forget,
> He shows you stars you never saw before,

He makes you share with him, for ever more,
The burden of the world's divine regret.
How wise you were to open not! And yet
How poor if you should turn him from the door!

(Source not traced)

CHAPTER 7

Communicator

Introduced by D Bruce Cannon

Hugh Douglas was a natural communicator. Had he never moved beyond a parish he would have earned a deserved reputation for effective communication from the pulpit and in counselling his parishioners. But he was a man for his time and was able to take these intuitive gifts and multiply them a thousandfold through the emerging media of radio and TV. And, if that were not enough, he achieved the rare distinction of being able to translate his spoken words to published print.

Fundamentally, Hugh communicated well at a personal level through the warmth and style of his personality. He enjoyed the benefit of a considerable powerful physical presence. A handsome man by any standards, he carried his tall frame with dignity and grace. Seldom has the traditional Moderatorial dress been worn with more panache and style than by him.

Hugh used his inherent gift for relating to people at all levels in his parish ministries where his abilities, backed by great good humour, won the respect and affection of churchgoers and non-churchgoers alike. His first encounters with broadcasting came in the 1940s when he was invited by the BBC to contribute to the old 'Lift up Your Hearts', the original religious 'morning spot'; to take prayers in the greatly beloved 'Children's Hour'; and to lead evening devotions in the quiet of 'Ere I Sleep'.

More significantly, however, he was involved in the remarkable 'Radio Mission', mounted by his media mentor and later close friend, the Revd Dr Ronald Falconer, Head of Religious Broadcasting with the BBC in Scotland. The Radio Mission was an imaginative attempt to harness the unique outreach of broadcasting to the outreach of the Scottish Churches. It was a pioneering event which led subsequently to the memorable 'Tell Scotland' Movement of the 1950s.

Inevitably, Hugh moved into the burgeoning new medium of television. Ronnie Falconer knew he had found a winner for this latest and potentially most powerful of media. In Hugh he had a communicator able to stand alongside Dr William Barclay, the Glasgow Professor of New Testament, whose skills in popular Biblical exposition had grabbed the imagination of ordinary viewers in their tens of thousands.

Together Hugh and Ronnie evolved a type of programme in which Hugh drew on his experience as a parish minister to talk on a variety of personal and social problems. These programmes, often broadcast on the United Kingdom network, not just in Scotland, brought an instant response from viewers, many of whom wrote to express their appreciation. Typical of many he received was one from a viewer in Cornwall who said she found it hard to believe that Hugh was so many hundreds of miles away because of the intimacy with which he spoke to her and her friends sitting round their TV set in St Ives. 'We simply hung on every word . . . and breathed a sigh of appreciation as you finished . . .' she wrote.

It was from these programmes that the highly successful 'Coping with Life' series emerged. Such was their success that Hugh went into print with a book of the same title (Arthur James: London 1964, second edition 1988). Like the programmes, the book was to achieve a wide popularity, proving—if by now proof were needed—his successful mastery of yet another communication skill, the written word.

It is by no means easy for the accomplished performer in one medium to make a transition to another. Of all the commendatory words written (and, no doubt, spoken) about

Hugh's book, none could have been more welcome to Hugh than a letter from the late Dr J W Stevenson, a distinguished former Editor of *Life and Work*, the Kirk's official magazine, in which he wrote: 'You have done it! Your book carries over into the different medium the qualities which have made your TV talks.'

Television, however, continued to play a large part in Hugh's life—and not just as a performer. In 1966 the BBC invited him to serve on their General Advisory Council, a gathering of selected individuals chosen to reflect a wide spectrum of interests and backgrounds for the guidance of BBC policy. How he reacted to this new involvement with broadcasting is not recorded, but one can be sure that the BBC did not regret their choice.

In 1970 Hugh found himself the subject of a TV programme when Ronnie Falconer made a documentary on the man who, at the age of 59, was about to become one of the Church of Scotland's youngest Moderators of Assembly. This feature won acclaim for its technical merit, but also for Hugh's frankness in talking about his life, particularly some early traumatic family experiences that must have influenced much of his subsequent speaking and preaching.

Hugh frequently drew on personal experience to illustrate his talks and sermons, but never more powerfully than when he returned to the TV screen and pulpit after a heart attack. His popular series 'Coping with Life' reappeared under the title 'Coping with Yourself', which, he explained in the first programme, was partly because he felt his Scottish countrymen were earning an unenviable reputation for their poor health and because of his own failure (as he put it) to 'cope with life' by succumbing to the heart attack.

How far that experience of a life-threatening illness continued to influence Hugh will never be known, but in the following few years he did not flinch from the toughest of topics for his programmes. For example, he did a short series of TV epilogues for the BBC on the theme of 'Victory over Death' in which he explored the ultimate questions of life and death, even attempting to answer for ordinary people questions about heaven and hell.

Hugh was in no doubt that the electronic media presented the Church with a great opportunity to communicate the Gospel. The growth of independent television alongside the BBC provided him with even more outlets for his broadcasting talents. He was a weel-kent figure in just about every TV studio in Scotland. Grampian Television, in particular, made good use of the minister of St Mary's, Dundee, as a good 'local' man for their regular evening prayers; Hugh, true to style, having adapted to the particular discipline of the short talk compared to the more expansive religious programme.

But, such were the communication skills of the man, that his pulpit performance revealed the same attention to professional skill. His preaching style and mannerisms were commended to divinity students as fine examples of how to hold the attention of a congregation. In a lecture to divinity students in Christ's College, Aberdeen, he cautioned against 'pretentious' pulpit accents and advocated diligent work in achieving effective voice projection.

Hugh coped with all the media in the service of his Master. From many letters and comments it is abundantly clear that his listeners, whether in the pew or in front of a radio or TV set, benefited greatly from his talks and sermons. The mail from fans, from University principal to incarcerated prisoner, reflects the remarkable achievement of Hugh Douglas, master communicator, since they all, in their own way and at their own level, 'got the message'.

In reading the scripts of Hugh's TV appearances, one has to remember that the words lack the essential television images that accompanied them and to that extent the scripts are only 'one dimensional'.

Much of Hugh's success as a broadcaster was his personal charisma. His handsome features were extremely 'tele-visual', while his voice was both gentle and comforting. Quite simply, it was not just what he said, but the *way* that he said it, that won such popular acclaim.

Sadly those of us who are now left with simply the words before us, can but try to imagine how they came across to viewers seated in the comfort of their own homes.

✻   ✻   ✻

IT CAN'T HAPPEN TO ME!

A BBC TV broadcast on Sunday evening 5 March 1965.

'It can't happen to me!' But what if it does?

The last time I spoke on television was almost a year ago, in the series which was called 'Coping with Life'. The reason why the title is now 'Coping with Yourself' is twofold.

For one thing, I've noticed recently that we Scots are getting an unenviable reputation in some respects. Apparently we are among the leaders (certainly in the top ten) of those who suffer from ulcers, heart attacks, lung cancer and alcoholism. As we've always had a 'guid conceit o' oorsel's', it is perhaps just as well that we should also think of 'seeing oorsel's as ithers see us' and ask why we should be advancing progressively backwards.

The second reason for changing the title is that having written a book called 'Coping with Life', I immediately proceeded to fail signally to do so by falling ill with a heart attack. It thus penetrated to my consciousness that, being now at the receiving end, I should have to take a long, hard look at coping with myself and try to discover just what the Christian faith could teach me in a situation like this.

So if we think in generalities about this subject, please be sure that I am not merely ladling out dollops of gratuitous advice. I've had to take a good deal of advice myself and make some discoveries which have not been altogether flattering. The general situation of which we are thinking certainly became very particularised for me when I was walking up the Mound to a meeting of the General Assembly in Edinburgh, and suddenly realised that while my heart was still presumably in the right place, it was behaving in a queer kind of way.

Since then I've talked with quite a number of people who have had heart attacks (or other illnesses like duodenal perforations) and I have been interested to discover that we have all shared a common experience. It has been one of shock, surprise and humiliation. The shock comes and we say, 'No! it can't be! It can't happen to me! I'm not that type! I'm not going to fall ill!' So we struggle on a bit, if we're able. But things don't get better. They get worse. We have to give in. We have to lie down to it. What a performance for us of all people to stage! How extremely humiliating!

I remember very clearly feeling like that. My morale was not raised as I lay in bed and read a certain newspaper which had included a notice of my illness in the column headed 'Obituaries'. Nor were the prophets of doom lacking, like the one who said to me, 'Haven't you got the same thing as so-and-so who died a fortnight ago?'

However, there are many fortunate people, like myself, who go on from this initial stage, unpleasant as it is, to make good recoveries, thanks to the skill and care of the medical and nursing professions. It's certainly not my job to talk about the treatment of illness like this. All I have to say to anyone in such a situation is, 'Get the best medical advice you can, and then do precisely what you are told'. There are many healthy-looking characters doing their normal jobs who have been glad to learn this lesson. So, raising a grateful hat to the doctors and nurses, let's move on to examine two main points.

The first is, why do so many people fall ill in these ways? The second is, what has the Christian Faith to tell us about coping with ourselves in illness and recovery?

So far as the causes of illness are concerned, we all talk very glibly today about the rush and bustle of modern life, over-work, over-conscientiousness, nervous strain and tension, anxiety-neurosis and all the rest. We seem to know all the reasons and we give the impression of knowing all the answers, especially when the popular digests are so good at publishing articles to guide us. But we are still remarkably slow to recognise the symptoms or the danger signals in ourselves.

This is no compendium of diagnoses, nor a *Guide to Happy Hypochondria*. But from talking with a variety of people I have found the following picture emerging. It might be entitled: 'How to be sure of making yourself ill'.

Get into the habit of working very hard all the time. Don't take any recreation unless it is quite unavoidable. Rush about in trains and cars as much as you possibly can. Don't on any account think of walking. This is quite out of date. Realise that if you try to relax you will (a) feel guilty and (b) in any case remain tensed like a coiled spring. This means that relaxation is a bad thing in a competitive society where so much depands upon your own invaluable efforts.

You will, of course, find that all this involves a certain degree of strain. However, not to worry! You have a good supply of cigarettes. Ah, how gladly the hand strays to the pocket, and how satisfying the drag on the filter-tip when the phone rings or a tricky situation develops!

You're feeling a bit down at the end of the day? Nothing like a quick drink to soothe the nerves! And if you find that you need more of it more often, why, the work's increasing isn't it? And people are more difficult, aren't they? What a job it is to get on with them! You need something to make them endurable.

So it's time to get off to bed. You were off your sleep for a time weren't you? But that was before you persuaded the doctor to give you the sleeping pills. It's true that they're losing their effect now, but those tranquillizers should make a difference during the day. Or will they? Not to worry! Not to worry! But it's strange how panicky you can get, especially about three or four o'clock in the morning.

This is a composite picture, of course, but perhaps we can recognise in it some parts of ourselves or our problems. I hope that we can also go on to recognise the answer which the Christian Faith can help us to find. I am quite convinced of the relevance of the Faith to the occupational diseases and the strains and stresses of today. I only wish I were a more successful practitioner of the Faith myself. But at least I can try to pass on some of the glimmerings of light of which I have been—sometimes painfully—made aware.

The first is the need to live a more disciplined life. I am sure that this is one of the really valuable things about daily prayer, morning and evening. It helps you to plan out and review your days regularly, and to see that you are using your time in a right and constructive way. St Paul knew a thing or two, in spite of all the clever blokes who try and knock him for six today. He was on the ball when he spoke about the need to go into strict training like an athlete and to buffet and master our bodies.

We may well need, for example, to discipline ourselves to take regular recreation and exercise, and to find our relaxation in this way rather than through the spurious satisfaction of drugs. Among drugs, of course, I include tobacco, and particularly cigarettes. They are a mild narcotic, and we should be as foolish to deny that, as we should be to be blind to their clearly established bad effects. I believe that anyone can stop smoking, provided they want badly enough to do so. I record the fact that it took an illness to teach me, and several others whom I knew, that simple lesson.

Going on from this stage, I believe that we can find a better answer to our strains and worries through Christ than through the escape routes which we are so often apt to try. One picture which I find particularly helpful is the contrast which we find in the New Testament between the powers of darkness and the light of God in Christ. The early Christians were always shouting for joy that they had passed from darkness into God's marvellous light. The trouble with us is that, after nineteen centuries of Christianity, we too often exist in a kind of dim artificial twilight. But God's light is still real.

It delivers us from fear. Of course, we are much too sophisticated to be afraid of the powers of darkness. The old gods of the pagans have gone for ever. Or have they? A good many frightened people are going about today. Many of them know only too well what it is to be the victims of unreasoning fear, of panic.

Panic, now there's an interesting word. It means the unreasoning fear associated with Pan, the cloven-hoofed piper of forests, mountains and valleys, one of the old powers of darkness, the forerunner of Auld Nick himself. And that's the kind of fear which grips you as you lie turning on your bed in the darkness of the small hours.

The answer to such dark fears is the light of Christ. It really is. If these fears seem to be vividly real we have to remember that Christ is literally much more real. His light assures us that evil is not in control. It is God who is in control. This is his world. We are part of it and we are under his care. This is true.

We all need this truth, even the best of us. In Chekhov's play *Uncle Vanya* the doctor, Astrov, explains the reason for his basic depression in spite of all his good works. It is, he says, because he is like a traveller going through a forest in the dark. The tempest rages, the wind drives the branches in his face, he has lost his way. If ahead of him he sees even a small light, he can carry on. 'But for me,' he says, 'there is no small light.' Nothing but the dark, and panic fear and ultimate hopelessness. That is why people need the light of Christ.

His light is unquenchable, because it is the light of God's love. And love casts out fear. It drives the power of darkness away.

Thus, again, the light of God means right relationships. You remember how St John brings us and all our brash pretensions down to earth with a bump. He writes, 'A man may say, "I am in the light"; but if he hates his brother, he is still in the dark . . . he walks in the dark and has no idea where he is going, because the darkness has made him blind' (1 John 2:9–11, NEB).

How sadly and fatally easy it is to be caught in the toils of bad relationships! They occur in the home, at daily work, in our professions, in our activities, in our Churches and congregations. Their effect is always evil. They make work frustrating instead of fulfilling, so that it becomes something to dread rather than welcome. They can make people actively and literally ill. They can lead to negativism and despair.

And one thing is certain: that to let bad relationships continue is to be in thrall to the power of darkness. This is where the light of God makes all the difference. To walk in the light means always trying to do the positive, friendly and helpful thing. Remember that most difficult people are also ordinary people; and that we can be the ones who seem difficult to others. If we pray for the people we find irritating or obstructive, our attitude towards them changes—it has to. And so can their approach to us. It is not easy. It takes time, but it can only happen in the light of friendship and love. It can never happen in the darkness of bad feeling and hatred.

Finally, light ends our separation from God and reconciles us to him. There is a profound truth in the great poem of creation in Genesis chapter 1. Before God's creative love went into action, there was nothing but purposeless and empty darkness. When God began to act, in creative love, he said, 'Let there be light'; and there was light.

Whenever, by our pride, selfishness and disobedience we separate ourselves from God, we bring the darkness down upon us. It is the story of the garden of Eden and the Fall all over again. There is no purpose in what we do. It is separation from God. Suppose we had to live in physical darkness all the time. How warped, stunted and dim-sighted we should become. But when we shut ourselves off from God, our personalities are condemned to the dark. We can never grow into mature persons apart from the light of God, deprived of his creative love.

This is why Jesus came, why he lived, taught, suffered and died. That is why the light always shines about His Cross. This was the deepest darkness of all. It was the most mistaken, foolish, wrong and evil thing men could do—to kill Jesus. It was the furthest they could get from God. And yet his love was there, seeking them on the Cross. His light shone, unquenched by the thickest darkness. And no matter how far we may think we have got from God, we cannot go beyond the range of his light. Many, if not all, of our frustrations and our consequent illnesses can have their roots in our separation from God.

It may have taken us a long time to get out of touch with

him, and it may take a long while before we make our way back where we belong. But if we know that he is light and in him there is no darkness at all, we can start on our journey with confidence.

God is light and God is reality. It is a great thing to know this and to depend on this instead of on any artificial substitutes or crutches. Jesus has taught us to live a day at a time and not to be morbidly anxious about the future. And indeed we only begin to live in the real sense of the word when we learn to be thankful each day simply for being alive, and know that we have to depend on him if we are to get through the day in the right way.

If I believe anything, I believe this.

THE MINISTER CALLS—
AT THE END OF THE YEAR

A BBC Television broadcast in the 'Meeting Point' series on Sunday evening, 29 December 1957. The programme was introduced with: 'On the last Sunday of the Old Year the Revd Hugh Douglas visits your home and conducts Family Worship'. It began with the singing of the Scripture Paraphrase 'O God of Bethel'.

Good evening! We're nearly at the end of another year, and as you look back on it, I wonder what you feel about it? Would you say it had been a good year, or a bad year for you? You may feel that you've had a pretty tough time. Perhaps you've had more than your share of illness, or you may have lost someone very dear to you, so that you feel that life can never be the same again. You may be at the stage where you're worried about making ends meet, or about the problems of bringing up your family. Or perhaps you're at the beginning of your married life and are finding not only the thrills but also the tensions of this new relationship. If you were making an assessment of what the year has brought you, how would things balance up? Would you think the year had brought you a profit or a loss?

I've been using the words profit and loss in a metaphorical sense, but I'll tell you one thing that worries me. I suspect that there are too many people who measure happiness and success in terms of the state of their bank books and of the material things which they possess. I also suspect that a good many people imagine that their happiness depends upon luck. I don't believe that either material possessions or luck are the things which really bring us happiness. And at this point I'd like to tell you a story about our Kirk Beadle.

Like most Beadles I have known, he has a lively sense of humour—and like most Beadles he certainly needs it. In our church we have some lovely old silver Communion Cups which we keep in the bank across the street. They are stored in large heavy boxes. One day the Beadle had to bring them to the church. He was standing outside the bank, weighed down with his load and waiting for a lull in the traffic, when a man who had seen him coming out of the bank said to him, 'What on earth have you got in those boxes you brought out of the bank?' 'Did you no' ken,' said the Beadle, 'that I'm efter winning the pools?'

A good many people would think that they were well on the way to happiness if they had won £75,000 in the pools. They would have all the material possessions that they want, and they would feel that they had been extraordinarily lucky. But I don't think that life works out in that way. The richest people I've known haven't been the happiest ones. The people who have trusted in nothing but luck, aren't—in my experience at least—the ones who make a real success of living.

Listen to what Jesus had to say about material possessions. The words come from the twelfth chapter of St Luke in a modern translation (Luke 12:15–20, RSV).

And he said to them, 'Take heed and beware of all covetousness; for a man's life does not consist in the abundance of his possessions'. And he told them a parable, saying, 'The land of a rich farmer brought forth plentifully; and he thought to himself, "What shall I do, for I have nowhere to store my crops?" And he said, "I will do this: I will pull down my barns and build larger ones; and there I will store all my grain and my goods. And I will say to my soul, Soul, you have ample goods laid up for many years: take your ease, eat, drink, be merry." But God said to him, "Fool! This night your soul is required of you; and the things you have prepared, whose will they be?"'

Not so long ago someone said to me, 'I've got all the money I need, but if there is one thing I'm sure of it is that material possessions can't bring me happiness'. That's true for everyone who makes material possessions their goal and their God.

And what about this business of luck? The other day I had a letter from someone who said, 'I can't see us getting on at all. I hope to God that next year brings us better luck'. I know the situation in that home, and it isn't luck that is going to make next year a better one for that family. Let me illustrate from my own experience.

Right at the beginning of this year I was sent one of those anonymous letters which tell you that if you don't send it on to someone else you'll break the lucky chain and have a run of bad luck for a year. It's most annoying to get a letter like that. You're annoyed at the mentality of the person who's sent it. And you're annoyed at yourself for getting annoyed and paying any attention to it, because there's a streak of superstition in most of us which makes us, even if just for a moment, wonder if there's anything in it.

Well, of course, I tore it up and threw it into the fire. But here's the point. Soon after that, several things happened which were peculiarly frustrating and disappointing. And simply because I'd had such a letter and destroyed it, the niggling question came up, 'Can there be anything in this wretched thing after all?' I quote the story not because I thought for a moment that there was anything in it at all, but because when things happen to us which hurt us or grieve us or trouble us, and we don't see any reason for their happening, the temptation is to doubt God and envy the people who seem to be so much luckier than we are.

If ever we feel like this we have to take a hold of ourselves and get back to the Gospel. You'll find no trace in the Bible of people believing that luck or fate or fortune is the guiding power in human life. The Bible tells us that everything which happens to us happens as part of the plan and purpose of God.

Here, for example, is what St Paul said in the eighth chapter of Romans:

> Likewise the Spirit helps us in our weakness; for we do not know how to pray as we ought, but the Spirit himself intercedes for us with sighs too deep for words. And he who searches the hearts of men knows what is the mind of the Spirit, because the Spirit intercedes for the saints according to the will of God.

And listen to this:

> We know that in everything God works for good with those who love him, who are called according to his purpose.
> (Romans 8: 26–28, RSV)

Now there's a belief which takes you beyond luck, and which tells you that in everything God is with you if you love him. In terms of what we're thinking about, it means that if you and I love God, then everything which has happened to us during this year can turn out to have been for good.

I don't pretend that's easy to believe. A statement like that reminds me of what Mark Twain made Huckleberry Finn say about the Bible. Huckleberry Finn was a homeless boy brought up on the banks of the Mississippi, and the story of his adventures is one of the great books of the world and contains some shrewd comments about life. About the Bible Huckleberry Finn said, 'The statements was interesting but tough'. And tonight you may be saying to yourself, 'Believe that in what's happened to me during this year God's purpose has been working out? No, it's a bit too tough to believe that'.

If you feel like that, then let me assure you that I've met quite a number of people during this past year who've felt the same as you, because this year has brought them sorrow or illness or trouble of one kind or another. And I have heard people say, 'What have I done to deserve this?' You know the feeling. Perhaps you've said the same kind of thing yourself.

Well, if you have felt like that or if you still are feeling like that, let me tell you not to give in to that feeling. What has happened to you is not due to fate nor is it due to a God who is waiting to pounce out on you whenever you slip up and slog you hard for it. What has happened to you has happened because you are a human being living in this world. It is part of life. And whatever it is it can be turned to good if you go on trusting and loving and serving God.

I know, because I've seen it happening. I've seen it with people in hospital, facing their illness with courage, finding it a deepening and enriching experience in the long run. I've seen it with a woman dying of cancer and who knew for three years that she would die of cancer, and whose faith and courage worked for good in her and in those who knew her. I've seen it with people whose lives have been darkened by disaster and sorrow, and who have not given in or allowed themselves to be embittered but who have still looked for what they could learn from their experience.

There are a lot of clever people who will go on for long enough arguing the toss about the unreasonableness of believing in God because of all the suffering and evil in the world. You've seen or heard some of them on television or steam radio. Well, I don't know if you'll get anywhere by arguing about this subject, no matter how clever you may be. A doctor doesn't argue about why there should be germs in the world. He tracks them down and deals with them. In the

same way you don't find much argument in the New
Testament as to why people should have a tough time in the
world. You simply find the record of men and women who
coped with the toughest times that anyone could have, and
coped with them victoriously.

And when we're measuring up what this year has meant to
us, I think that we'll do well to think of it in terms of what
we learn from the New Testament rather than in terms of
what this modern world of ours counts as being success or
happiness. You couldn't say that modern civilization has been
conspicuously successful in producing happy people, whereas
the Christians of the New Testament and the early Church
had most evidently found the secret of a full and happy life.
Part of their discovery was, surely, this: that this world is a
school of character in which with God's help we can grow and
develop. And if this year has made us men and women with
more sympathy, more faith, more kindness, courage, humour
and goodness—why then it has been a good year for us, and
it has been good because God has been with us, as he will be
in the year to come.

Well now, I've had the privilege, so to speak, of paying you
a visit tonight. I'd like to take further advantage of this
opportunity, and invite you to join with me in simple family
prayers. If you have a Bible and Hymnbook at hand, you may
like to use them for the readings and the praise which we're
going to have.

I don't think we could do better than begin with the 23rd
Psalm, and you won't need any book to remind you of the
words.

[Singing of the metrical version of Psalm 23, 'The Lord's my
Shepherd, I'll not want,' followed here.]

I'd like to read two short passages from the Bible which seem
to fit in with the thoughts and feelings which we have as we
stand at the watershed between one year and another. One
comes from the Old Testament and the other from the New

Testament, and they both speak of the goodness and the nearness of God and of Jesus.

First, some verses from the 139th Psalm:

> O LORD, thou hast searched me and known me. Thou knowest my downsitting and mine uprising, thou understandest my thoughts afar off. Thou searchest out my path and my lying down, and art acquainted with all my ways. For there is not a word in my tongue, but lo, O LORD, thou knowest it altogether. Thou hast beset me behind and before and laid thine hand upon me. Such knowledge is too wonderful for me; it is high, I cannot attain unto it. Whither shall I go from thy spirit? Or whither shall I flee from thy presence? If I ascend up into heaven, thou art there: if I make my bed in hell, behold, thou art there. If I take the wings of the morning, and dwell in the uttermost parts of the sea; even there shall thy hand lead me, and thy right hand shall hold me. If I say, surely the darkness shall overwhelm me, and the light about me shall be night; even the darkness hideth not from thee, but the night shineth as the day: the darkness and the light are both alike to thee.
>
> (Psalm 139:1–12, AV)

I must say that I find great comfort and encouragement in those words. We think that the darkness hides us from God and God from us. But that isn't true. God is there all the time. He's there when you're lying awake in the wee small hours not able to sleep, thinking about all the things that worry you. God is there then. He's there when something happens which seems to blot the sun out of the sky and the light out of your life, and when you think that both God and man have forgotten you. God hasn't forgotten you. He's there then. You may wonder about some of your family who are away from home, what's happening to that lad or girl, or that young couple who have ventured overseas. God is with them, wherever they are. Remember that.

And now the passage from the New Testament. I'm going to read the closing verses of the eighth chapter of the letter St Paul wrote to the Romans. This is what he says:

What then shall we say to this? If God is for us, who is against us? He who did not spare his own Son but gave him up for us all, will he not also give us all things with him? Who shall bring any charge against God's elect? It is God who justifies; who is to condemn? Is it Christ Jesus, who died, yes, who was raised from the dead, who is at the right hand of God, who indeed intercedes for us? Who shall separate us from the love of Christ? Shall tribulation, or distress, or persecution, or famine, or nakedness, or peril, or sword? . . . No, in all these things we are more than conquerors through him who loved us. For I am sure that neither death, nor life, nor angels, nor principalities, nor things present, nor things to come, nor powers, nor height, nor depth, nor anything else in all creation, will be able to separate us from the love of God in Christ Jesus our Lord.
(Romans 8:31–35, 37–39, RSV)

I think those words speak to us all in our modern situation and in the need which we all can experience. I know they speak to me. They remind me that the real level of living isn't touched by anything that can happen in the world. We're apt to be dazzled and bemused by scientific and technological progress, and to be scared stiff by the thought of what men might be mad enough to do with the power which they have unleashed. But when it comes to the bit, it isn't rockets and sputniks which make up real life for us, but our personal relationships. It's our family, our friends and all the people we meet who make up life for us. And deeper than all our human relationships is our relationship with God, for that is something which cannot be taken away from us, which cannot be destroyed.

With this in mind, let us join in a prayer to God, thanking him for the year past, asking his help for the year to come, and commending to him ourselves and all whom we love.

Let us pray:

We thank thee, O God, for all that has happened in the year now coming to its close. For all the good things which it brought us; the happiness of our families, of seeing young folk grow up in strength and grace; the gladness and the gaiety we have had, the gifts of laughter and of friendship.

We thank thee for the work we have had to do and for the satisfaction of doing it; for new knowledge and new experience, for a clearer understanding of ourselves and of others.

We thank thee for the faith of Jesus. We know that we haven't kept the faith as we should, or fought the good fight as he did, and we ask thy forgiveness for this. But we know that without him we could not have come through. Without him we could not have got over the hard and difficult times or seen the lessons we had to learn through them. We thank thee that he made it possible for us to go on believing, and so to grow in sympathy for others; that he kept us from bitterness and put more of his strength and goodness into our weak and imperfect lives.

And now we pray that always we may know and feel that thou art with us and all those whom we love. Be with our homes and families. Keep us from disharmony and let the light and freedom and joy of Jesus be with us every day. Be with any who are away from home just now. Keep them safe and well, and guard them from harm and evil.

Whatever happens in the future, keep us loyal and true. Help us to join our prayers with those of Christians everywhere for peace and prosperity and harmony among all men and all nations. And make us the kind of people who can do some good in thy world.

Give us truth in all our conversation; generosity in deed and word and thought; integrity and sincerity in all dealings; serenity when we are anxious and things go badly with us; thoroughness in our work and a worthwhile use of leisure, so that with the passing days we may become more like what thou meanest us to be: for Jesus' sake. Amen.

And now let's end our family prayers with the rest of the paraphrase we use so often at times like this—the one which began my visit to your homes.

[The programme ended with singing of the remaining verses of 'O God of Bethel', and with a Blessing.]

AFRAID TO DIE?

The first of a series of short BBC TV programmes, 'Victory over Death', broadcast during one week in July 1967. The titles of the other programmes were: 'In Fellowship with Others'; 'Stages on a Journey'; 'Disembodied Spirits or Recognisable Persons?'; and 'To Hell with Heaven?'

Good evening! One of the biggest differences between the early Christians and their pagan neighbours was in their attitude to death. It was not that the Christians were unafraid of death while all others feared it. The Stoics, for example, were extremely courageous in the face of death. No, the difference was that the Christians looked forward with hope beyond death. They believed that on the other side of the fires in which they might be burned stood their friend, Jesus. That was why they could die singing. But the non-Christians had no such certainty. There might be a world beyond and there might not. At the best they could speculate, at the worst they could only despair.

This difference still remains between Christians and non-Christians. It is not that Christians are better than others. It is simply that they can never look on death as being the end of everything. Rather do they see it as a gateway into a fuller life. Thus Dietrich Bonhoeffer could write of death, 'Come now, highest of feasts on the way to freedom eternal', and when the Gestapo took him from prison to execution, he said to a friend, 'This is the end. For me the beginning of life'.

In my experience I have found that a faith like this is shared by many ordinary Christians. It is not limited to the saints and heroes of the faith. An aunt of mine died at the age of 94. She knew that she was going, and she accepted the fact with serenity. She had always been accustomed to settling the household accounts, and she said to her daughter, 'I'll say good-bye, because I'm really going now; but I'll see you again. And isn't it a good thing that I'm dying after all the bills have been paid?'

Or again, I think of a younger man who was dying slowly and painfully of cancer. He also knew that he was dying, and it was better that he knew. There was no pretence. So often one sees a situation where the truth has not been told. Everybody is pretending. Sometimes even the patient is pretending, knowing full well that the illness is likely to be fatal. But in this case the man and his wife both knew what the trouble was, and they could talk openly to each other, saying all that was in their hearts to say. One could feel that because of this, some of the weight of the burden was lifted. It was an example of how the truth does set us free.

I found that in such an atmosphere I could stop using kindly platitudes, and begin to talk about the reality of the faith, about a Man tried and tested by suffering who died and rose again, who stands beside us in our pain, who died as we have to die, and who has won a victory over death, a victory in which we can share. The pain is still real in such a sick room. The sorrow at the prospect of separation has still to be endured. These are inevitably part of our human experience. But there is no despair. Christ has overcome death.

Good-night.

CHAPTER 8
Champion of Christian Marriage
Introduced by Jean Forrester-Paton

Every parish minister has to perform numerous marriages, but it seems that Hugh Douglas early felt called, not merely to uphold, but to *champion* Christian teaching on marriage and family life—certainly he gave it a central place in his ministry. From his student days he had contact with George MacLeod, and later with the Iona Community on Iona and at Community House in Glasgow. Both offered Hugh many opportunities to speak *informally* on this subject, especially with young people. So it was the Community which asked Hugh to write the pamphlet *What is Christian Marriage?* Selling at six old pence, it was published in 1944 and immediately became a best-seller of its kind. On bookstalls at camps, courses and conferences—abroad as well as in the UK—it caught the eye of enquiring youth who, with relief, found it called a spade a spade! Although some church people, of course, objected to its frank account of sexual intercourse, the pamphlet provided Hugh and other busy ministers with a tool when preparing couples for marriage. We know he took this task very seriously: he saw many couples at least twice, but when possible he arranged courses of six meetings for several couples together, at which there was often lively discussion. All would receive a copy of the booklet and the course outline. I know from correspondence that many couples greatly appreciated Hugh's teaching and friendship in these meetings.

It could almost be said that the publication of *What is*

Christian Marriage? affected Hugh's life as much as the lives of his readers, though in a different way. For from then on, he was marked as one who could communicate attractively, reverently and with authority on Christian attitudes to sex, marriage and family relationships. So he was invited to speak far beyond the bounds of his parish at conferences, summer schools, on radio and television.

It was not all words, however. Both Hugh and Isabel were deeply involved with others in starting the Edinburgh Marriage Guidance Council, and as counsellors for it. Then, when they moved to Dundee, Hugh saw the same pressing need there and worked hard as the first chairman of its Marriage Guidance Council. He was ahead of his time in regarding what were then new 'secular' bodies—the MGC and the Family Planning Association—as helpful agencies to which the parish minister could refer couples. Certainly the pioneers of MGC, such as Dr Herbert Gray, had a pastoral concern for couples in difficulty and a zeal for *positive education* before marriage, which Hugh fully shared. He regarded helping with marital problems as a major element in a minister's pastoral work; and as chaplain of Dundee High School he introduced, with help from doctors, graded annual talks on personal relationships.

It was further evidence of Hugh's strong commitment in this field that within two years of his first coronary he accepted an invitation from the Churches in Ghana to spend three months there in 1967. Lecturing at training courses for 'Family Advisers' was to be his main task, though he afterwards reckoned he had given 150 addresses of different kinds! Happily Isabel could accompany him and share this strenuous visit. The training courses were attended by 245 picked lay people and clergy—twice as many men as women—and were arranged by the Christian Council's Committee on Christian Marriage and Family Life, of which I was secretary. They also had full backing and participation from the Roman Catholic Church—and the general spirit of unity and co-operation between the Churches in Ghana was one of the things on which Hugh specially commented. There were five courses, held in different regions, with Hugh giving eight lectures at each. There were also lectures by Ghanaian doctors, social workers and others, as well as group discussion and worship.

In preparation for the visit, Hugh had read about Ghanaian customs and traditions, but, amazingly, he also managed to write his main lectures and epilogues before he left Dundee. As a result, he was relaxed and free to chat with the trainees, whenever time permitted. Ghanaians found him approachable. Any feelings of shyness were soon dispelled by Hugh's lighter touches and vivid stories, drawn from his own pastoral experience, which featured in the lectures or in the discussions that followed. With his fresh presentation of familiar Bible passages he, along with other speakers, inspired as well as informed the first Family Advisers. These courses led by Hugh, along with the wider publicity through press, radio and television which they engendered, laid foundations. A demand grew for fuller training in counselling, so two years later the British MGC sent tutors to conduct the first of several courses in marriage counselling. Now qualified Ghanaians conduct them for the Christian Council's Committee, and they are regularly used by Government social work and health staff.

After his return, Hugh often spoke about what he had heard one of Ghana's leading politicians say to the members of a Family Advisers Course.

> Professor K A Busia told them that they were preparing to do one of the most important tasks in the building of the new Ghana. He urged them to be active in . . . working against polygamy, easy divorce, concubinage . . . in replacing promiscuity and infidelity by true companionship and loyalty in the marriage relationship.

Hugh wryly contrasted this with the advocacy of permissiveness by some intellectuals in Britain.

Hugh's great contribution in this whole field was in presenting effectively, and championing courageously, what he saw as the best tradition of Christian teaching on sex and marriage. (We do not find him speaking or writing much about new issues raised by feminism or by fresh study on homosexuality.) So what were the chief features of Hugh's presentation?

After perusing the wealth of related papers, one appreciates, first of all, the empathy he has with his listeners. For instance, the sermon 'What it means to be Human' (printed below) clearly met the concern and anguish of church members, and not least of parents of students among them, over the sexual permissiveness which had come to prevail by 1972. Similarly, addressing a wider TV audience in the 'Coping with Life' programme on 'Bringing up the Family', he spoke as a parent who knew 'the tensions and worries which mingle with the joys of family life. . . . If you find your children . . . at one moment a lump in your throat and at another a pain in your neck, so do I.'

Second, he constantly urged couples to use the tensions which inevitably occur in every marriage as means of growing so as to achieve a mature relationship. He stressed the need for God's help to grow, to forgive one another after quarrels and to resist temptations to unfaithfulness.

Third, Hugh expounded in a positive and fascinating way the inner and abiding truths about the relations of men and women contained in Genesis, in Jesus' life and teaching, and in St Paul's letters.

Finally, if Hugh was an uncompromising champion of Christian standards he was not a harsh one. He often pointed to Jesus's compassionate dealing with people who had plainly broken God's law in their sexual behaviour, and he showed compassion in his own pastoral work. He loved to quote T W Manson:

> The Living Christ still has two hands, the one to point the way, the other held out to help us along. So the Christian ideal lies before us, not as a remote and austere mountain

peak, an ethical Everest which we must scale by our own skill and endurance, but as a road on which we may walk with Christ as guide and friend.

(*Ethics and the Gospel*: SCM, London, 1960, p. 68)

* * *

CHRISTIAN TEACHING ABOUT MARRIAGE TODAY

The second of two Sermons on Christian Marriage preached in St Mary's, Dundee, in November 1967.

What therefore God hath joined together, let not man put asunder.

(Mark 10:9, AV)

A fortnight ago we were thinking of the challenge and opposition which Christian marriage faces today. We saw that the choice with which we are faced is between the lifelong, monogamous union and more easy, casual and temporary liaisons. We considered the teaching of the Old Testament; and today we look at the teaching of Jesus, with special relation to some of our contemporary problems.

The difference made to the status of women

We should realise that over the centuries the person and teaching of Jesus have made a radical difference to the status of women. Reverence paid to Mary, his mother, and the example of the Holy Family, slowly made men think anew. The Christian emphasis on the unique value of each individual soul gradually did away with the notion that women were inferior to men, and that, for example, girl babies could be exposed to die because they were an economic burden to the family—which was sometimes the custom in pre-Christian and non-Christian societies.

Even in the Church, however, the conception of woman's equality and full partnership with man was slow to develop. Two scriptural passages were quoted to emphasise man's primacy: Genesis 2 and Ephesians 5.

In Genesis 2, woman was said to have been created out of man's rib. Therefore she was regarded as a side issue. But, as Robert Burns pointed out, another interpretation is that the Creator having made man, said, 'I can do better than this', and went on to create woman!

In Ephesians chapter 5 St Paul said that in marriage man is the head of the woman as Christ is head of the Church. This is quoted as justification for the husband's authority in his home. But the passage must be closely studied, and it shows the depth of a mutual respect and devotion in which there is no competition for mastery. Further, if the husband is to emulate Christ, let him remember that Christ 'loved the Church and gave himself for it'. Therefore the husband's headship does not mean domineering authority, but in fact he should be ready to lay down even his life for his wife. That should make husbands—and wives—think!

In this question we have to remember Paul said that in Christ 'there is neither male nor female' (Galatians 3:28, AV). And in the marriage relationship, I think one could safely say that Christian teaching implies that husband and wife should have equality of status, but difference of function.

The fact of the Incarnation

Another difference was made by the actual birth of Jesus. The fact that he was born in the flesh, that he was born of a woman, gave people a different view of the body. The idea that there was something inferior or even evil about the body because it was material, is not a Christian notion. It is pagan, coming from Greek philosophy. What Christians call the Incarnation, the coming of Jesus in the flesh as a fully human person, emphasised the doctrine of creation, namely that 'God saw all that he had made, and behold it was very good' (Genesis 1:31, AV).

Thus when Jesus spoke about marriage he re-stated and re-emphasised the unity of husband and wife as 'one flesh', in a unique relationship for life. In the words of our text: 'What God hath joined together, let not man put asunder'. Bodily union is God's purpose, and it is for life, at least in the primary intention.

The celibacy of Jesus

Of course, the fact that Jesus himself was not married has led to some people questioning the validity of what he has to say about marriage. But if we examine this argument it does not have a great deal of substance.

The worth of any teaching depends surely upon its intrinsic value and upon the person of the teacher. With Jesus there is a unique combination of teaching about personal relationships and a life which exemplified all that he taught. Jesus was the perfect man, in the sense that he was the most complete and mature person that the world has seen. The fact that he was not married does not lessen the authority of what he says about personal relationships. He is the supreme artist in living.

The fact that he was unmarried, however, does not mean that celibacy is a higher state than marriage. The Church was slow to recognize this and for centuries taught that true progress in spiritual growth was only possible for those who had forsworn marriage. It took the Reformation and indeed even later development to show that marriage is a state in which there can be real growth to spiritual maturity and to fulfilment of personality. In this connection it is significant that within the Roman Catholic Church there is a growing movement which is in favour of priests being allowed to marry.

Jesus' teaching on chastity and fidelity

In view of some of the recent statements about the Christian attitude to chastity before marriage and fidelity after it, there is need to underline the fact that there is no evidence at all that Jesus ever condoned unchastity or unfaithfulness. Indeed, what he said about husband and wife entering into the one-flesh relationship emphasised that this was a unique and lifelong relationship, within marriage, and between one man and one woman.

He also made it quite clear (in Mark 7:21) that what he bluntly called fornication and adultery were sinful acts.

At the same time he had complete compassion for sinful men and women. He was never shocked by anything or anyone. But he never lowered his standards. He did not condemn the woman taken in adultery, but he did not condone what she had done. He told her plainly not to do it again.

It would therefore seem to follow that in the Church we should never be pharisaical in our condemnation of the more obvious sins. We should not be shocked by what others may have done. But if we are to help them, we must be firm in maintaining the Christian standards while showing them all the love and charity that we are capable of.

Jesus and divorce

This leads us on to the issue of divorce.

(1) It is, I think, obvious that the purpose of marriage, in the mind of Jesus, is to provide a lifelong union between man and woman. Again we can refer to the words of our text: 'What God hath joined together, let not man put asunder'.

It follows from this that Christians who are loyal to their faith have an obligation to do everything possible to keep their marriages in being, not merely in outward form but in inward reality. It is the Christian belief that the love of 1 Corinthians chapter 13 does, under God, overcome the greatest difficulties. This is what G K Chesterton meant when he said that Christian marriage is founded on incompatibility of temperament. So often this is advanced as a reason for divorce, but for Christians it can be a means by which they can in the end reach a deeper and a richer relationship.

(2) It has to be recognized, however, that marriages do break down. What is the Christian attitude to be if this appears to be inevitable? What can be regarded as grounds for divorce?

(a) At the moment divorce is granted in this country on grounds of offence by one or other party in a marriage. These grounds have been extended but they are not regarded as finally satisfactory. The distinction made between the innocent and the guilty party is often far from accurate.

(b) It has therefore been urged that there should be divorce by consent. But, for Christians, this would appear to make divorce too easy and casual an act. We have the lamentable examples to warn us which we see in certain States in the USA.

(c) There is a growing body of Christian opinion which feels that although marriage for Christians is meant to be indissoluble, we must recognize that a stage can be reached when a couple find it impossible to continue living as husband and wife. It is therefore argued that if a marriage has ceased in any real sense to be a marriage at all, and if this can be plainly shown, then—as the lesser of two evils—Christians may have recourse to divorce.

(d) If this is so, obviously it follows that the Church must be concerned about any future marriage into which a divorced person may wish to enter. There is no time to deal with the practice of other Churches, but in the Church of Scotland divorced persons may be re-married in Church. Before this is possible, however, they have to satisfy the minister with regard to the circumstances of their divorce and their sincerity in seeking God's forgiveness and his blessing in their new marriage. This leaves the way open for people to learn from their experience and perhaps, in the end, to establish a better relationship within the fellowship of the Church.

In conclusion, in spite of all the movements of thought which assail us today, we can claim that the foundations and basic principles of Christian teaching about marriage remain firm. We are not going to serve the Christian cause, or indeed the welfare of society, by attempting to relax these principles. At the same time there is a great need for Christians to be urgently concerned with interpreting the spirit of Christ's teaching in relation to contemporary problems, rather than to be hidebound by the weight of dead traditions, or by the mere letter of custom. The Church has not always been true to Christ's spirit and has indeed misinterpreted his teaching. Today we need clear minds, resolute wills and loving hearts in our efforts to make men and women see that in marriage, as in all things, Jesus Christ is the Way, the Truth and the Life.

'YOU ARE THE MAN!'

A sermon preached at St Andrew's Church, Brisbane, Australia, on 21 August 1977. The sermon as printed here is taken from a recording of the service.

Then Nathan said to David, 'You are the man'.
(2 Samuel 12:7, NEB)

The Old Testament is a mine of wonderful stories and particularly of course when, in addition to the fascination of the narrative, we can see the impact of divine principles upon human character and behaviour. One of the greatest of these stories is the story of David, and one of the most vivid incidents in that story is his relationship with Bathsheba, Uriah her husband, and Nathan the prophet.

I hardly need to remind you of the details of the story: how David fell in love with Uriah's wife Bathsheba, how he saw to it that Uriah was killed in battle in order that he might marry Bathsheba himself. It raises some interesting points about David, because we always think of David as the sweet singer of Israel, as the author of the Book of Psalms, that wondrous treasure house of religious devotion; and here he was behaving in this sordid manner. But he was a great man, David. He was a fine leader, he had great loyalty and compassion for Saul whom he knew he was to displace; he had a deep lasting love for Jonathan; and above all he was himself profoundly religious. The trouble was that he was a king, and kings then and for centuries afterwards were accustomed to getting what they wanted. In this particular instance he wanted what he wasn't entitled to have, but none the less he was determined to get it. Of course in those days, 3,000 years ago, it was quite legitimate for a man to have more than one wife. But it was not permissible for him to have an adulterous relationship with another man's wife. This was precisely what David had had and Bathsheba was carrying his child while her husband was still alive.

I am sure that all of us in our own small ways have known the experience of trying to justify a somewhat dubious course of action. We are pretty sure that what we want to do isn't quite straight, it isn't entirely above board. But you may know the process by which we begin to work out excuses or reasons to justify what we really want to do, but which we know we ought not to be doing.

Well, this of course is precisely what David set about doing. He wanted to legalise the whole business in the eyes of the people, and the only way in which he could do it was by getting rid of Uriah, who was an honest to goodness, straightforward soldier. So David went about it in a very circumspect manner. He talked to nobody except Joab his Commander in Chief. He arranged everything with him so that Uriah was to be sent into the front of the battle where the fighting was thickest and most dangerous and where he was almost certain to be killed. If this happened, then Joab was to send back a message suitably cloaked and disguised, and when David heard that Uriah had been killed he was to show indignation at the loss of such a trusty warrior. Well, it all worked beautifully, and when the period of mourning had been accomplished, Bathsheba married David and it was entirely above board. Everything was all right. People said, 'What a wonderful relationship, what a beautiful love match!' But David and Bathsheba knew that the rules of morality had been rather badly bent.

Of course that was 3,000 years ago; that was just when the seeds of moral concern were being sown, which over the centuries were to grow and develop and bear fruit in the concept of marriage as a monogamous and life-long relationship. We know that today, and we know that today the rules can be pretty badly bent. We know that society, if it is to be sound and healthy, depends on the stability of home and family life, and we know equally that home and family life depends upon the foundation of the Christian moral standard. Sadly these standards are being widely disregarded today, the standards of chastity before marriage and fidelity after marriage. There is no evidence that the sum of human happiness has been increased or that society has in any way been benefited by these rules being disregarded. Indeed the reverse would seem to be obvious, judging by the statistics of broken homes, of problem children and of juvenile delinquency.

It's all the more surprising, therefore, that in the face of such evidence there are one or two modern theologians who would actually try to justify cases of premarital intercourse or post-marital infidelity, because of what they call the beauty of the relationship, like the beauty of the relationship between David and Bathsheba. Now there is absolutely nothing in the teaching of Jesus to justify such arguments, and I believe that views like this can only serve to produce more shallow and impermanent relationships, and we see far too many of them today. If we are to have maturity, fulfilment and lasting companionship within marriage, then these are the rewards of those who are obedient to the standards which have been shewn to us by Jesus and by the development of the concept of marriage over the centuries.

But you see, just as people today are inclined to try and bend the rules to suit themselves, so David and Bathsheba bent the rules to satisfy their own whims and passions, instead of realising that rules are there to guide and control human behaviour. So that was the situation, and you can be sure that most people in the city of Jerusalem knew exactly what had happened. Everybody would be talking about it beneath the surface, but nobody would like to bring it out into the open and challenge the king himself. My word, no, not when he had the power of life and death. But there was one man, the prophet Nathan; and the Word of the Lord came to Nathan. It's a great phrase that, 'the Word of the Lord'. The Word of God, we read in the New Testament, is alive and powerful and sharper than any two-edged sword, and Nathan felt this compulsion that he had to go and have it out with the King face to face about his behaviour.

He was a wise man was Nathan, as well as a courageous one, and you remember that parable in which he cloaked his first approach to David. He knew that David was a compassionate man; he knew that he was a deeply religious man; he knew that he sought justice in his dealings as a king. So he told him this parable about the rich man who took the poor man's little ewe lamb to which the poor man was so utterly devoted, and killed it in order to satisfy the hunger of a passing traveller. And of course, as he had guessed, David's anger was kindled and he said, 'This is terrible, this is iniquitous, this man must be punished'. And then the courage of Nathan: he said to David, 'You are the man'. Just imagine the silence that fell on that colloquy at that point: 'You are the man'.

Now Nathan was in the true tradition of prophets from Moses to Jesus. They were under the compulsion of the Word of God, they had to speak out what they believed to be true. But there were two distinctive qualities about such prophets. The first was that they always spoke out face to face. They didn't say things behind other people's backs; they had it out with those whom they wished to challenge or rebuke. And the second quality was they never did it to hurt, they always did it to heal, which again is different from the kind of gossip which is spoken behind anybody's back.

This produced a unique reaction in David, and this is what makes the Bible a unique book. It doesn't seek to gloss over the faults and the iniquities of human nature. There you see men and women in their true colours, warts, faults and all. And this is why David is such an attractive character in spite of all his sordid behaviour. That's why we can feel an affinity with a man like him, although I hope we don't emulate him in some of his worst actions. But here was a man who not only was a sinner but—this is the important point—realized what he had done. The great passage in that story is not just Nathan saying to David, 'You are the man', it's also David saying, 'Yes, I have sinned. I have sinned against God and I have sinned against my neighbours and I realize what I have done'. That is self-knowledge, self-realization; and that is why we can think of David as an inspiring example of progress and of growth, and why we can sincerely look to him as one of the great religious leaders of the Old Testament.

When you come to think of it, my friends, isn't this what life itself is all about, this whole process of learning and making progress? We do it not just when we are young, we do it right on through our life towards death itself. That great old Victorian preacher in Edinburgh, Alexander Whyte, speaking once of how temptation could dog your footsteps right through your life, said, 'Yes, the hounds of hell could pursue you right through the course of your lives to the very gates of heaven itself and leave their slaver on the golden bars'. Well, we go on learning all the time, and we only learn in the right way when we learn not only about God but also about ourselves. I am sure you have heard the story of the American philosopher Emerson, of how he came back from Church one Sunday and wrote in the diary which he kept every day: 'Went to Church this morning, heard a good sermon, applied it to myself'. Well, I can assure you that preachers very rarely know whether they have preached a good sermon or not. But

I think most faithful preachers try to start by preaching to themselves; that is the beginning of a sermon. And the end of it is that they hope that, if they have said anything of the truth, then both they and their hearers will apply it not just to other people but to themselves.

WHAT IT MEANS TO BE HUMAN

A sermon preached in St Mary's, Dundee, on 8 October 1972.

Now we see only puzzling reflections in a mirror.
(1 Corinthians 13:12, NEB)

When we look into a mirror it is, of course, ourselves that we see. And Paul rightly calls this a puzzling reflection. For as we look at ourselves, who and what are we? Animals or persons? Amalgams of genes and chromosomes, or immortal souls? Life is a search for identity. It is a mystery, and so long as we live we may feel that we have never found any clear answer. But there is an all-important clue given in this chapter, and it is Love.

(1) In brief, love is the Christian answer to the present debate about the alternative society, pornography and permissiveness. Love, in its Christian meaning, is about the total relationship of persons. For that reason it is opposed to the current campaign for what can only be called the dehumanization of personal relationships.

Let me give you a very recent example of this. I have here a cutting from last Wednesday's *Scotsman* newspaper. It gives details of a centre page spread in the Edinburgh University Magazine *The Student* which provides information for first year students. It details contraception methods saying of the Pill that 'it has the advantage of allowing you to leap abandonedly into bed'.

But this is the imposition of a point of view which may not be accepted by large numbers of first year students. Why should it be assumed that they all wish to leap into bed with the first accommodating member of the opposite sex? Why should they be encouraged to do so?

The article goes on to advise about abortions and recommends a certain Pregnancy Advisory Service as being kind, helpful and cheap. Why should it be assumed that students will be so promiscuous as to run the risk of becoming pregnant? Why impose the attitude that abortion is safe and easy, when the psychological effects on the girl are unknown and when many of the nursing staff are increasingly unable to bear the destruction of tiny life-forms? Is this attitude about the creation and destruction of babies typical of first year students or is it relentlessly plugged by a determined minority?

I suggest that this is only one more example of a determined effort to dehumanize personal relationships. This is not love which is being described. It is the isolation of sex, of the physical act. It reduces love to casual sexual contact. It trivializes it, and it does not help the young in their search for identity. Those who write such articles should be reminded of certain curious facts.

(a) The more technical knowledge about sex there is purveyed, the less fun and happiness seem to result. There is endless information about how to sleep together. But this does not help to solve the puzzle of living together, which is a much more complicated, demanding and personal relationship.

(b) The more information about contraception that is made available, the greater the number of illegitimate pregnancies. And along with this goes the epidemic escalation of VD. None of this gives any joy.

(c) The greater the licence that is practised, the more is society in bondage to violence, anarchy, crime and delinquency.

In short, this is nothing but a sad and dusty answer to the

search for identity. It leaves the reflection in the mirror painfully frustrated and distorted.

(2) This chapter on love (1 Corinthians chapter 13) repays the closest reading and a lifetime of study. It is about our relationships as human beings—total and all-inclusive, unity of mind, body and spirit. This is what distinguishes human beings from animals. But the modern approach does violence to this. It diminishes our human stature. Here is an extract from an autobiography by John Masters, in which he has been praising the American way of life. He is describing a young couple. 'Their mating', he writes, 'had been amazingly public and the marvel was only that her husband and his wife had not come across them, locked like dogs, at various spots along South Mountain Road.' And that is a mild example of the kind of stuff that is increasingly being written and published today. It is being done in the name of what someone has called 'the new puritanism' which insists violently that everything must be open and public; and its advocates demand that their point of view must express itself not merely in their own behaviour, but in books and magazines, in plays and films, in the press and on the TV screen. This, they claim, is liberation from the restraints of the old puritanism.

The Christian answer is that this does not liberate people. It reduces them.

As human beings we have *a need for and the right to privacy* in the deep and intimate relationships we have with each other. It reduces our humanity when this privacy is abandoned by stage and screen representations. Privacy is related to our dignity as human beings, and it does violence to this human dignity to have men and women reduced to the level of animals. It must also do grave damage to the actors and actresses who are paid to behave in these ways.

As human beings we seek fulfilment in and through each other. This means that we *treat each other as persons*, not as objects to be used for mere selfish or passing enjoyment. In the BBC TV presentation of 'Casanova' which was viewed by twelve million people, the attitude was that of persons being used as things or instruments for physical pleasure. This is to trivialize what is the greatest of God's gifts to the human race. The more that sex is trivialized, indeed, the less fulfilling and enjoyable it becomes, the less meaning it has.

As human beings we have *a right to honour this relationship.* The whole range of modern permissiveness, from pornography and strip tease to the public use of four letter words, shows contempt for the man–woman relationship. It reduces it to the level of drunken obscenities shouted on the terracing of football grounds. It makes something which has produced some of the greatest literature and poetry in the world fit only for the gutter.

(3) Finally, the Christian view is that as human beings *we need the family* for our development in responsibility and maturity. You may remember the name of Richard Neville, the editor of *Oz.* Recently he was asked if the reading of his magazine by a fifteen year old girl would encourage her to be promiscuous. He replied that this was the whole point of the magazine, and that his aim was also to get rid of the old-fashioned family. He had nothing definite to put in place of the family, and in this he was typical of the nihilistic approach which destroys but does not try to construct.

The Christian answer is that it is in the family that the love of 1 Corinthians chapter 13 is both tested and given full play. If indeed 'love is very patient, very kind . . . never rude, never selfish, never irritated, never resentful' (1 Corinthians 13:4–5, Moffatt), it is obviously required in the relationships of the family—between husband and wife, between parents and children, between sisters and brothers. The family is a community in miniature. It is a microcosm of the world. It is where we learn to live together so that we may be people of integrity who can be useful members of society. Attack the family and you attack the very foundations of any civilized society; and, of course, that is why the family is being attacked today. Its enemies have a contempt and hatred for what makes us human, and they want to destroy it.

During the last war an Austrian called Viktor Frankl was sent to the concentration camp at Auschwitz. He said that he survived Auschwitz because of his love for those dear to him whom he never expected to see again. In a situation where Jews were liquidated and slaughtered like animals, there was born in him a desire to help human beings to be human, to find a meaning in life, to seek a clue to the puzzling reflection in a mirror. And he has this to say about the problem he seeks to solve:

> No one should be surprised today that young people behave as if they did not know anything about responsibility, option, choice, sacrifice, self-devotion, dedication to a higher goal in life and the like. Parents and teachers, scientists and philosophers, have taught them all too long a time that man is 'nothing but' [the product of evolution]. [The result is that] man becomes more and more like the image of man he has been taught about.

And that image is *less than human.*

The battle going on today is in very truth a battle for humanity. That is why in the Church we must be aware of it and be ready to meet the challenge. We have a holding operation to carry through, preserving the Christian values and the Christian family. But the time shall come when we shall advance again, if it has not begun already. For Christian love is still the only valid clue to the problems of our identity, to the puzzling reflections of ourselves in the mirror.

CHAPTER 9

Speaker to
Community and Nation
Introduced by D H Whiteford

As the Parishes of Scotland from the Solway to the Shetlands
need ministers to speak to their people about Jesus Christ, so
do the great cities of Scotland in their civic identities need
ministers to speak to the public life of Scotland, so that the
Christian tradition in civic life is preserved, and the standards
to which civic or national institutions adhere continue to be
judged by Christian principles.

Hugh's predecessors in the old city charge of Dundee
Parish Church (St Mary's) were men who had spoken to the
many shifts and changes which make up the story of Scottish
city life. Into this inheritance of civic ministry Hugh came
when he moved from North Leith to Dundee in 1951. As his
predecessors had done, he made his own mark on the life of
the city, exercising an influence which was to go far beyond
its civic boundaries.

To speak to men and women in their civic roles about their
public duties, to encourage, compliment or rebuke, demands
of the preacher an understanding of the nature of government,
both local and national, its function and its limitations, and
an ability to make relevant the principles which the Christian
conscience believes are of first importance to its performance.

From the sermons which Hugh preached at the traditional
Kirkin' Services, which the City Council, and later the
District Council, attended as a body, the 1974 sermon which
is printed in this chapter provides an example of both style
and content. Was he listened to? What effect did this civic side

of his ministry have? Such questions are best answered by a quotation from a letter he received after the 1977 Kirkin':

> As on all previous Kirkin' Services which I have attended over the past twenty years . . . your message was relevant, thought-provoking and inspiring. I feel that as parish minister and civic chaplain you have provided an example of devotion and dedication which has permeated and enriched our lives. I have just returned to duty after a long and serious illness, during which I have had time to think afresh and re-assess my life and the blessings I have enjoyed.

In July 1974 Hugh preached at the dedication of the King Robert the Bruce window in Dunfermline Abbey on the 700th Anniversary of Bruce's birth. It was an appropriate occasion on which to consider the needs of the nation. He quoted from the 'Declaration of Arbroath' (1320): 'It is not for glory or for riches or for honour that we fight, but simply and solely for freedom, which no good man surrenders but with his life'. 'Once again,' he said, 'Scotland is in search of her soul. If patriotism means anything, surely it means that we seek freedom to be the best that we can be. Above all we need freedom from the things which sully our name and debase our standards.'

He then went on to plead for four essentials, and here are excerpts from what he said about them:

1 A Revival of Faith:

> We need to recover what has been bred deeply into the Scottish religious tradition, namely, the sense that God is concerned with the whole of life, that Christ is the Lord of the nation as well as of the Church, and that the soul of a people is more important than their money-bags.

2 A Revival of Democracy:

As with Christianity, it is the substance of democracy rather than the form of its party manifestation that matters. . . . It is less important which party has a majority in Scotland than that the Scottish people as a whole should have a responsible concern for the way in which the country is governed at national and local level. Politicians come and go, but it is the people who are the final arbiters. It is for them to take the responsibility of ensuring that the affairs of the country are conducted with honesty, integrity and efficiency.

3 A Revival of Patriotism:

Like other noble qualities, patriotism can be exploited and degraded. It can be confused with less worthy attributes such as arrogance and greed. In its purest form patriotism desires the best for its country.

(He expands this theme in his 1974 Kirkin' Sermon below.)

4 A Revival of Leadership:

We get the leaders we deserve. A self indulgent and mean-spirited people will throw up leaders like itself. It is only a nation with some degree of courage and resolution which will produce the men able to match the needs of the hour.

On the Devolution Bill (1979), which proposed to establish a Scottish Assembly to handle many Scottish affairs, Hugh asked: 'Will it in any real sense bring government nearer to the people? Will it simply make the government of Scotland more complicated and expensive?'—questions which many today still ask about devolution. 'Merely to have a Scots

Parliament will not cure our ills—we had one in the sixteenth and seventeenth centuries and little good it did us!'

Because Hugh saw this as part of his wider ministry, he served on the committees of a number of civic bodies in Dundee and for many years on the Law Society of Scotland's Legal Aid Central Committee of which he was one of the first two lay members. He also undertook speaking engagements to a whole range of clubs and societies—Rotary, Trade Guilds, Curling Club, Glasgow Academy Dinners, School Prizegivings, and so on. He prepared carefully for each one. His speech at the Annual Meeting of the Dundee Savings Bank in 1970 shows how he could use such occasions to say something relevant and important and say it in an interesting way.

Although Hugh had no personal military background, at the laying up of colours at St Mary's by Scots Guards and the Black Watch (1966), he spoke with singular insight into the nature of military duty, and the place of the Forces of the Crown in our national life. Much of what he said then is included in his last sermon on Remembrance which he preached at St Andrews in 1985 and which is printed below.

There are two kingdoms in Scotland, as Andrew Melville contended in the sixteenth century, reminding King James VI that he was a subject of Christ Jesus the King. How we relate the affairs of the two kingdoms, and our duties in respect of each in twentieth century democratic Scotland, is a constant challenge to our Christian conscience. This challenge Hugh was always ready to face—and to answer.

*　　*　　*

THE WORK OF A CENTRAL CITY PARISH

An article contributed to the University of Glasgow Faculty of Divinity and Trinity College Bulletin, November 1966.

One might describe the centre of Dundee, in a memorable phrase of Sean O'Casey, as being 'in a state of chassis'. The pessimists say that it is even worse since the opening of the Tay Road Bridge. Be that as it may, there has been a mounting fury of demolition which, even after several years, has not reached its climax. Ancient and dilapidated buildings have been steadily disappearing to be replaced by the usual modern erections of concrete and glass. In the midst of the gradually developing city centre stands the historic pile known locally as the City Churches and the Old Steeple (more accurately, the Parish and Burgh Churches and St Mary's Tower). As one of my elders emerged recently from St Mary's, a Dundee wifie hailed him, pointing to the churches, 'And when,' she asked him, 'are they gaun tae knock doon that lot?'

Probably she had no idea of how often churches on the same site had been knocked down before. Four times by the English—by Edward I, Richard II, Protector Somerset and General Monk. Once (in 1841) fire destroyed three of the four churches which stood on the site of the single great church, the largest in Scotland. The St Mary's Tower is the only relic of former architectural glories. But if the buildings lack the highest aesthetic merit at least they speak of the ability of the Church to survive and to adapt itself as the generations pass.

This is indeed the challenge faced by a central city parish today. Is it going to survive? Can it adapt itself to a changing situation? Has it a vital function to fulfil? After nearly fifteen years in St Mary's I cannot claim to know all the answers. I can only note down some of the points which appear to be relevant.

Obviously the Church must always be represented visibly in the centre of the community. There ought to be a building which provides the permanent and official link with the City, the University and all kinds of other bodies. It stands there as a witness to the foundation on which our society has been built, however post-Christian we may have become for the time being. The doors are open daily, and there is always someone on the spot to welcome visitors and answer questions. It is the proper setting for the formal services in which our people still indulge, ranging from the Kirkin' of the Council to a Church Parade of Brownies (whom a friend once dubbed 'The Little Flowers of St Vitus'). Its incumbent has to be prepared to take on many non-congregational engagements, as a kind of PRO for the Church.

He is, however, first and foremost the minister and pastor of a congregation, and here he may well feel that the problems which are shared by every parish in the land are accentuated in his own case. People are increasingly moving away from the centre of the city. Despite every encouragement many refuse to break their ties with 'the old church' although they rarely attend it. Coming as they do from a' the airts, they may know few others in the congregation and (even after years of membership) feel strangely isolated. A City Kirk is very different from one in a new housing area or in a residential suburb, where the members share the same background and where much of their social life may centre round the church hall during the week. A difference which I found particularly notice-able when I came from North Leith to St Mary's was in hall accommodation. There can be few churches which have better halls than North Leith and there can be few which have smaller or more inadequate accommodation than St Mary's. Our old 'mission' hall gave some scope for youth activity, but it perpe-tuated the division between the Two Cultures which flourish as actively (although in different form) in the Church as they do in society. Thus, before I united them, I found that the Mission and the St Mary's Sunday Schools went to the same park for their picnic, but the children from the Mission went to one small corner while the children of St Mary'a shone in another. The main problem was therefore fairly clear. It was to seek ways of expressing our fellowship as Christ's people in spite of our social differences, and to do something about our hall.

In the campaign to break down the barriers two occasions stand out. The first was a resounding defeat, when a proposal to abolish seat rents was thrown out by the forces of reaction. I remember being heavily depressed as I listened to nice people expressing what seemed to me to be the most stupid and unchristian arguments I had ever heard. However, another day was to dawn. Four years later the proposer of the motion to retain seat rents became the Convener of our Stewardship Committee.

We needed a Stewardship Campaign in St Mary's, and it did us a lot of good. Seat rents, incidentally, were swept away by the mounting tide of interest and good will, without anybody seeming to bother. A large number of the membership was mobilized to take part. The congregational meal was a great success. The finances went up. There was a new spirit in the congregation, and several new forms of service emerged. The pattern and the results were much the same as those of any other Stewardship Campaign which has been carefully planned and carried through. The point is that it was particuarly useful for our type of congregation, not least in bringing together many people who came from widely varying backgrounds and who, in spite of their common membership in St Mary's, had never even spoken to one another before.

This variation in the social background of our membership remains as a constant and stimulating factor. It is reflected in the Kirk Session and in all our congregational activities. Thus the Youth Fellowship contains a university lecturer who was a scholar of Christ Church, and a nice but rather dim-witted lassie who works in a factory. The Woman's Guild have seen a lady who still possesses a resident cook dancing Strip the Willow with the said cook at a Christmas party. And so on. There are plenty of tensions, but the family feeling is growing.

One experiment in family living which we carried through recently was when we took over the whole of Carberry Tower and its newly-opened annexe for a congregational week-end. My wife and I had seen this done in Queensland by one of the Brisbane congregations, and we thought the experiment was worth trying here. It was a resounding success. As always, the secret lay in the sharing out of the planning and the work among the membership. We were fortunate in having a former assistant-adjutant of the Argylls as our secretary, and he directed the whole operation with military precision.

In the event, over eighty of us, our ages ranging from nineteen months to seventy-five years, descended upon Carberry Tower in a downpour of rain which continued without intermission for three days. If anything, it only helped the success of the weekend. The programme followed the normal pattern for any informal conference, but the encouraging thing was the way in which representatives of all age-groups, from the oldest member of the Woman's Guild to the youngest (and white-booted) member of the Youth Fellowship mixed happily together.

We have also continued to go some way towards solving the problem of hall accommodation. At first it seemed intractable. Because of the central redevelopment in Dundee there were no buildings near the church which could be taken over, and the prospect of renting space at an exorbitant price was obviously out of the question. We were unable to build any addition to our hall because (a) it was scheduled as an historic building and (b) no planning permission would be granted in view of its position in the new city centre. Fortunately the old hall had a high roof. An able architect produced an intelligent plan for the insertion of a mezzanine floor, and as a result we have more than doubled our previous accommodation. What we have is still insufficient for our needs, but it is a compact and efficient unit of its kind. It has allowed us to provide a coffee bar after services which has been much used and greatly appreciated.

So the work goes on. On this ancient site the Church is still surviving and still adapting itself to the changing situation. There is no success story to tell. Plenty of problems remain, and their number is not likely to diminish. But there is a worthwhile job to be done.

THRIFT AND GENEROSITY

Dr Douglas was invited to speak at the Annual Meeting of the Dundee Savings Bank in December 1970 during his Moderatorial year. After introductory remarks, which included some jokes at his own expense, he said:

It is none the less perhaps fitting that a minister should at least occasionally second the adoption of this Report, because I don't need to remind you that the founder of the Trustee Savings Bank Movement in Scotland was the Revd Henry Duncan. In July of this year I found myself officially visiting Annandale Presbytery, and I took the occasion to pay a dutiful pilgrimage to Ruthwell, and when I was there I saw two things of note. I saw the cottage in which the Revd Henry Duncan began the first savings bank in this country, and I saw in the parish kirk the Ruthwell Cross, a magnificent eighth century preaching cross, a carved Celtic cross. Its central panel is interesting in that there is a carving of Mary Magdalene anointing the feet of Our Lord with precious ointment in that extravagant and nobly generous gesture. At first sight it seemed a strange juxtaposition in this tiny village that you should have a memorial to the Savings Bank not so far away from a memorial to Mary Magdalene, quite a contrast between thrift and extravagant generosity. And yet as I thought about the juxtaposition it seemed to me that there was something here to remind us about the basic unity of strands in our national history.

It was appropriate that a minister should have started the Savings Bank Movement in Scotland, because after the Reformation the Queen and the lairds kept the bulk of the Church's wealth, and for many years ministers were comparatively speaking poor men among comparatively speaking a poor community. Over the years in Scotland there grew up a tradition of three words: God, and duty, and work, which were basic to our endeavour in this nation. Scots people had to save, and to save hard, and for that reason some have dubbed them as mean. But this is not really a true criticism, because wherever one goes in the world one finds that rightly or wrongly the Scots have a reputation for hospitality and friendship. The Scots have never been niggardly for example in paying for education without counting the cost, so that you have had a strand of giving as well as of getting.

You may remember the parable of the two seas in Palestine, the Sea of Galilee and the Dead Sea: the Sea of Galilee which is bright and sparkling because rivers run into it and rivers run out—it gets to give; and the Dead Sea, into which rivers run but from which none emerge, and which is dead and bitter because it gets to keep.

I wonder if this is not something to challenge us at this particular stage in our national economy. We are all aware of the fact that it needs to be revived and put on a sounder basis. Now, as you well know, I am no expert in economic affairs, but as the Moderator moves about the country he has the privilege of meeting a great many interesting, influential and capable people, and if he keeps his ears open he hears some interesting comments, not least on the situation of the country today. I remember for example a high executive in the British Steel Corporation saying that it would not probably be long before we had to buy coal from America to keep the British Steel Corporation going, and yet, he said, in Lanarkshire we are sitting on top of thousands and thousands of tons of coal. But the mines were ruined by the greed of those who tore the coal recklessly from the bowels of the earth without giving any further thought to the future.

I have also heard people condemning—and I must say I thought with very good reason—outrageous demands made by certain unions. And again, in contrast, I have listened to a person occupying a very high position indeed in the Ministry of Defence who knows a great deal about business firms in this country and has dealt extensively with them, saying that it seemed to him to be almost a tragedy that so many leading managers or heads of firms not only seemed to be totally unaware of what their workers felt and thought, but worse still, didn't seem to care.

Obviously we have a certain sickness in our society which needs to be healed. We have barriers which need to be overcome, we have relationships which need to be put on a sounder basis, and we need to have ethical guidance, if I may dare to make this suggestion, for the management of our economy. So that it does seem to me that it is of importance that at this particular stage in our national history we should be concerned not simply with getting but also with giving, that along with thrift there should go generosity. And again, if I may with some hesitation venture to say so, as one has moved about the country it has been encouraging to see many firms—because the Moderator does visit quite a number of industrial concerns—many firms where there is a good atmosphere, where it is possible, as I did, to sit round the table for forty-five minutes with representatives of management and of labour and to hear them talking frankly about their problems and their hopes. And it is encouraging to know that this tradition has existed and still continues to exist in our own city and its environs.

In all of this it is a good thing to have the example of the Dundee Savings Bank and its associated Banks in this area, and to know that the Trustee Savings Bank Movement is playing such a vital part in the health of our nation's economy. . . .

CITIZENS OF HEAVEN

A sermon preached in St Mary's, Dundee, at the Kirking of Dundee City Council on 12 May, 1974.

We, by contrast, are citizens of heaven.
(Philippians 3:20, NEB)

At this transitional stage in local government it is important that the traditional Kirkin' Services should be continued in Scotland. They remind us that structural changes are less important than basic principles. A new system is unlikely to be any better than its predecessor if it is badly manned and inefficiently managed. A Kirkin' Service faces us with the challenging idea that responsible citizenship needs the help and guidance of God.

To be citizens of heaven does not mean that our minds are to be set only on the other world. It does mean that earthly citizenship is to be penetrated, inspired and upheld by belief in God. This is an exceedingly practical matter. There is nothing airy-fairy about it at all. Consider three areas in which we can see a need for higher standards than at present obtain.

We need a higher standard of behaviour

There is a crisis of confidence in our country today. It is a sad and sorry business when trust in local and national government is undermined. An unhealthy atmosphere in public life is only worsened by the weary and cynical disillusionment which prevails. What is the remedy?

With the evidence of how the American press uncovered the Watergate scandal, some would say that if corruption is to be prevented then there must be a press which is entirely free and unfettered in its reporting of the facts. No one, to be sure, would deny the need for such a press, but is it itself either infallible or incorruptible? Is it free from the prejudice which will lead it to suppress some facts and suggest a slanted interpretation of others?

Will it put things right if we have Royal Commissions to enquire into the press as well as corruption? They may indeed serve some useful purposes, but unfortunately the facts they uncover and the good they do have too often proved to be severely limited.

It would be much simpler and very much more worth while if there could be a revival of the belief that God is concerned with how we behave as citizens, both in our private and in our public lives. This is a belief which was brought into the world by the Bible with much greater force and effect than has been achieved by any other ethical system. Ethics are unpopular today, because they prevent people from following their uncontrolled desires. That is why both Christianity and Christian Ethics are attacked and disregarded, with the results that we have been considering.

It is time we all realized that we cannot have confidence and trust in our institutions unless it is recognized that there are certain absolutes on which society depends, and that these absolutes come from God. Nor need we plead ignorance as to what is right and what is wrong. If we want a description of what is wrong with our society today we have it in the words of Jesus himself: 'evil thoughts, acts of fornication, of theft, murder, adultery, ruthless greed and malice; fraud, indecency, envy, slander, arrogance and folly' (Mark 7: 22–23, NEB). To be citizens of heaven means that we behave in the right way not for fear that the press will pillory us if we don't, but because this is what God requires us to do.

We need a revival of true patriotism

Scottish people can be fiercely patriotic. They are not slow to proclaim their pride in their native land—in its beauty, in its traditions of friendship and hospitality, of plain living and high thinking, in its achievements in education and industry, and in the work done by Scots all over the world. Along with this patriotism there has increasingly been associated the demand that the Scottish people should have greater control over the management of their own affairs. This is a demand that the General Assembly of the Church of Scotland have consistently supported, and long before North Sea oil hit the headlines. At the same time the Church exists to remind the nation that patriotism is not enough and that our citizenship is not only in Scotland but in heaven.

It is not enough to have a patriotism which springs from

hate. We have seen what this can do in Ulster, for all that they have had a government of their own.

We must beware of a patriotism based on a sense of inferiority and frustration, which makes Scots loud-mouthed and aggressive while they remain deficient in talent and ability.

We must reject a patriotism based on greed. A country which is poor may too easily be deluded by dreams of wealth. If indeed oil is going to bring better days to Scotland, this will only happen if we reject the selfish exploitation of our natural resources and face up to the responsibility of being good stewards, so that the riches of the sea do not leave the land disfigured and defiled.

We must be realistic enough in our patriotism to rid ourselves of the habits which tarnish our reputation. There is no cause for pride in having the highest figures in these islands for alcoholism and violence or in having football supporters who make strangers think that drunkenness and obscenity are Scottish characteristics.

We Scots are at heart a religious people. It has been popular recently to blame the Kirk for being hypocritical, puritanical and kill-joy. This is only partly true, and only applicable to a limited period in the history of the Scottish Kirk. What the critics conveniently—and unfortunately—forget is the part played by Christianity in producing steadfastness of character, honesty in craftsmanship, courage in adversity and the sound democratic spirit which assesses a man not by his rank or by his wealth but by his worth as a human being. If we are to be proud of anything, it is of facts like these, which derive less from the native genius of the Scots than from their debt to the Gospel of Jesus Christ.

We need a greater concern for individuals

One of the delusions from which our western civilization has been suffering is that the bigger an organization is the more efficient it becomes and the better are its results. Fortunately we are beginning to see that the unrestricted development of vast corporations has its dangers, not least in the exhaustion of the earth's resources and the pollution of the human environment.

One would hope that more attention will also be paid to the lot of the individuals who are caught up in the gigantic industrial machine. As the former Economic Adviser to the National Coal Board, Dr E F Schumacher, has said, we need to evolve a technology 'with a human face', so that people have a chance to enjoy themselves while they are working instead of being mere cogs in an entirely impersonal process.

Further, if we claim to be a democracy, something will have to be done to make people feel that they matter and that they have a voice in democratic processes which has some effect. Recent events have made a nonsense of democracy, when the decision of seven men, and in particular the casting vote of one of them, brought hundreds of thousands out on strike, many of them against their will, all of them without having been consulted; when members of other unions were thrown out of work, industry was threatened with paralysis, and Parliament seemed powerless to do anything.

What has citizenship in heaven got to do with all this? Simply that if your eyes are not fixed merely on earth, it is possible that you may take a saner and longer view of the human situation. It is also possible that wisdom may prevail rather than the competing selfish and sectional interests which tear our society apart. Here is a quotation which is applicable to our present plight:

> With jealousy and ambition come disorder and evil of every kind. But the wisdom from above is in the first place pure; and then peace-loving, considerate and open to reason; it is straightforward and sincere, rich in mercy and in the kindly deeds that are its fruit. True justice is the harvest reaped by peacemakers from seeds sown in a spirit of peace.

Wisdom like that would make a vast difference to our political and industrial disputes today. And the description comes from the New Testament, from the Letter of James (3:16–18, NEB). Wisdom reminds us that individuals matter.

There are no more familiar words in the Christian tradition than the petition from the Lord's Prayer: 'Thy will be done in earth, as it is in heaven' (Matthew 6:10, AV). Would that more of us said these words with faith and sincerity and did our best to follow them up in our daily lives. For it is being written ever more clearly in the record of these troublous days that it is only when men are motivated and guided by the enduring principles of heaven that they will be able to make earth a more just, fair and happy place.

THE POLICE, THE LAW, AND GOD'S LAW

A sermon preached in St Mary's, Dundee, on Sunday, 1 September, 1974 at a service marking the 150th Anniversary of the founding of Dundee City Police.

> Then I surveyed the position and at once addressed the nobles, the magistrates, and all the people. 'Do not be afraid of them,' I said. 'Remember the Lord, great and terrible, and fight for your brothers, your sons and daughters, your wives and your homes.'
>
> (Nehemiah 4:14, NEB)

There are people and things which we are too ready to take for granted. We take God for granted, until we are frightened. We take our health for granted, until we lose it. We take the police for granted, until our homes are burgled.

One welcomes a service like this, to mark the 150th Anniversary of the Dundee City Police. It gives an opportunity of showing that we do not take the police for granted, and that we are grateful for all that they do for the citizens of Dundee.

I find it difficult to imagine the people of some totalitarian countries coming together to show their appreciation of the police. In a totalitarian system, or in a corrupt society, the police are not respected. They are hated and feared, because they are the agents of oppression and evil. If we are to continue to regard the police as one of the reliable and welcome bulwarks of our democratic society, certain conditions must be fulfilled.

The police must deserve and receive the support of the people

No doubt it would be very pleasant if there were no evildoers to be restrained, but things being as they are, society must be protected from the criminal. In Dundee public demand was responsible for the beginning of the police force. Before statutory provisions had come into operation, some of the merchants and citizens banded together to pay the wages of a few stalwart men who kept watch over their shops and their homes.

A century and a half later, it is impossible to think of our country without the police. There are pacifists who deplore the use of force, but I have yet to meet a pacifist who leaves his house unlocked when he is away from home and who would seek to abolish the police force. We have many advocates of the permissive society who resent the enforcement of the law by the police, but they are quick to invoke the aid of the law, and of the police, on their own behalf. The truth is that the police are necessary; that they have a difficult task to perform; that on the whole they carry out their duties admirably; and that they often deserve more support and co-operation than they receive.

Our Old Testament lesson from Nehemiah described a small society which was threatened by enemies from without. Nehemiah called on the people to fight for the preservation of their society—for their brothers, their sons and daughters, their wives and their homes. Today our society is threatened from within, rather than from without. For that very reason, perhaps, the battle to preserve it is more urgent. We must fight for our homes, our way of life, our recreations and our institutions. Our homes are threatened by the breakdown of personal relationships; our recreations are threatened by the escalation of violence; our institutions are threatened by corrupt practices and by blatant and organized crime. In all these areas of life the police are involved. If they and the public can work together more effectively, the present battle for honesty, decency, peace and happiness is all the more likely to be successful.

The police must be servants of the law, not of the politicians

We have already noted that we can be thankful that in this country we do not suffer from the activities of a secret police force which operates under the control of the dictators and politicians rather than of the law. Let us for that very reason beware of the voices which tell us that our present political confusion and disarray show the need for a strong leader who will sweep away party strife and pull the country together. This was the way in which Hitler and the Gestapo came into being.

Equally we must beware of any powerful group which seeks to disregard the law in its own interests. The difficulties which the police have had to face with picket lines, with what are called 'aggros' and 'demos', with bomb scares and explosions, are all symptoms of the effort made by such groups to get their own way by force, in spite of the ordinances of the law. In such situations it is all the more important that the police should act, and should be seen to act, with the rigour and impartiality which the law demands. The universal relief which is now felt throughout the United States of America [after the resignation of President Nixon because of the Watergate affair—Ed.] is an example of how a great democracy can be thankful for having been released from a situation in which political power sought to manipulate both the law and the police. Let us be warned by what has happened across the Atlantic.

There must be principles by which the guardians of society are guided

'Who will guard the guardians themselves?' asked the Roman poet Juvenal. The answer given by the Christian Faith is that we need the truth of Jesus Christ to be our guide. The law must be the servant of the truth. Justice depends upon the truth being revealed, and therefore neither evidence nor the law itself should be 'bent', even if it appears that justice might be served by doing so.

This is not an age which pays much attention to the principles of the Christian Faith, and indeed this is part of its sickness. Society cannot remain strong and healthy unless it recognizes and is regulated by good and unchanging principles. We have seen what happens when men make up their own principles to suit their own ends. Their efforts are self-destructive, whether they follow the pattern of a Hitler, a Stalin or a Nixon. 'If there were no God', said Voltaire, 'it would be necessary to invent him'. In the same way, even if we are doubtful about absolute principles, we require to behave as if they existed. Otherwise our society will crumble and fall as so many others have done.

This is a time of challenge for all who are concerned about the future of our country. Let us be grateful for the part which the police have played in making and keeping it a land in which we are glad to live. And let us pray that it may be possible for them to continue as one of the wholesome and strengthening elements in a democracy which will remain faithful to its Christian heritage, at the same time as it seeks to regain its wholeness and its health.

WHY GO ON KEEPING
REMEMBRANCE SUNDAY

A sermon preached in Hope Park Church, St Andrews, on 10 November, 1985

> Remove not the ancient landmark, which thy fathers have set.
>
> (Proverbs 22:28, AV)

It is coming on for seventy years since the First World War ended and over forty years since the close of the Second World War. The majority of those present this morning were not even born before 11 November 1918, and many of the younger people in the congregation have only heard vaguely about the Second World War. What is the point of being told to remember something which is entirely remote from your experience? This morning I would try to say why I believe that Remembrance Day is an ancient landmark which should not be removed.

We should keep it, not because we want in any way at all to glorify war, but because we wish above all to preserve peace. Both World Wars have been terrible and dreadful; a third and nuclear war would be the end of what we call civilization, if not of life itself. And there are many still today whose hearts are sore when they remember the men and women who lost their lives because of war, whether in the forces or in the bombing of the civilian population.

But while we rightly remember the awful penalties which war brings with it, paradoxically there are lessons which war teaches us which we urgently need to remember today.

War taught us something about *Love of Country*. We tend to take many things for granted, like health. It is only when we are ill that we realize how much we depend on our health and how much we miss it. And it is when our country is

threatened that we begin to realize how much we love it—
and above all that special part of it which we hold most dear.

> God gives all men all earth to love.
>   But, since man's heart is small,
> Ordained for each one spot shall prove
>   Beloved over all.   (Rudyard Kipling: 'Sussex')

For all of us there is some particular place which focuses
the love we have for our native land. I know a farm house, at
the foot of a West Highland glen, from which a younger son
went to serve in the Fourteenth Army in Burma. A friend told
his family that, as he lay dying of wounds in the torrid heat,
he said that the one thing he wanted above anything else was
a drink of cold water from the well at the head of the glen
from which he could see his home.

For all its horrors, war taught people something about love
of country. And is that not something which we need to
recover today, not least in Scotland? This Scotland of ours is
a small country, but to loyal Scots it is still the fairest land
beneath the sky. If we love it as we ought, we should be sad
and sorry to see its cities laid waste with bad housing,
unemployment, squalor and deprivation. It should grieve us
to see the inroads that vice and drink and drugs are making
upon the lives of so many young girls and boys, youths and
maidens. The casualties of peace are the broken homes, the
disturbed children, the juvenile delinquents, the battered
wives and babies, the queues for abortions and VD treatment,
and the growing number of those who cause violence—and
their victims. There is just as much urgency to defend our
native land today as in either of the World Wars; but the
enemy is within our own gates and the battle is a spiritual one
against the power of evil. If we love our country we should be
fighting the good fight on its behalf, armed with the sword of
the Spirit, the shield of faith, and the helmet of salvation, not
with bullets and bombs.

Paradoxically again, war taught us something about *Love*

of Neighbour. I did not serve in the armed forces, only in the humbler role of running a Church of Scotland Hut for the Forces, but I could see and to some extent share in the warmth of fellowship which was engendered in army regiments, naval vessels and Air Force squadrons. And as civilians the whole population of these embattled islands found, during the war, that in a real sense they could only survive by learning to love their neighbours as themselves; they had to love each other or die.

There were no barriers of race or class or wealth when the bombs were falling, when people had to sleep in air raid shelters, help to rescue those who were caught in the rubble of bombed buildings or give shelter to any who had lost their homes.

These are lessons, taught by war, which we should do well to remember and act on in our torn and divided society today. It is sad to see our country and our people bleeding from so many self-inflicted wounds. And, of course, it is always someone else's fault. It is because of the black immigrants, or because of white indifference and superiority, or because of the police, or because of the criminal element in the inner cities. We forget that we are all brothers and sisters under our different skins, members of the one family of citizens of the United Kingdom; and that we must learn to love each other and work together to solve these hard and grievous problems or they will overwhelm us and we shall be destroyed.

But I do not believe that in this country we are as weak in will and feeble in resolve as to allow this to happen. We are not just the people who stood alone in 1940 against the evil power of Adolf Hitler. We are the people whose forebears abolished slavery, pioneered the Welfare State, disbanded the greatest empire the world had known and formed a world-wide Commonwealth of free and independent nations. Many of us are tiring of the politics of class and confrontation and conflict. We long for a vision and a spirit that will unite and enable us as a nation. And as Christians we should indeed be faithless if we did not believe that God can still give us the vision and endow us with the power to bring it nearer to fulfilment.

For, and again paradoxically, the very awfulness of war can teach us something about the *Love of God*. In times of crisis people turn to God. They are faced with ultimate realities of life and death. They realize that they are weak and powerless, afraid and in need of help from above.

Today an affluent society can cushion us from any sense of crisis. But the crisis is there, not in one nation but world-wide. Read Mark's Gospel, chapter 13, and see how apposite is the picture Jesus paints of the end of all things, ushered in by famine and earthquakes.

Many of the sects seek to frighten people into their folds by concentrating on the imminent end of the world. This is not my aim today. But the fact remains that human life is threatened all over the world in new and alarming ways—by destruction of the environment through exploitation for gain, by the spread of radioactivity, and by the overhanging threat of nuclear warfare. In a real sense all men everywhere—Christians, Muslims, Buddhists, Pantheists, whatever their religion—need to turn to God: to affirm that this is his world, that we are his stewards and must seek to work in it according to his laws. Without such a vision mankind may perish.

In this Scotland of ours our religion has sometimes been as rugged as our hills, but it goes as deep as our lochs. Scratch a Scot, men said, and you will find a theologian. This may not be so true as once it was, but note how a drunk man will often head straight for a clerical collar, claiming that he once attended Sunday School or was a loyal member of the Boys' Brigade. The roots of the Faith are still deep in our land. But people need to be awakened to their need of God. And if we keep Remembrance Day positively, this may help to stir the grey embers of faith to a living flame. For we should remember today in order that we may fight for peace; that we may show that we love our country, not in any narrow way but so that it may be a worthy member of the world family;

that we should seek for a fellowship in which we can work together with our neighbours of all races and classes; and that we may turn again to God who has made us for himself and without whom we are helpless.

CHAPTER 10

Churchman in the Wider Church

Introduced by R A S Barbour

Hugh Douglas was nothing if not a churchman. He could not have imagined a Gospel that was not enfleshed in the living-and-dying body of Christ which we know as the Church. But his loyalty to the Church of Christ, and to the Church of Scotland in particular, was not an uncritical one. In the 1960s and 1970s he saw that the Church was losing its influence in the life of the people of Scotland, numerically and in other ways, and he summoned it to new life and new effort. During his year as Moderator of the General Assembly he spoke on a number of occasions of the need for Scotland to be re-evangelized, and in an address to the Dundee College of Education in the Spring of 1971 he called for 'determined and constructive rebels within the organized church'.

But renewal rather than rebellion, mission rather than protest, remained his main theme. His attitude to the Church and to its place in society is well summed up in the sermon 'Foundations for a Christian Democracy' which is printed below.

He believed in a comprehensive Church and a broad Christian charity and sympathy. Another sermon, from the Moderatorial year, based on the story of Jesus and the Samaritan woman in John's Gospel (chapter 4), stressed that Jesus began where she was, and continued:

One wishes fervently that this was common practice for more Christians today, namely that they should establish

human contact with those who do not share their view.
But too often, at least to those outside the Church, there
appears to be a great gulf fixed between them, across which
Christians regard the others with a chilly and self-
righteous disapproval. In the Church we may forget too
easily that whether men are Christians or not we are all
human beings, and that we are united by many natural
bonds and can share many meeting points which a too
rigid righteousness might neglect. We need the insight of
Jesus to realize that many whom we regard as outsiders
might even be ready and willing to do us a good turn, and
in that event we should, like Jesus, be humble enough to
accept it.

But if Hugh knew the Church's weaknesses, he also had a
ready appreciation of its continuing strengths in relating to
Scottish society. He noted that in his Moderatorial year all
five Lord Provosts of Scottish cities were elders of the Kirk,
and he saw the influence of Christian principles and ideals in
our national institutions as something that was far from spent.
That very fact only made it all the more true that because the
Church is for all, we must have not just the Church which
some of us want, but the Church which all of us *need*. This
was one theme of his address to the General Assembly in 1970
as its Moderator, and another was a strong statement of
Hugh's constant belief that the parish ministry is at the centre
of the Church's life and can be a most exciting, as well as
demanding, form of service.

Hugh's vision of the Church and its mission reached
far beyond Scotland. He was excited and impressed by
experiences he had on visits to Churches in India and Ghana,
and in South Africa which he visited as Moderator of the
General Assembly. Hugh had often spoken vigorously against
the evils of apartheid; now he and his wife were able to see
its effects in practice. Visiting the Bantu Presbyterian Church
in connection with its 150th anniversary, he made good
friends among people who sang some of the Scottish psalm

tunes to words in the Xhosa language, and who combined a Scottish sense of the priesthood of all believers with a lively involvement of all believers in song and dance and worship that could put any contemporary Scottish congregation to shame. The writer of these paragraphs followed in his footsteps nine years later, and discovered what a deep impression Hugh and his wife had made in South Africa. They called him the 'red bull' because he usually wore his scarlet Queen's Chaplain's cassock, and they loved him all the more for that.

Within Britain one notable occasion in which Hugh took part during his Moderatorial year was the Inauguration of the newly established General Synod of the Church of England. In giving the greetings of the General Assembly, he pointed to the different course the Reformation had taken in the two countries. In the 1970s Hugh served for five years on the British Council of Churches, and his lively sense of the differing gifts which the varied Church traditions must bring to the 'coming great Church' (a phrase he espoused) made him a discerning supporter of the movement to recover Christian unity. With that he combined a sharp awareness of the value of a Church–State link of the kind which had been happily established in Scotland after long struggles, and also an appreciation of the part which the monarchy played in the preservation of a healthy community in Scotland and throughout the Commonwealth.

It was a sign of the esteem in which he was widely held that by the time he was fifty he had become both an honorary Doctor of Divinity (from the University of St Andrews) and a Commander of the Order of the British Empire, as well as a Chaplain to the Queen. All these honours reflect the value given to a man who himself above all valued the service he could give as a parish minister. The Queen has ten chaplains in Scotland who represent the life of the Established Church and constitute the Chapel Royal, headed by a Dean. Hugh succeeded to the office of Dean in 1974 and soon made his mark as a wise and trusted counsellor with the Royal

Household—as indeed he was to many in less exalted walks of life. On his retiral from the Deanship, the Queen made him a Knight Commander of the Royal Victorian Order.

But the value of the man is not only or even primarily shown by the honours which he received. The Church of Scotland also used him well, and he served on many important committees of the General Assembly. Perhaps his spirit and qualities are best summed up by a brief consideration of the part he played in the celebration of the quatercentenary of the Scottish Reformation in 1960. It is significant that it was Hugh who was appointed in 1955 to head the committee making preparations for the celebration: here was a man whom all could trust to celebrate the past in such a way as not to devalue or misread the present and the future. And so it turned out to be. The details of the celebration need concern us no longer. But it is one small sign of the spirit in which the whole venture was carried out that, after it was over, Hugh received a letter from Cardinal Gordon Gray (as he later became), Archbishop of St Andrews and Edinburgh in the Roman Catholic Church, in which he recounted the worry that had existed in that Church before the celebrations that they might become divisive and unhappy for the Catholics, and told Hugh how deeply grateful he was that the very opposite had been the case. So it came about that great gifts given to the Kirk in Scotland at the time of the Reformation could begin to be seen as gifts even by those of the Roman Catholic Church; and one hopes also that Presbyterians were helped to see that a new vision of the *Una Sancta* could thereby rise before their eyes. And then, perhaps, that commemorative General Assembly of 1960 could even be seen as a kind of small foretaste of 'the getherin an assemblie o God's firstborn, whase names staunds i the burgess-row o heiven' (Hebrews 12:23, Lorimer translation in Scots). It was above all in that sense, as a member of Christ's Church on earth who looked forward to its consummation beyond all imagining in a world to come, that Hugh Douglas lived his life here and prepared so many for something even larger and better. His family, and the great numbers of those who were and are influenced by him, are his true memorial.

*   *   *

THE CHURCH WE WANT OR THE CHURCH WE NEED?

The first part of Dr Douglas's address to the 1970 General Assembly of the Church of Scotland as its Moderator.

Right Reverend and Right Honourable,

If I venture to speak of the task and the responsibilities which face the Church of Scotland today, I can only do so from the point of view of a parish minister. At least it means that I shall speak from my own experience; and I am encouraged by the thought that this will not differ, in any marked degree, from the experience of the majority of Commissioners, who represent parishes throughout the length and breadth of Scotland.

I read recently an assessment of the Church in Denmark by a Danish Churchman, Professor P G Lindhardt. In it he wrote that the Danish Church 'is now no longer regarded as a divine institution—"a salvation home"—but as a reasonable function in a welfare society . . . where every reasonable public demand has a right to be satisfied, including the one that a Church should be available to those who want it'. He added that if this was so, the question would arise as to whether one always got the Church one needed when one got that which one wanted.

What kind of Church is wanted in Scotland today? There are only a few who are so opposed to the Church as to wish to see its claim disregarded and its authority removed. Even many who have nothing to do with the Church, and never go near it, would like to see it continue. One doubts if there are large numbers who would, as in Denmark, regard the Church as merely another function of the welfare state; but there is a wide variety of opinions as to what kind of Church is wanted. Some want a formal Church, suitable for ceremonial occasions. Others want a pietist Church which will mind its own business and keep quiet about political or controversial issues. Others, again, want a Church which is relentlessly modern, both in its belief and in its ethics. The fact remains, however, that if people seek to remould the Church according to their desires, they may well find that they get the Church they want but not the Church they need.

In the Church of Scotland our tradition has ensured that we have clear guidance about our loyalty as a Church. It is to the Lord Jesus Christ who is sole King and Head of the Church, and not to any current whim or fashion. Admittedly, succeeding generations see new and different facets of his truth; but this is quite different from attempting to accommodate that truth to the limited area of one's private predilections. If we are to be loyal to our King and Head then we have a duty to proclaim the Gospel to Scotland; to be (to the best of our ability) the conscience of the people; and to show the example of the Christian life. This may not indeed give Scotland the Church she wants, but it will be more likely to give her the Church she needs.

Thus when the climate of opinion is affected by secular and humanistic thinking, we have all the greater need to proclaim our belief in terms which people can understand and which show the relevance of the Gospel to their daily lives. This is a task in which the best intellects of the Church should be actively engaged.

Again, when there has been a subtle erosion of Christian principles leading to less integrity in public life and increasing decadence in private morality; when in spite of all the good causes which are canvassed there seems to be more selfishness abroad and less compassion—has the Church not a duty then to appeal to the conscience of what is still basically a Christian country?

Mere negative denunciation will have little effect. But even if, when we speak our minds, we are called puritans, this does not matter if we can show the example of a puritanism which is both glad and positive. We have to make it plain that modern permissiveness is not the new freedom, but the old slavery; that there is more happiness in being dependent upon God than upon drugs; that it is the discipline of love and not the licence of lust which leads to maturity; and that while selfishness spells death, self-giving means life abundant.

[The original address continued beyond this point.]

THE FOURTH CENTENARY OF THE SCOTTISH REFORMATION

Dr Douglas, as Convener of the Committee planning the celebration of this event, presented its proposals to the General Assembly in May 1960. This is the opening section of his address.

There are, I think, three fundamental points about the Scottish Reformation which the Committee has sought to keep in mind during its planning for the worthy celebration of the fourth centenary.

In the first place, the Reformation was an event of outstanding importance in the history of Scotland. It affected not only the Church but the life of the whole nation. It was essentially a people's movement, and this was recognized by James VI and I when he wrote that 'the reformation of religion in Scotland was made by a popular tumult and rebellion and did not proceed from the Prince's orders as it did in England'.

In the second place, the results of the Scottish Reformation were not confined to this country. It is not, perhaps, as widely recognized as it might be how many Presbyterians throughout the world regard the Church of Scotland as in a very real sense their mother Church. There are, it is estimated, some forty million Presbyterians in the world today, and for many of them the central features of their national liberty are closely connected with the Scottish Reformation.

In the third place, the commemoration of such an event can never be a pious recollection of past glories any more than it should be an attempt to revive the bitterness of past conflicts. If we believe, as we do, that the Reformation was due to the work of the Holy Spirit in men's hearts, then as a Reformed Church we must always be looking for the ways in which the same Spirit is guiding us in the contemporary situation.

In celebrating the Fourth Centenary we are not seeking to escape into the past. Rather are we, by looking to the rock whence we were hewn, endeavouring to meet the challenge of the present with the same scriptural faith as did our forefathers four hundred years ago.

The plans which we have made, of which we hope the General Assembly will approve, are designed to be in harmony with these strands in our heritage.

There could be no more fitting way of celebrating the Fourth Centenary of so historic an event than by a special meeting of the General Assembly. On 20 December 1560, a handful of ministers and elders met in the little Magdalen Chapel as the first General Assembly of the Church of Scotland. When the commissioners and delegates from overseas go to the High Kirk of Edinburgh for the Service of Thanksgiving on 11 October 1960, they will remember with humble gladness what the General Assembly has meant for Scotland and what, under God, it still may mean in the future. In the proposed Resolution of Solemn Thanksgiving which is now submitted to the Assembly we have endeavoured to set down within reasonable compass and in plain language those things for which we can sincerely thank God, along with something of our aspirations and prayers for the Church today . . .

A GREETING FROM GENERAL ASSEMBLY TO GENERAL SYNOD

Dr Douglas, as Moderator of the General Assembly, repre-sented the Church of Scotland at the Inauguration of the new General Synod of the Church of England on 4 November 1970. After introductory words, he said:

I come to bring you the fraternal greetings of the General Assembly of the Church of Scotland on the inauguration of the General Synod of the Church of England, and I am sure that the General Assembly would wish me also to add their warm good wishes and their prayers that Almighty God may bless the General Synod in its work for the advancement of Christ's Kingdom.

It is interesting to see how the course of Church history has run in our separate lands. In Scotland, the Reformation was a revolution in the name of religion against the State. In England it was a reformation which was carried through by the civil power. In consequence, our struggles in the sixteenth and seventeenth centuries were very different. In Scotland we fought for the independence of the kirk. In England you fought for the independence of Parliament. In England they held the Speaker of the House of Commons down in his chair. In Scotland, we are told, a stool was hurled at the head of the Dean in St Giles, and when the two countries were, strangely enough, united in their opposition to Charles I, their alliance was termed a Solemn League and Covenant because the English wanted a civil League and the Scots insisted on a religious Covenant. In these ecclesiastically less violent days we think more of the things which unite us than of the things which divide us.

It is a good thing that Churches should revise their constitutions and forms of government. We may have to do the same in Scotland some time too, but in the meantime you will probably regard it as typical of the Scots that they take it as a tribute to their own sagacity, if to nothing higher, that the constitution and powers of the General Synod of the Church of England now approximate to the constitution and powers of the General Assembly of the Church of Scotland. You will also no doubt regard it as a regrettably typical instance of Scottish obstinacy that we have not so far seen our way to incorporate the benefits of episcopacy within the somewhat rigid framework of Presbyterianism. Be that as it may, I am sure I speak for the Church of Scotland when I say that we have much to learn from each other and will be enriched by doing so.

It is a good thing that we should review our constitutions, and we will be united in this: that our main task and function in this particular age is to make the message of our Lord Jesus, the good news for the new age, relevant and alive today. That the Church of England may be enabled to do this more effectively through the General Synod now so happily inaugurated is, I can assure you, the fervent and continuing prayer of the General Assembly of the Church of Scotland.

THE CHURCH OF THE ETERNAL JESUS

A sermon preached in the Cathedral, Brechin, on 17 April 1977 during the celebrations marking the 750th Anniversary of the building of the Cathedral and the 75th Anniversary of its restoration.

Jesus Christ, the same yesterday and today and for ever.
(Hebrews 13:8, NEB)

I am honoured to have been asked to be with you on this great day of Celebration and Thanksgiving. I bring with me the congratulations and good wishes of my own Kirk Session and congregation. Like yours, our roots go deep into the past, so that we can all the more sincerely share in the spirit of your festal day.

I have chosen as my text these great words from the Letter to the Hebrews. On such a day as this there must be—

Thanksgiving for the past;

Faith for the present;

Hope for the future.

And surely all these are summed up in the clarion call of the proclamation: 'Jesus Christ, the same yesterday and today and for ever'.

Thanksgiving for the past—yesterday

You have a great heritage and tradition in this Cathedral, for which you can all give thanks. It is our part of all our yesterdays. It is the heritage of the Christian Faith, of Jesus Christ.

If a visitor from outer space were to fly the length and breadth of this land, one feature would impress him as demanding explanation. Everywhere, whether in city, town, village or open country, he would see the Church spires and towers pointing heavenwards. (You remember G K Chesterton's description of how 'all over Europe Gothic spires sprang up like a flight of arrows'.) Whatever the state of Church-going today, no matter whether men are humanists, atheists or agnostics, if they live in the United Kingdom they cannot reject their Christian past.

We today have no wish to reject it. We give thanks for it, remembering all we owe to Jesus Christ and his servants of yesterday. Our laws, our education, our hospitals, our social services—all these have Christian foundations. Our homes and families—how great a blessing to have had the love, discipline and security of Christian parents in Christian homes. Consider all that has been given to us, undeserving as we may be, through Jesus Christ—and be thankful!

Be determined also to hold on to it and maintain it—this heritage from the past. There are strong voices raised against the Christian faith, sometimes in scorn and derision. Let them only confirm your resolution to hold to the truth as you have known it in Jesus. Because you have proved the truth in your own experience—there is the test!—no one can wrest it from you. And you know that it is as relevant today as it was 2,000 years ago.

Faith for the present—today

Jesus Christ is the same today. He is the Good News for the new age.

It matters not that he lived and taught in an obscure corner of the Roman Empire. His words have stood the test of time. They are eternally true. Nor have the basic needs and nature of mankind changed. Whether they lived in first century Palestine or in twentieth century Britain they are the same wayward, selfish, and potentially splendid beings today as they were then. Years ago a Chinese teacher was telling his students how it used to take him three weeks to go home from University. 'Today,' he said, 'I am a fool when I step into the aeroplane and I am still a fool when I step out of it. What benefit if my folly is spread abroad more quickly?' So much for mechanical and technological progress. It is no answer to the cry of a despairing or repentant human being.

But Jesus is. He is the same today. See how, even when his Church is attacked or neglected, men cannot fight him. Think even of how they put him on stage or screen or television, in programmes like 'Jesus Christ Superstar'; 'Godspell'; 'Jesus of Nazareth'; 'Who is Jesus?' A sign that so many hearts are restless until they rest in him. His is the love of God that will not let us go. He has made his home in the world and nothing can drive him from it. The vacuum in the lives of millions is waiting to be filled by him. With him is reality.

Hold on to that faith today. I read the other day of an American organization called COYOTE—Call Off Your Old Tired Ethics. The ethics of Jesus may be old but they are not tired. They have not been tried. My thoughts turned to an article I read in a Geographical Magazine. It described a visit by the writer to a Soviet village where the church had been turned into a school. To the astonishment of the villagers the old frescoes of the saints had begun to appear again on the walls through the overlay of crude green paint. The superstitious read this as a sign of divine intervention. The local commissar was more practical, saying that the explanation was simple—the old paint was of a better quality. He spoke the truth, not knowing what he said. The Word of God in Jesus is the truth: it is reality. However thickly men try to cover it up with their shoddy modern substitutes, it will shine through in the end, as it has always done and as it will always do. Have that faith today in a time of testing.

And remember our resources. You can go to the edge of the limitless ocean and, if you have only a thimble with you, it is only a thimbleful that you will carry away. How much of God's love and grace will you ask for—a thimbleful or full measure, pressed down and running over?

> We are coming to a King;
> Large petitions let us bring.
> For his grace and power are such
> None can ever ask too much.
>
> (RCH:450)

Have faith in Jesus who is the same today.

Hope for the future—for ever

Jesus Christ is the same for ever—therefore have hope for the future.

Do you ever tremble for the ark of God? Are you ever fearful for the future of the Church? One is tempted to be so sometimes but it is wrong to be like that; it is a denial of our belief in God and the fact that it is not our Church, but his Church.

Remember what the old priest said to the young man who asked: 'Father, what did the Church do in the French Revolution?' 'My son,' was the answer, 'the Church survived the French Revolution'. And so it will survive whatever comes. Not because it is an anvil which has worn out many hammers, but because it is an organic, living body. Think of how the New Testament describes it—as the Bride of Christ, as the Body of Christ, as the Vine of which he is the Head, as the Temple built of living stones. You rejoice in your building today, and rightly so, but what gives the Church here life is God—through Jesus and his Sacraments, and through you, the living stones in the building of God's house.

Nor need we fear that because Jesus is the same he will be insufficient for the needs of the future. Always his treasure will be like the man who brings out of it things new and old. It is inexhaustible, because it is God's treasure. Or Jesus and his truth are like a wonderful jewel with innumerable facets; and each generation sees different facets, new aspects of the eternal truth.

Yes, Jesus is the same. But so is the Spring every year. Always the same, and always new. Always bringing the message of new life—and we would welcome it in no other way, than because it is always the same and it is always new.

Have confidence, then, and hope for the Church. Like other living organisms the Church may be subject to seasonal changes. At times the Springtime of new life floods through it, in reformation or revival, to be followed by the luxuriance of Summer growth and flower. Then may come the melancholy of the Autumn and the apparent death of Winter. Even on the barest bough the buds have been forming and the Spring is coming. And there are stirrings of new life today.

So with the Church of Jesus. Be it Autumn or Winter for

the Church, his life is always surging through it, and Spring and Summer are still to come.

> So be it, Lord! thy throne shall never,
> Like earth's proud empires, pass away;
> Thy Kingdom stands and grows for ever,
> Till all thy creatures own thy sway.
>
> (CH3: 646)

For Jesus Christ is the same, yesterday and today and for ever.

FOUNDATIONS FOR A CHRISTIAN
DEMOCRACY

A sermon preached in St Machar's Cathedral, Aberdeen, on 14 February 1982. The opening paragraph explains the special nature of the occasion.

> Honour all men. Love the brotherhood. Fear God. Honour the king.
>
> (1 Peter 2:17, AV)

I count it a privilege to be in this historic Cathedral today, with a double purpose in mind. The first is to have a part in the celebration of the 850th Anniversary of St Machar's; and the second is to be present at the dedication of my successor in office as Dean of the Chapel Royal in Scotland. Each occasion is congruous with the other. We are reminded by the one of the enduring power of the Christian Faith in our country: and in the other we see the equally long tradition of a link between the Crown and the Church which has been preserved in unbroken succession to the present day.

Remembering these facts, let me draw your attention to the words of our text in 1 Peter chapter 2 verse 17: 'Honour all men. Love the brotherhood. Fear God. Honour the king'. I would suggest that here, in brief compass, we have a clear outline of certain elements which are basic to a Christian democracy, and which must always challenge us.

'Honour all men'

We are proud of our democratic tradition in this country. And indeed there is no other land in which I should choose to live. But—do we indeed honour all men in our society today? We are glib in our protestations about the freedom and values of western democracy, but do we show due respect and honour to all individuals therein?

We have, of course, made some progress since the bad old days which followed the Industrial Revolution and which produced living conditions for human beings which I can remember and which were worse than those which I have seen among the primitive tribes in the north of Ghana. But how are we doing, as we stand at the beginning of the Technological Revolution and with the early effects of this and of that other revolution in human relationships plainly visible?

Do we honour all men in our society when we condemn increasing millions to 'stand idle in the market place' because no-one has hired them? We cannot be complacent about that.

Do we honour all men when we have seen the deliberate dehumanization and trivialization of the most intimate and rewarding human relationship between men and women?—a trivialization which has resulted in the break up of families, in lasting wounds to children and in the attitude among some violent men which regards rape as a matter of small consequence.

Do we honour all men when 'the covetous greed which is idolatry' seems well set to turn us into a nation of dishonest fiddlers, whose concern is for personal aggrandisement, at whatever cost to the wellbeing of others?

Our so-called Christian democracy has still a very long way

to go in showing respect for the individual, but we have a good foundation on which to build.

'Love the brotherhood'

Peter was writing for the Early Church. And indeed there is eloquent testimony that these Christians, set in the midst of a pagan society, were seen to 'love one another whole-heartedly' (1 Peter 1:22, NEB) as they faced trials, persecution and death.

But how do we stand in the Church today? In our society the Christian Church should not only be the example of fellowship. It should also, through its members, be the salt and the leaven, spreading its savour and its influence through the outside world.

The older I grow the more I find myself able to thank God most sincerely for the fellowship of the Church, which is deeper and stronger than that of any other group or community that I have known. Nor do I have any doubt that the Church still gives stability, purpose and fulfilment to countless individuals; that it still underpins and exercises its leavening power in society.

But how far we still have to go, in loving the brotherhood! I am not unduly concerned with much of the criticism and unpopularity of the organized Church as an institution. Those who attack the Church in this way almost always base their criticisms upon the standards which the Church itself has preserved. Rather is it my concern that, as in our democracy, so in the Church we should not be prone to complacency.

Can we not be complacent in thinking that a modicum of efficient restructuring of our organization is enough to go on with?

Are we not complacent in accepting a steady decline in our membership without girding ourselves adequately to go out in mission to the lapsed and the seemingly indifferent?

May we not be complacent in thinking that the barriers which still separate us from those of other communions are as impervious to change as some South African politicians would like the man-made barriers of apartheid to be?

Let the call to love the brotherhood be a challenge to us in the Church today. Such love is no easy thing; but while it is hard and demanding, it is also exhilarating and fulfilling.

'Fear God'

Here we come to the heart of our text and the nub of the whole matter.

It is all very well to have ideals and to be aware of challenge. The test comes when we have to put our ideals into practice and overcome the difficulties which challenge us. The Christian position is basically very simple: it is that apart from our belief in God, our awe and reverence before him, there is no real hope that we shall consistently be able to honour all men and love the brotherhood.

Of course we all have benevolent instincts and good qualities. We are made for neighbourliness, companionship and love. But however one may choose to define or explain them, we also have inborn in us other instincts and qualities which militate against what is good. The great virtue and compelling power of the Christian Faith is that it confidently proclaims that God himself has shown us a way out of this impasse, in the life, death, resurrection and continuing love of Jesus Christ. We are thus enabled, when we respond to this seeking of us by God, to find the way in which we can not only control our baleful instincts but discover how they can be transformed and released, unto our freedom and fulfilment, as the persons God means us to be.

The danger in our modern society is that we tend to imagine that the desired results can be obtained by human ingenuity and skill alone. In contrast, the Christian claim is that we must be obedient to the purpose and love of God before we can begin to build the kind of democracy of which we dream.

'Honour the king'

Peter recognized the need of a symbol to give stability to society, even if it was a pagan and oppressive one in his time. Christians should honour Caesar even if they were prepared to go to their deaths for refusing to *worship* him.

After centuries in which the Church in our country has gone through tribulation in its relationship with the Crown, we have reached the situation in which the first thing a Monarch does after accession to the throne is to take an oath to uphold the Presbyterian worship, government and discipline of the Church of Scotland. The Church of Scotland is firmly loyal to the Crown, but acknowledges its primary allegiance to the supreme and sole King and Head of the Church, the Lord Jesus Christ.

In this relationship the office of Dean of the Chapel Royal is a small but significant link. It can remind us that the Crown and the Church both depend upon God; that after the extraordinary developments in science and technology, in spite of the severity and the grave consequences of economic depression, the British monarchy has remained remarkably firm and stable. Its power may have greatly diminished, but the force of its example and the affection it inspires have notably increased. This is in no small measure due to the personal qualities of Her Majesty the Queen and her own devotion for over thirty years to the unchanging values of the Christian Faith, not least in her own home and family life.

So, while in our British democracy today there are flaws and faults of which it would be folly to remain unaware, there are signs of hope which should inspire and encourage us as we face the uncertain future. Let us remember, then, these words from the past which have stood the test of the centuries and are as relevant for us today as ever they have been: 'Honour all men. Love the brotherhood, Fear God. Honour the king'.

CHAPTER 11

Coping with Retirement

An introduction to this chapter is provided by what Professor James Whyte has written on the Retirement Years in the Biography (pp. 56 ff).

In 1979 Dr Douglas was invited to give three talks at an In-Service Training Course attended by ministers who might retire before very long, and he was asked to repeat these talks at a similar Course in 1980.

1 Taking the step

'Coping with Retirement' was not my title, but was the subject on which I was asked to speak to you. And on thinking it over, I felt that I should dispel any idea that retirement is some awful fate which lies in wait for us. I have not found it to be so, nor have the vast majority of those other ministers with whom I have discussed their experience of leaving their charges.

It does not help, of course, to be termed one of the aged and infirm. [A reference to the Aged and Infirm Ministers Fund, as the Church's main pension fund was then called—Ed.] Perhaps this was in the mind of our elder daughter, who has always taken a keen interest in seeing that her parents tread the right paths. On hearing that my wife and I, after settling in St Andrews, had become members of the Church in whose parish we live, namely Hope Park, and on further hearing that Bill Henney was going to be our minister, said to her mother, 'I'm delighted to hear that. How nice it is that you will have someone you know to see you through your last rites'.

Our younger daughter, quite separately, also showed some anxiety that we should miss no opportunity of properly adjusting ourselves to a new situation. She takes an active interest in the work of that admirable institution, St Columba's Hospice in Edinburgh, which deals with terminally ill patients in a relaxed and happy atmosphere. Possibly with this in mind she said to me one day, 'I hope, father, that now you are retired you are gearing your reading to the prospect of departing this life'. A case, one supposes, of reading for one's finals!

Be that as it may, retirement is obviously not a state into which one should drift without some not inconsiderable thought and preparation. It means leaving the work for which you had a lengthy training and in which you may have been engaged for some forty years or more. It means digging up your roots, which is always a painful process. It means separating yourself from a home which you have grown to love, even if it has most probably been nothing more than a tied house. It means, in many cases, leaving a great many friends on whose close companionship you have come to depend. And, of course, it means that you no longer have the inestimable privilege of being the minister of a church which has a host of memories in its very stones, and the pastor of a congregation in whose joys and sorrows you have shared so intimately.

For these and other reasons there are ministers who find it difficult to face the prospect of retirement. Also, in our profession we are given a fair amount of latitude compared with others. Ministers are not obliged to retire before the age of seventy, and there must still be a sizeable number who can soldier on *ad vitam aut culpam*, as they used to do in the more spacious days of yesteryear. Then, of course, in *quoad omnia* charges men could retire with one third of the stipend, leaving their colleagues and successors to make the best of the remaining two-thirds, plus any congregational supplement. And there was one scholarly incumbent of a country kirk in north-east Fife who went off to Crieff with the whole stipend, to pursue his researches, leaving a *locum*, who was paid a mere pittance, to care for the parish and congregation. But times change and we change with them. It is no longer even the case that ministers are sent first to the country to break them in, then to the city to break them down, and again to the country to break them up. With linked and united charges in the depopulated areas, a man will think twice or thrice before deciding to leave an urban for a rural charge. Thus his mind is apt to be wonderfully concentrated, as Dr Samuel Johnson said in another context, on the prospect of retirement.

I am conscious that what I have to say on this subject is very far from being spiritual direction, and is very much 'of the earth, earthy'. But it would be wrong if I failed to emphasise that one's retirement should obviously be a question of making a moral decision as to what is the right thing to do in a particular situation. And in this, as in all else, we must look for the help and guidance of God.

Consideration for the congregation

It is not only ourselves whom we have to consider. If we have a certain latitude in choosing the date of our retirement, then we also have a responsibility for the welfare of our congregations. This means, I suggest, that there are some questions which we should ask ourselves.

Are things going as well as they should be in the congregation? Clearly, things are never going as well as they should be, but in this instance might it be that they would be better if we were away and a younger man with a fresher outlook were doing the job?

Are we still looking and planning ahead, trying to see how

the congregational life should be adjusted and directed to changing situations, or are we content simply to jog along in the settled groove, keeping things ticking over in the usual way? Is there any progress or only a gradual running down?

On the other hand, if we can in all honesty say that things are going not badly, pretty well in fact, is this indeed the right time to leave, so that one's successor can find a people in good heart; with leaders of the right quality in the right places; with the finances sound and a good fabric fund built up; and with the Kirk Session ready to face up to new challenges and take bold steps? Is it a good time at which to hand over a going concern?

When we have decided on a date for our retirement, consideration for the congregation also requires that we give due notice to the Presbytery, so that the vacancy procedure can begin in good time and the congregation be spared an unnecessarily long vacancy.

Consideration for oneself (and one's wife)

Is the work still enjoyable and fulfilling, or is it becoming increasingly a worry and a burden? As we know, and so often tell other people, work is what we should enjoy doing. Is it so with ourselves?

Similarly, are we slowing down so much that it is less possible to cope with a full work load? Are essentials being left undone—that second visit we promised to make, that case of marital trouble which needs more and more time spent on it, that office-bearer who has missed so many meetings without obvious reason—is it becoming too wearisome to tackle all these, too easy to leave them to the next convenient opportunity in the future—which never comes?

Do we hold on, again, simply because it is so much more comfortable to do so than to face up to traumatic changes?

Is the burden of a large manse, and the kind of hospitality which one likes to give, becoming too heavy for a wife who has to run the house with a minimum of domestic help?

Financial considerations

Inevitably these come strongly and forcibly into the picture in modern times—much more than they did in the old days. Can we literally afford to retire?

One has an immense amount of sympathy for the man who has been on a low stipend level all his working life, who has little or no private means, whose wife has not been working, and who has been unable to make any substantial savings. Although things are beginning to improve for him now—at long last—neither individual congregations nor the Church committees responsible have done anything like what they should to provide him with adequate means for his retirement. As you know, the Church of Scotland has lagged behind most other churches—and some much smaller churches—in this field. You will be able to question the Maintenance of the Ministry Committee Secretary on this matter and discover from him what improvements are being made.

The situation is relieved, as you know, where a man retires in the interests of union, and is given the life tenancy of a manse which reverts to his widow so long as she does not marry again. That man is also fortunate who has been able to purchase a house in the time when prices were relatively cheap. But what of those who are unable to take such steps?

We know the central committees are beginning to take action. But one would also hope that congregations would, where possible, do more in the way of planning for their ministers' retirement than having a whip round before the farewell social. I am no expert in these matters, but in my first presbytery forty years ago there was one far-seeing minister who had arranged with his Kirk Session to take out an insurance policy on his life, the premium on which the church paid, and which stood him in excellent stead when the time came for him to demit office.

[At this point Dr Douglas became, as he said, severely practical and gave facts and figures, now out of date, about the basic financial position of ministerial pensioners and their wives, both their annuity from the Church and the State Old Age Pension. He also mentioned possible income from pulpit supply, and the price reductions on trains and buses and other perks that all pensioners enjoy. He concluded: 'All in all, retired ministers seem to get along not too badly'.]

Clearing the manse

I remember when I went to my first charge I was told how my predecessor, who had been there all his active ministry, spent days in the bottom of his garden before he left, burning his old sermons. In my youthful and critical mood I thought this was sad and pathetic. But when I came to retire I found it was all too necessary an exercise. Naturally, one needs to keep a certain number at hand so that they can be used or revised when occasion arises. But the greater part of my collection was soon reduced to ashes blowing in the wind.

I found also that it was advisable to start the whole process of clearing out and tidying papers in good time. It is, as I expect all of you except the specially tidy and well organized characters know, fatally easy to accumulate all kinds of things over the years, and all the more so in days when one cannot belong to a committee of any kind without being steadily submerged beneath a flood of paper. At the same time make your plans about the furniture and fittings which you are going to take with you or dispose of when the time comes. It is possible that some articles which are no longer of use may prove quite valuable in the sale rooms. On the other hand, be prepared for pieces which you regard with affection being treated as junk by the dealers.

Books and their disposal are quite a problem. Each individual will have his own plan of dealing with this. I can only record what I did. First of all, I went through all my books and decided upon those which I really could not do without. This had to be calculated in relation to the space which would be available for them in our new home. Having come to a decision—and I warn you that it is far from easy to make—I laid the chosen books on one side, and let my son, my sons-in-law and my assistant have their pick of the rest. With the remainder I approached a shop in St Andrews, where the lady in charge came across and took practically everything that I had to offer, and paid me what seemed to be a reasonable sum for them. She also removed the lot in her van, thus making it all a reasonably easy operation.

Of course one misses some of the volumes which were taken away or sold. The purchaser of my books told me of how some ministers went round the shelves with her, almost with tears and groans, saying: 'No, I don't think you can have that one after all'. Others, she said, appeared weeks later at her shop asking if they might buy back again some of the books which they had sold. I can understand that feeling all too well. On the other hand, we are lucky in St Andrews with the excellent University Library which graduates of all the older Scottish Universities can join; and where I have found it convenient to borrow books which I want and which I have never had in my own library.

Taking precautions

Finally, if I may give a further bit of advice, I would say that it is worth while planning for some interesting bit of work, if this is possible, for the time immediately after retiring. There is always sure to be some emotional trauma in the experience. A man is bound to be rather strung up and busier than usual with all the preparation for departure, the farewell service and social gathering, the leaving of the manse, the removal to the new home. And after the excitement has worn off there can be quite a reaction and a horrible feeling of a vacuum when one realizes that one's life work has quite definitely ended and one has to begin something quite new and different. If it is possible, therefore, to arrange for some sort of gradual easing into the new state, it will be well worth while. I myself was exceptionally fortunate, in being invited to fill a vacancy in Australia for six months immediately after I left St Mary's. I do not want to enlarge on my good fortune but it was an immense advantage to be on the other side of the world when my successor was being chosen!

To sum up: it is an exceedingly big step to retire. Be sure that you plan it well in advance and make all the preparations that you reasonably can before taking it.

2 Immediate adjustments

Where should one retire? This is a large and important question, and obviously one to which no general answer can be given. All sorts of considerations must dictate a man's decision. Some men have little choice because of finance. They must go where they can afford to find a resting place. Others feel that their roots have gone down so deeply in the place of their ministry that they cannot face the prospect of digging them up. Individuals must have their preference—and their wives especially will have their preferences—and their own grounds for making their decisions and their choices.

My own general preference was clear in my mind over a long period. It was that I should not stay too close to the scene of my former labours. I was also determined that, much as I loved Glasgow where I had been born and brought up, to go back there would, for me, be to return to a ghost city haunted by the memories of forty and fifty years ago. I have seen examples of those who, moved by sentiment or even by sentimentality, have tried such experiments and have found them to be unhappy in their consequences. So my wife and I, some years before we had fixed on any date for retirement, decided that we should look for a house in St Andrews. Our reasons were that we both liked the place and knew many people there; it had interests which appealed to both of us; and it was far enough away from Dundee to keep me from sitting on my successor's doorstep, but not too far to prevent us from keeping in touch, in a social as distinct from a pastoral capacity, with our friends in the city and congregation.

On reflection, the only definite guidance that I should care to give on this particular issue is that a man and his wife ought to consider it reasonably far in advance, and be moved by reason rather than by emotion in making their decision.

Adjusting to the new scene

Imagine yourself, then, in your new location. You wake up each morning to find that the routine of many year's duration has been suddenly changed. There is a big adjustment to be made. No longer are you in the familiar surroundings of the manse, with the well-trodden carpet leading to your study. No longer do you have the familiar setting of the weekly services in the well-loved church, with all those people that you know so well sitting in the pews. No longer can you move through the streets and be greeted as the minister; no longer can you go to the doors of your people and receive the friendly welcome—or be helped so strongly by the very folk you had come to comfort in their time of trouble. Your thoughts, your prayers, your efforts have all been geared and directed towards this one area of concern and activity—and now you are removed from it, you have no real place in it.

It is not by any means a pleasant experience, and it is precisely for that reason that my own firm view is that it is better for a minister to make a clean break with his congregation and parish. After retirement, to put it at the lowest level, he is no longer being paid to do this work. The pastoral tie has been severed. The church still stands and the congregation is still there, but ministers are birds of passage. One can see this every time one looks at the photographs in the vestry or the board in the vestibule bearing the names of former incumbents. When a man leaves his charge he is no longer the minister. He has no rights or responsibilities there, and it is necessary to face up to the realities of the situation. Indeed it is false and useless to take any other course.

Therefore I would say, eschew sentimentality; respect scrupulously the position and the rights of your successor.

Even if you have to live in the same town or district, join another congregation. Do not visit your former members unless you and they clearly understand that this is in a social capacity. Do not gossip about your successor with them, but be as pleased as you honestly can be when they have good things to say about him.

This will be better for your successor. It gives him a chance to be himself and take his own way. In our own imagination we must think of what we should have felt like if we had had our predecessor looking over our shoulder or breathing down our neck. And even if we had this experience, surely this is all the greater reason why we should not inflict it upon anyone else.

And, I suggest, it will also be better for you as a retired man to take this course. When a man is retired he has done his job, good or bad. It is not possible to put the clock back. There is no point whatsoever in pretending that he has still any responsibility as minister, preacher or pastor. Protocol, good manners, commonsense—they all indicate that, to put it brutally, a man must clear out and stay out, until invited to return. I can only say that I should find it unbearable to be a member of my former congregation, to see changes made of which I did not approve, to feel that I might be a hindrance or an excrescence or a nuisance, to be in any sense a barrier between the man in charge and the proper doing of his job.

But it will probably be inevitable that you will feel that you cannot turn a blind eye to your friends and their troubles. Certainly not. You can write to them if they are bereaved. You can attend the funerals. But you ought not, in my view, in any way to infringe upon pastoral responsibility. Thus if one is invited to take part in a wedding or a funeral, one can only say that the request must be made in the first instance to the parish minister, that the decision is his and that you will comply with whatever he may decide. This keeps all parties right; and in due course the problem will cease to arise.

Adjustments that are inevitable, and severe

Undoubtedly some men find these adjustments, which have been outlined in a general way, very hard to take. Most of us, I am sure, have known cases of ministers who have become quite ill, either nervously or physically, because of their retirement. Often this is precisely because of their very devotion and involvement in their charges. They are men who have, perhaps, been so conscientious that they have not made time for recreation or relaxation. They have had little or no experience of what to do with their leisure time. Even on holiday they have just collapsed into a kind of weary inertia, trying to recharge the batteries in time for when the unremitting round of duties begins again. And when they retire, especially if in new or unfamiliar surroundings, they find themselves in a kind of vacuum, which they abhor.

I do not suggest that such men are lacking in faith or in spiritual qualities; often the reverse is true. But they may to some extent be lacking in forethought and commonsense. They have not made time—as you can now make time—to prepare themselves for the days which are not filled from early till late with sermon preparation, committee meetings, the pastoral round and all the multitude of concerns which assail a busy minister, and to which some men even seek to add without due reasons. In retirement, one must realize, there is a new stage to be faced, a new routine to be established, a new tempo to be found—and perhaps new values to be discovered.

There are also some things which retired ministers more than some other retired men will miss. There are no more ministerial perks. No more listed expenses: you have to buy your own notepaper and envelopes, your own stamps; you have to pay all your telephone bills and all your car expenses and repairs. No longer can you call in the fabric convener to deal with the leaks or the electrical failure or the dry rot. All these, along with the rates or the rent, are your responsibility. If you had secretarial help, you have it no longer, and you have to write or type all your own letters. It will be little consolation to you that you receive fewer letters than before, because this will simply remind you of your diminished status and importance.

Is it all, therefore, a gloomy prospect? No indeed! Far from it!

There is much on the credit side

The pressure is lifted. No longer need you be tensed up day after day with the sense of so much to do and so little time in which to do it. No longer do you need to wonder how long can you possibly keep up the pace. There is a lesser burden of responsibility. You do not have to look anxiously at the figures of the weekly offerings, wondering if all the requirements and assessments are going to be met, or if it is once again going to be a matter of letting the Mission and Service allocation fall short. You do not have to chase round trying to find someone to take over the leadership of the Boys' Brigade or other youth organization, or to see if your long-serving Sunday School Superintendent is prepared to carry on for another term.

Much as you love your church hall, and in spite of all the improvements you have so carefully carried out, it is going to be a relief not to have to put in an appearance night after night, especially during the winter. You are not sorry that the recurrent problems with the organist and choir will no longer be yours to solve. There are also the really tiresome and difficult cases you no longer have to deal with. I don't mean the serious upsets or tragedies which have strained your resources to the utmost and in which somehow you have been able to give some help, but the irritating people, the boring folk whom it is hard to help because they never will understand that they *are* boring; the elders or office-bearers like the man who said after a session meeting: 'There's ae thing Ah'll tell ye, and that is, so long as Ah'm a member of this kirk session there'll never be a unanimous decision'. While all these events and individuals have been part of our development, training and (under God) our growth in grace, it would be dishonest not to admit that it can be a relief no longer to have a responsibility towards them.

Also, once you have begun to relax and settle down, you will find that you can call more of your days your own, in the sense that there is a greater opportunity to plan out your time as you would like to, instead of being compelled to conform to a strict timetable.

I think it is also true to say that ministers in some respects are more fortunate than those of other professions in that, on the whole, they have a greater opportunity of exercising their skills and talents in retirement. I find that there are few of the retired men I meet who have not had a fair share of preaching engagements. Admittedly, preaching in strange churches Sunday after Sunday is not as rewarding as preaching to one's own congregation. But there may be a series of engagements in the same place over a holiday period or in a vacancy. There may also be a *locum's* job, which can be more demanding but also, perhaps, more rewarding through its contact with a friendly group of people. There is no point in hiding the fact that the strain of writing sermons week after week is lifted, and that old sermons can often be given a fresh setting or contemporary slant, while there is the satisfaction of exercising such talents as one has in preaching.

For those who have friends or contacts overseas there may be the opportunity of doing a stint as a visiting or exchange preacher. Certainly more and more men seem to have engagements in America, although I myself have not been able to go there on the occasions when I have been asked to do so. In any case, and in one way or the other, the majority of retired men with whom I come into contact appear to have plenty to keep them interested and active. There appears to be no real reason why any retired minister should sit down and allow himself to be the victim of self-pity. More often you hear it said: 'I am more busy in retirement than I was before'. I can understand that statement, although I do not believe that it is normally strictly accurate. I incline to believe that what happens is that retired men are pleasantly surprised to find that contrary, perhaps, to their expectations, they really have quite a lot to do. And the fact that this is not part of a compulsory duty but rather because they are exercising a free choice, makes them imagine that they are busier than they were before, when they simply had to do their duty, their daily darg. One has therefore to make allowances for these elderly characters and smile indulgently at remarks like that of one of my older friends who, when asked if he was enjoying his retirement, answered: 'Yes, of course, but I miss my holidays'.

Finally then, let me suggest that retirement can be regarded with a sense of anticipation and even of adventure. It is not a relapse into a backwater—or it need not necessarily be so. Rather should it be seen not only as a new stage of life, but also as something of an exciting and testing experience, a challenge to one's adaptability and one's character. One is going to be set in a new environment. There is possibly going to be a new community with different ways of doing things. There will be new people to be met and new friends to make. Life goes on. And if you have found life interesting and rewarding so far, why should you not find it even more so when you have more time to savour it? Once again we are faced with the fact that we, who have spent so much time in advising and indeed in telling people what they should do, are faced with the task of putting into practice our precepts. And why should this not be rewarding and exciting?

3 Long term prospects

One cannot expect, in ministerial retirement, to have a constant round of *locums* and preaching engagements continuing indefinitely into the future. In any case, there may be those who do not wish to involve themselves in much of such activity from the beginning of their retirement. So what of a future in which a man sits in the pew instead of occupying the pulpit?

Being a member of a congregation

Having made your round of the various churches you will no doubt decide to join one particular congregation. Several men I know of have delayed such decisions for a surprisingly long time. Others have joined churches in which they have, for one reason or another, not felt at home, and then have had to face the embarrassment of going and asking for their 'lines'. [The certificate for transferring their membership to another congregation—*Ed.*] In St Andrews my wife and I found that the decision was much more easy than we had expected. I had never worshipped or preached in Hope Park Church until we came to live in St Andrews. As it happened, our house is two minutes' walk from Hope Park; and before we had made any decision at all I was asked to be *locum* in the vacancy there. I enjoyed the experience and found that we both felt at home in the congregation and received a warm welcome. So rather than delay the decision we became members, even before Bill Henney was called as minister.

Once again a member of my family cut me down to size. My wife, after Bill Henney had been in Hope Park for some time, said to him one day: 'I must tell you how nice it is for me, after all these years, to have a minister of my own'.

I must say, however, that it is a good thing to find yourself as an ordinary member of a congregation worshipping from the pew instead of leading the worship from the sanctuary. Mind you, one still enjoys preaching, even if one is never wholly certain if this enjoyment is always shared by those to whom one preaches. And one would hope to be privileged to go on preaching for a while yet. But it is nice to be part of the fellowship, and to see from the other end, so to speak, what the fellowship means to its members; and also to savour the advantage of belonging to such a fellowship in a new environment—in the sense that soon you are being greeted in the streets by those with whom you have worshipped in the church. When you are in a strange setting, as we have always tried to emphasize to others, the Church helps you to feel at home. And it is salutary for a minister to find this to be so in his own experience.

Kirk Session, presbytery and committee work

You may also be asked to become a member of a Kirk Session, not of course as an elder, but in the sense of being associated with the work of the Kirk Session. For various reasons I have not yet become thoroughly involved in the work of the Kirk Session at Hope Park. But I have found it a useful discipline to attend meetings when I am able to and to keep quiet—not without some effort after being accustomed to doing most of talking at Kirk Session meetings.

Then there is the new Presbytery, perhaps, to which you find yourself attached. Here again it is necessary, I think, to take a back seat and speak sparingly to begin with—or speak sparingly at any time, now or in the future. I think I prefer not to have to belong to the Presbytery to which I belonged for so long, not because I think St Andrews is a better or worse Presbytery than Dundee, but because I am now in a new stage of my life, and Dundee is associated with a stage which is past and done with.

And what about Edinburgh committees? I have never been overfond of travelling from my parish to Edinburgh. And after I had a coronary in 1964 I deliberately stayed out of Edinburgh committee work for quite a number of years—and, quite honestly, was glad to do so. I did not miss them one little bit, nor did they appear to miss me, and it was very useful to have more time for work in one's parish. Now, however, I have one or two committees to attend, and more than I had expected. In fact I should be at a meeting today— and perhaps you wish that I were—but I am not altogether sorry that I am not. I find it a two-edged question, this committee business. On the whole I am glad that I am still in touch with a certain amount of discussion at the administration centre of the Church. On the other hand I am quite certain, and I have been pressing this for some years now, that our committee system is top-heavy and ridiculously expensive and over-manned. The whole structure is going to collapse one day if it is not drastically pruned. So perhaps OAPs should be all the more ready to step aside, in spite of the wisdom and experience that they might be expected to have accumulated. When I see, as I have done, a prominent and respected minister of the Church falling asleep at a committee meeting (to be sure not without some justification) and snoring gently, I am sure that, however much he loves the committee scene, it is time for him to hang up his boots.

Various interests

There is one organization in St Andrews which, as yet, I do not seem to have had time to join, although it is specially designed for the likes of me. It is Probus, an organization for retired professional and business men. They have fortnightly meetings, usually at coffee time in the mornings, with speakers; and I am told by those who are members that it is worth joining. It must exist in a good many other towns too.

It seems strange to speak about not having enough time for this or for that, but it actually does work out like that. For one thing, a man ought to be spending, on average, more time in doing his share of the housework than he may have done formerly. And if so, then it does take up a bit of time. And then there is, at least in a good many cases, the garden to look after. I have always been a reluctant gardener. My great-grandfather was a landscape gardener, but since then we have all been ministers, and there seem to be no genes left over which, as yet, have enabled me to face the prospect of a morning among the weeds with any real sense of joy or uplift. To be sure, there is a satisfaction in seeing something one has planted actually growing, in spite of the depredations of frost, drought, pigeons or slugs. And after facing a veritable wilderness of weeds it is pleasing to see little oases of tidiness and flowers gradually emerging. But if anyone is seriously concerned about having time hanging heavily on his hands in retirement, let him go to a house with a garden, and he will be permanently deprived of any excuse for sitting staring vacantly into space.

In fact, as at the present time, I have to pick and choose with some care which of the various recreations I had promised myself I would take up, I am going to be able to enjoy. I know some men who play golf two or three times a week. I don't seem to be able to manage more than once a week at the most, and not always that. And if anything my golf is worse than it used to be. The ball doesn't go so far when I hit it; Henry Cotton says that you lose two or three yards for each year after forty. And just when, to compensate, one's short game should improve, I have been afflicted, after forty years, by a persistent attack of shanking which has shattered my confidence completely. But then, for the golfer of my calibre, golf is less a recreation than a spiritual discipline.

I had also meant to read so much more, and once again it isn't working out like that. Too often one finds that one's main reading is done when one goes to bed at night; there isn't even time to get through the Sunday *Observer* before the next one comes along. And when one reads in bed it doesn't seem so long before the print starts swimming before one's eyes. One thing I have done is to dig up some of the rusty remains of my classical training, and start reading the NT in the original. This I really enjoy doing. By contrast, alas, the delights of reading the OT in the original have never been remotely within my grasp.

And then I was going to try and do some writing. As yet the articles, or even the book which had been hovering on the horizon of my imagination, seem even more remote. Those masterpieces which I had planned seem likely to remain for ever unwritten. At least I shall be spared the experience of papering my room with rejection slips. Which reminds me that I really must get down to the job of painting the various objects, walls or doors in house and garden which are showing signs of wear and tear. There doesn't seem to be time to do this either; but then, in all honesty, this is probably because

I don't want to make time for painting. Since I fell off a step ladder along with a pot of paint in my first manse, painting has been one of my lesser enthusiasms.

Learning acceptance

As one grows older—and this is something one senses perhaps with more force in retirement—one has to learn the lesson of acceptance.

On the physical level this soon becomes obvious. I have already spoken of the ageing golfer who loses distance in his driving. This applies in other directions also. One is more aware of aches and pains, what the doctor reassuringly speaks of as 'signs of wear and tear'. Young people seem to walk past you at an extraordinary rate and with consummate ease leave you labouring in their wake. The Waverley Steps, as you start walking to 121 George Street, seem to have increased in number. Quite unexpectedly you have sudden spells of tiredness. I have known myself, full of the joys of life, setting out to take part in a wedding service. And then, halfway through the reception, I have been exhausted beyond belief. So that, literally, as I went in to the reception someone said: 'You're looking ten years younger,' and as I said my goodbyes another said: 'My word, you are looking tired'. In the same way I find that conducting a service takes more out of me than it used to in the days when I had five services or meetings to conduct on a Sunday. On a Sunday afternoon I go to bed with the *Observer* newspaper to read, and in no time I am sleeping. Only in this way do I face up to taking a second service in the evening. Which may all be rather humiliating, but it has to be accepted—and accepted, if possible, with good grace.

And then there is mental slowness. I do not try to think about how many millions of my brain cells are dying steadily as I grow older. To worry about that would probably increase the death rate among them. It is sufficient to try and deal with the effects of the deterioration. It becomes more difficult to remember the names of people and places. What seems to happen is that one's private computer takes more time to whizz into action. One has to wait a little longer, think of someone or something else, let the subterranean depths swirl round a bit, however slowly, and then, if one is fortunate, the name or the place or the incident comes slowly floating to the top. Yes, one has to accept increasing mental slowness; but one should not, I suggest, give in to it. There is much to be said for keeping one's mind, or what is left of it, as active as possible. We should not lapse into any kind of vegetable incuriousness, but be thankful that there are so many interesting things and people to occupy one's attention. A friend of mine is fond of quoting the jingle which runs as follows:

I can toddle up the staircase;
To my deafness I'm resigned.
I can manage my bi-focals,
But how I miss my mind!

Well, so long as we are free of the encroachments of senility—and surely these are the most pathetic of all the signs of old age—it is worth while keeping our minds open to all that is happening around us. I stress the word open, because as one grows older one is more resistant to and irritated by some new ideas and fashions. It is so much easier to remain with the ideas and the practices with which we are familiar and which we like precisely because we are accustomed to them. This is not to say that the new is anything like always the best. We should be prepared to give the young lions in their roaring a good run for their money before we gracefully acknowledge that there may be something good in what they are making so much noise about.

The credit side of old age

There are, of course, advantages in growing old—and not least in the fact that it is in itself a new experience from which there is always something to be learned.

There is an added richness in companionship and friendship, and all the more so because there may well be a little more leisure in which to appreciate these personal relationships, which are at the very heart of our living.

There is, one hopes, something more of experience and wisdom accumulated over the years, which can be passed on— but one should say, only to those who want to hear it or who specifically ask for such advice as we can give them.

There is more time to look objectively at the world scene, when we are not so actively involved, and try to trace a pattern in history as well as a pattern in our own infinitesimal lives. By the same token, as we look back over the course of our own existence we may be able to see if there has been any development or growth to maturity for which we can be thankful. Such an exercise, so far from leading to self-satisfaction or complacency, can help us to realize how much further we have still to go before we can be the kind of persons that we are meant to be.

And inevitably we become aware of the shortness of human life and the frailty of our mortal bodies. There is not so very much more time for us to go on seeing the sun rising and setting on our familiar surroundings. We know that there is going to be parting and a bit of heartbreak and the hard process of readjustment before our own time comes. Rather than allow such facts to cast a gloom over our lives, let me end by saying that when the time becomes shorter, there is all the more reason for us to make the most of it and enjoy it to the full. And this is what I hope most sincerely you will all find it possible to do when the day comes for you too to retire and start another stage in this fascinating life which is our heritage as human beings.

EPILOGUE

John McIntyre

So we come to the end of the story of the ministry and the message of Hugh Douglas, by all accounts and on all the evidence we have seen, a comprehensively representative churchman of the twentieth century. But if we have reached the end of the story, we have not reached the end of the ministry or the message. For it remains to consider the points at which, in their wealth and variety, they still have light to throw upon the problems and opportunities before the Church as that twentieth century draws to a close. Several such points of contact spring to mind.

In the very forefront of such an assessment must surely be Hugh's understanding of the nature of ministry in its primary essence as *parish* ministry. He would not have been slow to acknowledge the validity of the proliferation of ministries which we have witnessed in the past quarter of a century— ministries in which the Church seeks to concentrate its resources of caring, of evangelism and of leadership in areas where an especial need or opportunity reveals itself. Theologically the General Assembly has made several attempts to rationalize this proliferation in recent years, but Hugh's dedication to parish ministry has perhaps to be re-affirmed as the anchor of whatever other ministries the Church implements. The parish is where God's people, all of them, churched and un-churched, employed and unemployed, white-collared and blue-collared are to be found. So it is hard to imagine a time when the ordinances of God will not be administered within a parish context, as the ultimate home of all else that the Church seeks to accomplish.

This conviction of the importance of parish ministry on Hugh's part is the key to so many of the features of his ministry which have been emphasized, and which, it is being argued, continue to have relevance to a Church in a world so swiftly changing by the day. For example, there was his devotion to sermon construction as to a craft, which extended to careful design of the structure and to the selection of the appropriate substance, with right balance between the parts and a selection of relevant and integrated quotations and illustrations. In face of a market-place overcrowded with many forms of media presentation, the Church dare not be found to be careless or unprepared in the word that it preaches, or to speak other than in a distinctive voice. In face of a Church that seems at times to wonder about the continuing importance of the sermon, it has to be said that no more effective way has yet been found to break God's Word to men and women Sunday by Sunday, or with such immediacy to extend the range of their responsibilities, through an understanding of the implications of the Incarnation for their lives and this lost world.

But for Hugh, the sermon for all its importance was only a part of the total act of worship, which he saw as a spiritual progression from one phase of worship, the praise or the prayers or the readings, to another, in a manner which answered to the needs of the human soul, as they had been charted across the centuries. Formalism it may be, but at a time when some diets of worship are in danger of collapsing in chaos or anarchy, form is what is required. Nor is it form for form's sake, but form which eases the path of the soul into the presence of God, and does not side-track it into the excesses of emotionalism, the narcissism of self-contemplation or the banalities of ecstatic utterance.

The act of worship, however, whether on Sundays or midweek, the ordinary diet or the full sacramental occasion, in school assembly or in the panoply of a royal visit, never for Hugh occurred in a sterilised vacuum. It was fed from two sources, which have a continuing significance for this generation. First, maintaining a regular programme of parish visitation, he was in constant touch with the needs, the problems and the longings of ordinary folks, in their homes or at work. Parish visitation, it is increasingly asserted, has now fallen out of regular practice, and there are many reasons why that is so: television soaps and series and sportsnights, the breakdown of the family as a stable social unit, uncertainties about what the minister should 'do' when he does visit, the interesting modern range of extra-domiciliar attractions for young and old, and so on. It all seems so inevitable, but the price could be high, if the result is that the connection is severed between the pulpit and the homes of the congregation. Hugh's diligence in this respect is a signal to our contemporaries. The second source feeding worship for Hugh was the private worship of daily devotion. There was a phrase which recurred in books of daily devotion in use fifty years ago, which described such devotion as 'practising the presence of God'. The phrase has some odd overtones now, but at its heart was the idea that devotion was something that the Christian had to practise; it was never simply a case of 'doing the what comes naturally', to quote the words of a song popular around that same time. If spirituality is to be one of the dominant religious expressions in the 1990s, then maybe we should be looking afresh at the structures and the practice of Christian devotion, as the form which our spirituality is to take. We have a great deal to learn and maybe also to re-learn.

There is another interest of Hugh's which spans the century and which has as great relevance as it originally had. It is nearly fifty years since he published the Iona Community pamphlet, *What is Christian Marriage?*, and in few areas has there been greater change than in the subjects dealt with in that pamphlet. Free love, so called, and trial marriages were about the only departures from the sexual norm openly debated, even though there may have been much else going on. Today widespread advocacy and acceptance of alternative sexual practices call for the kind of definition of Christian stand-points which Hugh did not hesitate to offer fifty years ago, not least in the area of Christian marriage and the values which it enshrines and expresses. Maybe we are being sidetracked from that affirmation of faith by an all too legitimate concern for the overwhelming medical and social tragedies and problems which have been multiplying largely because of promiscuous sexual behaviour. Yet in the midst of increasing confusion, the obligation remains for the Christian Church to offer a positive, creative and redemptive vision of the life which God intended when he created 'man and woman' in his image.

We turn now to one aspect of this 'one man's ministry' which extended that ministry far beyond the bounds of the parish where he worked, namely, his radio and television presentations. Not only did Hugh perform these broadcasts, as we have read, with consummate professional skill and deep Christian understanding of the needs of his listeners and viewers, he was also sharply aware of the potential of both of these media to provide a rich diversity of new methods of communicating the Gospel to our generation. But the lead which Hugh, and, in a different way, Willie Barclay gave in the 1960s, has never seriously and systematically been followed up. If someone had told us sixty years ago that there would in the twentieth century be provided an opportunity to communicate the Gospel to tens of thousands, with the immediacy and the intimacy of personal evangelism and counselling, we would have been staggered by the immensity of that opportunity. We might even have been moved to place the opportunity on a par with that provided by the invention of printing in the fifteenth century. When we come to assess the achievements and failures of the Church in the second half of the twentieth century, close to the top of the failures will have to be its incompetence in the field of media communication, notably in television more than in radio. Some of the failure has been due to a certain poverty of substance and content, or undue reliance on established favourites such as 'Songs of Praise'. But mainly the failure is attributable to the inability of the Church or its representatives to discover the form and the message appropriate to these new media. Sadly, there does not appear to be any group which is addressing that question; we are still after fifty years in the trial-and-error mode.

Finally, if we are considering the ways in which Hugh's ministry is continuing, and in which his insights remain valid and operative, then account has to be taken of those whose lives and personal ministries have been touched by him. Mention has been made of his own family—Molly and her husband John Harvey, Ruth and her husband Norman Shanks, and Colin; and it is clear that many of Hugh's interests, as of Isabel's, have surfaced again in the commitments of the family—in the Iona Community, in recognition of the wide-ranging social, political, economic and bio-medical responsibilities of the Church, in the need to nurture the young in the faith, and in concern for the homeless, the underprivileged and the poor. Hugh's vision has not perished. It has been implemented also in the ministries of the ministers who, as his assistants, affectionately called him their 'bishop' and who have given us their own perspectives upon what he achieved and what he imparted to them. Conjointly they witness to the immense value of the system of probationer–assistantships as an essential part of education for the ministry, or 'ministerial formation' as we now call it. But whatever we call it, *praxis* of the kind which Hugh exhibited imparted life-blood to a *theoria*, which, however intellectually and academically impeccable, would otherwise become increasingly irrelevant to the needs of the Church and its members and to the challenge of contemporary society.

Measured in these terms, of influence and of inspiration, this ministry upon which we have been reflecting is still with us and is still in the service of the Church.